WHY WARS HAPPEN

Why Wars Happen

JEREMY BLACK

NEW YORK UNIVERSITY PRESS
Washington Square, New York

© Jeremy Black, 1998

First published in the U.S.A. in 1998 by
NEW YORK UNIVERSITY PRESS
Washington Square
New York, N. Y. 10003

Originally published in Great Britain in 1998
by Reaktion Books Ltd, London

CIP data available from the Library of Congress
ISBN 0-8147-1333-5

Printed in Great Britain

Contents

List of Abbreviations

Add.   Additional Manuscripts

Ang.   Angleterre

AE   Paris, Ministère des Affaires Etrangères

BL   London, British Library, Department of
        Manuscripts

CP   Correspondance Politique

FO   Foreign Office papers

PRO   London, Public Record Office

SP   State Papers

Preface

He said, *at once*, and with an animated tone – you
seem to calculate probabilities (as I have often done)
by weighing the great considerations of state policy,
national honour, and national advantages. This thing
cannot be true, because it would be impolitic, – that
event must happen because all our *data* are in favour
of it. But you forget that in the present crisis, it is not
the interests of France, of England, or of Holland
which holds the balance, but the personal wishes,
and hopes of John, Andrew, or Peter, the ministers of
those different countries. Mr Fox had his views in
accelerating peace – Msr. de Vergennes [French
foreign minister] believes he can attain the pinnacle
of favour by concluding that work – we must now see
what Lord Shelburne [British First Lord of the
Treasury] thinks, and if the establishment of his
administration requires peace or war.

Emperor Joseph II, ruler of Austria, as
reported by British envoy in Vienna,
Sir Robert Murray Keith, 1782.[1]

International relations, war and constitutional developments
were three of the major topics of historical study and teaching
within the European world in the late nineteenth and early
twentieth centuries. Each, however, went into a decline in the
interwar period, and this has remained the position since. Much
excellent work continues to be produced in these fields, but they
are not as central to historical enquiry as previously. This is
especially the case for study of the centuries prior to 1900, and
is true of scholarship in the leading countries of historical
research, such as the USA, Britain, France and Germany.

This lack of attention is misleading. War was a central activity of societies and states, and the conduct of international relations has been integral to political history. Furthermore, the overwhelming emphasis on conflicts in the twentieth and, to a lesser extent, nineteenth centuries in studies on the causes, and, indeed, nature and consequences, of war, limits the basis for theoretical and general reflections. This is rendered even more serious by a concentration on war (and peace) within the European world, with the addition of the USA, a state founded by Europeans, and Japan, once it had Europeanized. In addition, too little attention has been devoted to cultural and social factors in the literature on the origins of war.

In order to understand the present age, it is necessary to search for continuities and changes from the past. This study seeks to do so and, also, to raise a number of related questions: What is war? Do wars primarily reflect bellicosity in societies and states, or do they, largely, arise as a consequence of the breakdown of the diplomatic system. Are they deliberate or accidents? How far are the causes of war and war aims related to changes in the nature of warfare, of the international system, and also of the internal character of states?

In one volume it is not possible to study all types of war, but a major effort has been made to include a consideration of the situation outside Europe, as part of an attempt to tackle the subject from a broad historical perspective while maintaining fairly even coverage across time and space. The empirical domain is extended far beyond the European states system commonly discussed in such studies. A comparative scope is necessary in order to challenge Eurocentric perspectives.

The adoption of a chronological approach is designed to encourage a focus on the extent and causes of change. It is necessary to stress the relativity of circumstances, cultures and periods. The periodization of the chapters reflects the importance of the American War of Independence, as the first of the modern wars of revolution, and of World War One, as the first total war engaging much, but by no means all, of the world's population. The years 1450 and 1650 are not seen as turning-points, and, indeed, there are important continuities across both dates. They have been selected in order to examine the situation in a period somewhat unhelpfully described as 'early modern'. This was a period in which it is pertinent to consider the causes of war in light of such developments as transoceanic empires and the widespread use of gunpowder.

Throughout the book there is an emphasis on context, the contingent, choice and the individual attitudes, views and reasoning of political leaders, and scepticism about determinants, arguments based on concepts such as structure, and the abstractions of much international relations writing on the subject. It is difficult to formulate arguments about causation in a socio-political context, but, while accepting that any single interpretation or approach is open to endless qualification and that it is necessary to see the origins of war from multiple perspectives, this work emphasizes the role of cultural predispositions and bellicosity.

I am most grateful for the opportunities to develop arguments provided by writing the introduction to *The Origins of War in Early Modern Europe* (Edinburgh, 1987) and by subsequent invitations to speak at Illinois–Urbana, Indiana–Bloomington, Rutgers and Vanderbilt universities and the Institute for European History at Mainz, and would like to thank those who invited me to speak and who contributed to the discussion. I am most grateful to Ronald Asch, Chris Bartlett, George Boyce, John Darwin, Jerry De Groot, Kal Holsti, Trevor Johnson, Harald Kleinschmidt, Michael Leaman, Peter Morris, Charles Reynolds, Matthew Seligmann, David Sturdy, David Weigall and Peter Wilson for comments on earlier drafts of all or part of the volume. This book is dedicated to two old and good friends.

Introduction

> ... the rapacious appetites, the avarice and ambition
> of the human race, interrupts the general felicity, and
> render man an enemy to man. Injustice arms herself
> with force, to enrich herself with the spoils of her
> brethren. He who, moderate in his desires, confines
> himself within the bounds of what he possesses, and
> at the same time is unwilling to repel force by force,
> will soon become the prey of others ... Thus war
> becomes necessary to man ... There is no principle
> more generally received, than that which considers
> war, as never to be undertaken but from just and
> lawful reasons; nor hardly any one more generally
> violated.
>
> Anon., 'An Historical Account of the Rise and Progress of
> the Arts and Sciences', *Royal Magazine*, December 1761.

The causes of war, the causes of wars, the causes of specific wars: the three are connected, yet different. They all raise questions about the nature of political societies and also about the character and operation of international systems. Indeed, one of the most interesting aspects of the study of war is that it offers an approach to these questions, and does so by, and through, considering societies and systems in an important dimension of their activity.

The causes of war can be discussed with reference to anthropological, psychological and sociological perspectives, but it is helpful to complement general accounts of human, and indeed animal, propensities to violence with understandings of the varied nature of war and of why individual conflicts or groups of wars broke out. A general propensity to violence cannot readily explain peace or the decision to engage in particular wars.[1] This problem is accentuated if peace is treated as more than just a period of preparing for war, and also if wars that were prevented are considered.[2]

Nevertheless, general accounts of propensities to violence are of great value, because they clarify the question of human responses to disputes, and focus on the importance of arousing, channelling and legitimating violent urges, and of persuading people to fight, kill and run the risk of being killed, without which there is, and can be, no war. The willingness to kill is crucial to the causes of war, even if it may play little role in the reasons for particular wars; a preparedness to gamble with lives is more important in diplomatic confrontation. This willingness to kill is a conflation of long-term anthropological and psychological characteristics and more specific societal and cultural situations.[3] It is necessary to consider how far, and to what effect, these propensities to organized conflict have altered over time, an historical question.

This is not simply a question of whether settled societies have been more warlike than 'primitive' peoples, and, indeed, more specifically, whether there has been a particular propensity in Western society to make warfare more organized, destructive and ruthless.[4] This charge has aroused some controversy and now appears more problematic than was the case in scholarly argument twenty years ago. Whereas, for example, in the 1960s and 1970s scholars overlooked pre-Columbian inter-pueblo warfare and focused on Native Americans' supposedly peaceful relationships with nature and with one another, that approach now seems less convincing.[5]

There is also the issue of how far changes in society, culture and political organizations over the last half-millennium have affected bellicosity, not only in general but also in the particular case of the ability of governments to obtain support for war. This is not simply a matter of the decision to begin conflict or to take warlike steps, but also of the willingness to support wars once they have started. War – organized conflict – is not possible without manpower and resources, both their presence and their use, and these have been greatly affected by the changes already referred to. Thus, any account of the causes of war is, in part, an aspect of the totality of history. Furthermore, the difference of the past and the contingent nature of past circumstances limit the value of explanatory models that do not incorporate a temporal dimension.

The model of war as organized conflict between sovereign states, begun deliberately by a specific act of policy, is that which has been discussed most fully by theorists of the causes of war and by historians who have examined the question. Thus, the grand title of Donald Kagan's interesting *On the Origins of War and the Preservation of Peace* (London, 1995) reveals a study only of the Peloponnesian, Second Punic, First World and Second World wars and of the Cuban Missile Crisis. Kagan explains,

> I am interested in the outbreak of wars between states in an international system, such as we find in the world today. The Greeks and the Romans of the republican era lived in that kind of a world, and so has the West since the time of the Renaissance. Most other peoples have lived either in a world without states, or in great empires where the only armed conflicts were civil wars or attempts to defend the realm against bands of invaders.[6]

Such an overly restricted scope ensures that, as a discussion of the origins of war, this work is far too limited, although Kagan's stress on 'honour' is useful.

There has been insufficient discussion of the problem, for contemporaries and historians, of establishing what war is and thus of determining when wars begin. By treating war as a phenomenon, the generalization and generalizations involved in the definition become central to its explanation, although that process is often disguised. The more restrictive the definition of war, the easier it is to date it. A.J.P. Taylor, a prominent British expert on nineteenth- and early-twentieth-century European international relations, wrote of 'the more prosaic origin of war: the precise moment when a statesman sets his name to the declaration of it'.[7] This model corresponds closely to the reality of many wars within Europe in the nineteenth century, for example the Franco-Prussian War of 1870–71, but it is inappropriate for some conflicts in the Balkans or for much of the warfare arising from European imperialism in that century, and is, anyway, inapplicable for many wars over the preceding three centuries. It is also unclear that the distinction between peace and war was clear-cut in the twentieth century, for example during the late 1930s, in the so-called Cold War, and subsequently.[8]

Indeed the very difficulty of defining war, and thus determining the number and starting-point of particular wars, makes it hard to turn with confidence to statistical studies of the origins of wars, although they have been important and valuable in much theoretical discussion of the subject. For example, in early 1700 Augustus II of Saxony-Poland invaded Livonia and Frederick IV of Denmark invaded Holstein-Gottorp, but neither declared war. In 1726–7 the British blockaded the Spanish treasure fleet in Porto Bello and kept another fleet off Cádiz, dislocating the financial structure of the Spanish imperial system, while the Spaniards besieged Gibraltar, but neither power declared war and the conflict did not spread. The two powers signed a treaty in 1729. Chinese intervention against the American-led United Nations forces in the Korean War (1950–53) did not lead to any declaration of war, and there were no hostile operations on Chinese soil.

It is also difficult to characterize or classify wars. Much analytical, including statistical, work on warfare rests on such characterization, but it is open to empirical and theoretical qualification. For example, Philip Curtin suggested that wars in eighteenth-century Senegambia in West Africa be classified in terms of an economic or a political model, the former characterized by a quest for slaves. He accepted that these models were ideal types and that particular wars could contain a mix of motives, but, nevertheless, thought the political model dominant.[9] However, more recently, John Thornton has emphasized the difficulty of distinguishing between the two, and has stressed the multiple nature of wars in early-modern Africa,[10] a practice that makes statistical analysis difficult.

This is not an isolated instance, and, indeed, the problem of classification more generally affects not only the entire subject but also the situation, whichever period, area or level of conflict is under discussion. For example, Sanjay Subrahmanyam notes, 'it might seem that we are arguing that the Portuguese expansion enterprise of the fifteenth century was conceived in compartments: in one resided rational calculation and commerce, and in another the atavistic passions of anti-Muslim feeling were to be found. But this was not really the case, and in fact royal mercantilism itself cannot be found in Dom Manuel's reign [1495–1521] without its strange bedfellow – Messianism'.[11]

Furthermore, it is possible to add the problems of distinguishing war from force, to the difficulty of assessing causes of conflict. In eighteenth-century India military operations were related to revenue collections, often dictated by the need to seize or protect revenue,[12] but it is not easy to separate such operational aspects of wars from the use of force to collect or seize revenue. The same point is relevant for many other societies.

Thornton's comment on early-modern warfare on the Gold Coast of West Africa is even more challenging for such analysis: '... a complicated series of wars between the local states, whose motives are not clear to us and were equally unclear to the Europeans'.[13] The problematic relationship between knowledge and analysis has also been highlighted, although in a very different context, in a recent study of the Cuban Missile Crisis that argues that greater knowledge has complicated analysis.[14]

At the other extreme there is a lack of information on pre-[European] contact warfare between Native North Americans, and it is very difficult to define what war meant to the Natives. There was 'public' warfare, in the form of conflict between tribes, and 'private' warfare, raids with no particular sanction, often designed to prove manhood. Furthermore, there appears to have been no sharp distinction between raiding and hunting, the latter an economic necessity. They merged. In part, this may be because non-tribal members were not viewed as human beings, or at least as full persons.[15] The treatment of enemies as beasts or as subhuman can also be seen in European conflict, especially civil warfare, as for example the religious wars of the sixteenth and seventeenth centuries, and also in the genocidal drive of 'modern' states, most obviously Hitler's Germany.

Ignoring conflicts similar to those between North American tribes, and concentrating for analytical purposes on wars between European powers, as is the case in most theoretical work, risks offering a very partial account of the causes of war, and this is even more the case if the field for study is restricted to wars deemed 'hegemonic'. Circular arguments frequently play a large role in such definitions.

A concentration on wars deemed hegemonic avoids the definitional problem of war as an aspect of state sovereignty because, by their very nature, such conflicts can only be waged by major states and alliances of states. However, the problem of the relationship between war-making and legitimate authority becomes acute once less widespread struggles are considered. Any definition of war in terms of a public monopoly of the use of force has to face both the contested nature of the public sphere and the role and resilience of 'private' warfare.[16] As yet, there has been relatively little theoretical work on the causes of internal warfare.[17]

Although most quantitative work aims to be fairly general, the great majority of the studies are confined to data after 1815. In addition, a few are hesitant to apply their explanations to the pre-industrial era.[18] The only two major schools of thought that take an empirical approach that explicitly extend their analysis to the pre-1815 period are those involving long cycles – the work of George Modelski and William Thompson[19] – and studies by Jack Levy.[20] Both treat the period since 1495 as a single, but evolving, system. Kalevi Holsti went back to 1648 in a study that emphasized the role of human intention rather than structural considerations, although, again, the focus was heavily Eurocentric.[21]

In addition, there has been work examining economic explanations of war, specifically Kondratieff cycles.[22] However, it can be argued that, instead of such cycles producing war, war and the preparation for war generate price upswings.[23] Nevertheless, this approach has been given global range and a long-term perspective by Modelski and Thompson. In an attempt to elucidate the connections between structural processes in economics and politics, they link Kondratieff cycles to warfare.[24] Levy has produced some excellent analytical surveys of the various theories on the origins of war,[25] while Charles Reynolds has offered a cogent warning about the danger of explaining wars without basing the explanation in terms of the views and perceptions of those who waged them.[26] An example is provided by geopolitical accounts of German policy that focus on the country's central position within Europe, for example the thesis of Imanuel Geiss that Germany fluctuates between being a power centre and a power vacuum, fluctuations that have their own dynamic and to which the pragmatic Bismarck accommodated himself.[27]

A standard way to explain a war is to discuss which amongst a number of disputes and attitudes, each of which was regarded by different contemporaries or scholars as the cause of the conflict, was in fact the crucial issue. There is an alternative: the consideration of why, at a given moment, the range of hostilities and issues that made war a constant possibility, and conflict often a continual reality, led to serious hostilities, and also, by extension, why, for the most part, there was no such result. In short, in a situation of constant uncertainty, an international 'anarchy', there was a multitude of causes, but they were not the reason for the outbreak of war. Instead, it was necessary to concentrate on what have been termed triggers or precipitants, but to do so within a context that notes the degree to which such triggers are best discussed in terms of a cultural world that focused on conflict – in other words, bellicosity.

This was true of both international and civil war. Thus, in the case of England and Spain a whole series of hostile acts by both powers, including Francis Drake's attacks on Spanish trade, could have precipitated war long before it broke out in 1585. In Lebanon, in 1841,

> a Christian from Dayr al-Qamar was hunting with his gun on B'aqlīn land, and a Druze from there objected. Bad blood surfaced between them, and helpers came to both sides, the fray ending in the discharge of weapons. The cry reached Dayr al-Qamar that the people of B'aqlīn had killed their men, so the Nakad shaykhs got on their horses and rode to the place to quell the disturbance, and the men of Dayr al-Qamar too came armed and running. When they arrived they found the men of B'aqlīn gathered together and some men slain. Shots were fired and a fierce battle was fought until the B'aqlīn men were driven back with all those who had come to help them. The Dayr al-Qamar men did not leave until they had penned the B'aqlīn men in their village. Even after all this the shaykhs were still able to separate the two parties . . . The B'aqlīn Druze had been particularly

friendly with the Christians of Dayr al-Qamar, but this incident changed that and provoked all the Druze to take revenge.[28]

This they did, and Druze attacks on the Christians spread, although the major massacres did not occur until 1860. Lebanon was then part of the Ottoman (Turkish) Empire, so conflict between Christians and Druze did not count as war, in the sense of organized hostilities between sovereign states. Furthermore, at this level, it was not easy to distinguish between brawls or feuds and civil wars. However, any definition that requires sovereignty is not only excessively legalistic but also adopts a nineteenth-century Eurocentric view of the subject. There was a distinction between war begun by an imperial power, such as Ottoman Turkey, Safavid Persia, Mughal India and Ming or Manchu China, and war within the empire, but the latter could be large-scale, more so than external conflict, and could be regarded by contemporaries as war. Since each of these states rested on conquest, it is difficult to see why major attempts to overthrow them or to deny their authority should be regarded as sufficiently functionally and intellectually different not to be classed as wars.

In some cases the outbreak of serious hostilities within a country or, more commonly, between countries was clearly due to an act of state policy whose intended result was a major war. This was true, for example, of the Turkish invasion of Hungary in 1526. Suleiman the Magnificent was successful in provoking a major battle, Mohacs, in which Louis II and the bulk of the Hungarian elite were killed. The distribution of power in southeast Europe was radically altered, the way opened for the Turkish conquest of most of Hungary, and the decision to go to war amply vindicated.

However, it could be argued that war frequently happened, and happens, as a result of a series of acts whose intention was not to cause a major conflict or, at times, any conflict, and, indeed, the point at which these acts became a war was and is often unclear. A case could be made for discussing in these terms such major European conflicts as the Thirty Years' War (1618–48), the War of the League of Augsburg or Nine Years'

War (1688–97) and the War of the Spanish Succession (1701–14), each of which plays an important role in statistical and other accounts of major wars.

When Louis XIV invaded the Rhineland in 1688, he only intended a display of power that would compensate for diplomatic setbacks in the Palatinate and the Electorate of Cologne. These issues had become important tests of determination in a Europe where the respective strengths of the major rulers appeared to be altering considerably. There had already been a brief war between France and Spain in 1683–4, and by December 1686 circumstances were propitious for a war in the Rhineland.[29] What is interesting about the crisis of 1688 is not so much that it led to war but that the conflict proved to be a major one, and that despite the fact that the Austrians remained at war with the Turks. This was not what Louis wanted, and to a considerable extent it can be attributed to chance factors, in particular William III's seizure of Britain. His subsequent commitment of British resources to the defence of the Spanish Netherlands, a defence that Spain was no longer able to provide, played a central role in the continuation of the anti-French coalition. Thus, the crucial issue was not why Louis XIV intervened in the Rhineland in 1688, but why this had a response he had not anticipated. It has, also, been argued that Hitler did not intend to embark upon a major war when he invaded Poland in 1939, but, instead, that he was an opportunist seeking an easy gain.[30]

In such a perspective, war requires resistance, and a major war significant resistance. Thus Hitler's opportunism caused war in the autumn of 1939, but not that spring or the previous year, because the *Anschluss* and the overthrow of Czechoslovakia had not been resisted. Furthermore, the Anglo-French decision to continue the war after the conquest of Poland ensured that it remained a major conflict. This might be regarded as a foolish decision, although the impossibility of trusting Hitler suggests otherwise. The decision certainly helped to ensure that what might have been a limited war escalated.

In contrast, in 1788 the British Governor-General in India sent troops into the Circar, or fief, of Guntoor (Guntur), to which the East India Company had a claim, and, because the

Nizam of Hyderabad did not resist, there was no war. When Germany invaded Denmark in 1940, its vulnerable victim rapidly surrendered. In military terms, this was scarcely a war: a surprise attack by far-greater forces overwhelmed a pacifist government. A native government remained in office until 1943, and it was only then that resistance began.

An emphasis on the response to aggression does not imply an equality of responsibility or even, in judgemental terms, guilt. In 1914 France and Britain did not have to fight Germany, but the choice between doing so and accepting German hegemony had been forced on them by Austrian aggression and German willingness to support it.[31] Similar points could be made about the conflicts involving Napoleon[32] and Hitler.

If bellicosity and prudent consideration could both be involved in a decision to fight, they could also both be significant in the response. Bellicosity and other domestic factors ensure that relationships between means and ends cannot be comprehensively calculated. In addition, an apparent willingness to fight was crucial to the effectiveness of deterrence, but this effectiveness depended not so much on the documentation of alliances, that is, on their legal character, as on the sense that powers would be willing to fight – in short, their apparent bellicosity. Thus, the USA under Ronald Reagan (1981–9) appeared more likely to fight than under his predecessor, Jimmy Carter (1977–81).

The variation between intention and result is even more apparent in the case of civil, rather than international, wars. In the latter, what were often intended as shows of force, more akin to police actions or organized shows of defiance, became major steps in the outbreak of war. This was exacerbated by the possibility of governments using force without having to make, or intend, any declaration of war. More particularly, the absence of police forces ensured that troops were used to maintain order, as in Britain's North American colonies.

The argument of limited, if any, intentionality for war does not imply that the study of specific triggers of conflict should be discarded, but, rather, that it is necessary to match it by a full consideration of whatever is held to constitute the international 'system'. The latter comprised not only the range of interests and issues that divided and united states but also the attitudes that affected the conduct of policy, or, rather, the attitudes whose furtherance policies were designed to obtain. Furthermore, the 'system' can be seen as having a dimension that was less directly a product of the views and acts of individuals, still less under their ready control. This dimension can be usefully discussed in terms of structural – in other words, inherent – characteristics of the state system of the period, provided that it is not adopted as a mechanistic or reductionist analysis.[33]

One major problem with a systemic/structural approach is that it can lead to the argument of inevitable conflict. It is at this point that the crucial distinction between hostility and war is so useful. Hostile interests, whether economic, political, religious or ideological, do not have to lead to war. The conflicting political interests of Austria and France between 1648 and 1756, and their colonial and commercial counterparts between England and the United Provinces (Dutch) between 1609 and 1688, were both important in the wars between the respective powers, but they did not prevent peace. Furthermore, periods of peace between recent rivals were not simply opportunities to prepare for a fresh war. They could witness close co-operation, as between England and the Dutch in 1668 or Britain and France between 1716 and 1731. The co-operation did not have to be so close, but it could be such as to make it unclear that conflict was bound to occur. This was the case with Nazi Germany and the Soviet Union in 1939–41. Such developments cannot be fully explained by reference to a model that concentrates on systemic reasons for conflict or, instead, on clashing interests on the part of the two powers. If political differences drove Louis XIV to invade the United Provinces in 1672, they did not prevent close co-operation between him and William III of Orange in replanning the map of Europe in the partition treaties of 1698 and 1700.

Hitler's obsessive hatreds were more important in his decision to attack in 1941 than any more 'rational' explanation. Stalin had allowed Hitler to expand his control over much of eastern Europe, although not to the extent Hitler wanted, while the Soviet Union was supplying the German economy with valuable and valued raw materials that allowed it to lessen greatly the impact of the British blockade and to offset British economic strength. There were differences between Germany and the Soviet Union, particularly over Finland, Romania and Bulgaria, over each of which the two powers competed. However, it would not have been impossible to have arranged compromises or a *modus vivendi* based on spheres of influence, possibly rather similar to those which prevailed in Central and Eastern Europe from the late 1940s. Confrontation over an unstable intermediate zone between Germany and the Soviet Union did not have to lead to war. Their very ruthlessness made it easier to compromise at the expense of others.

Instead, the 'cultural' factor of Hitler's obsessive notions of racial and ideological superiority and inferiority was crucial. An attempt to establish a *modus vivendi* was made – led by the German foreign minister von Ribbentrop – in the autumn of 1940, but Hitler refused to provide consistent support. He was infuriated by the tough line taken by Molotov, the Soviet foreign minister, and subsequent Soviet proposals were ignored. Stalin took a firm line, perhaps because he thought the existing balance of forces could be exploited to improve the Soviet position in eastern Europe, and because he did not appreciate the imminence of German attack: insufficient allowance was made for Hitler's obsessional hatreds and wilfulness.[34]

Aside from the problem that systemic interpretations are better at accounting for rivalry than war, there is also the difficulty of establishing how a system is supposed to work. If a system and its development are defined, then it is all too easy to assume that events that correspond to the system are explained by it and prove it, and that those that do not are due to deviations from the model. In the case of international relations, such deviations can be explained in terms of the personal idiosyncrasies of particular rulers. Such an interpretation was employed in eighteenth-century Europe when accounting for the analytical faults of the contemporary model of international relations, one based on the concepts of natural interests and the balance of power.

To regard a war as a structural crisis in the international system because it occurred in a period of transition within that system, as is suggested in some systemic accounts of warfare, especially those that focus on the rise and fall of hegemonic powers, is to beg several questions. What if the war had not occurred? Are not all systems continually in a period of transition? Aside from being conceptually questionable, such theories are possibly too general to be of any particular use, and when they do descend to issues that can be discussed factually the results are often unfortunate. Britain was replaced as the leading maritime power by the USA without the two states waging war against one other. Tensions over Britain's colonial position did not prevent wartime alliances against other powers. Earlier, Britain had replaced the United Provinces in the same position without waging war between 1674 and 1780; again, the two powers had been allied. Furthermore, a model that places an emphasis on changes in one particular variable faces the difficulty that no one variable can indicate, let alone explain, state policy. There is, also, need for caution in the selection of individual variables, such as particular types of military spending, as crucial determinants of national strength.[35]

One of the more worrying aspects of the use of models is that they are sometimes employed by those who have clearly little interest in the surviving evidence concerning the conduct of affairs, evidence understood in terms of records of the views and policies of contemporaries. This may owe something to the impact of economic reductionism, or to the view of politics as epiphenomena, matters of limited and essentially transient significance, or to a sense, whether inspired by postmodernism or not, that contemporaries were unaware of the factors dominating and determining international relations.

Such an approach is of debatable value. A failure to consult archival material can lead to a schematic interpretation. Archival sources suggest that such interpretations are misleading, especially if more than one run of documents is read. The principal impression is that of the ignorance, uncertainty and unease of contemporaries, whether concerning the aspirations of other powers and their likely response to moves, or, indeed, the circumstances and characteristics of the state in question, the latter an important corrective to any subsequent concentration on ascertaining them. In place of glib assumptions about policy, archives permit us to glimpse the hesitations of the past, the choice between possible steps whose impact could not be assessed.

While eschewing determinist viewpoints, such an approach does not necessarily lead to a perspective in which it is assumed that policy depends exclusively on the views of governments. Nevertheless, it is these views that emerge as most significant in a study of the available documentation, necessarily so as it was produced by, for and about governments and was preserved by them. The Saxon envoy in Spain, for example, was instructed in 1725 to investigate ministerial views on foreign policy, court cabals, and the financial and military affairs of Spain, and was told that without understanding the internal state of a court it was impossible to form a sound judgement of its foreign policy.[36]

The crucial role of a small group of individuals ensures that in assessing the significance of *mentalités*, the effects of concepts such as glory and honour, and of ideas such as national interests and the balance of power, it is necessary to ascertain what they meant to specific individuals or groups at particular junctures.[37] Such concepts were neither uniform nor unchanging in their impact. Such specificity can subvert long-term models. It is difficult to incorporate in systemic models. More generally, it is difficult to locate *mentalités* in such models.

Study of these attitudes faces a number of problems. First, there is the tendency, in searching for long-term patterns and development, to offer a simplistic, not to say teleological, account. Secondly, there is the danger that modern criteria will be employed excessively. Thirdly, study of attitudes tends to concentrate on major European figures such as Erasmus and More, Grotius and Hobbes, Montesquieu and Rousseau, Clausewitz and Kant, and less effort has been devoted to assessing their impact. Arguably the subject suffers, as so many others do, from the great man obsession, the concentration on the ideas of a small number of usually atypical thinkers, a study facilitated by, and in some measure due to, the availability of their writings in print. A concentration on the views of political thinkers, rather than those of political actors, is particularly misleading.

Instead, it is more profitable to turn to governmental documentation in order to study shifts in attitudes towards international relations. Diplomatic archives are not usually regarded as a promising field for studies of political thought. They are exceedingly bulky; poorly, if at all, indexed; and the theoretical reflections they contain are fragmentary and peripheral to the often ephemeral nature of the reports. However, far from being unreflective, most diplomats were able and perceptive, and it was their job and their interest to understand the source, use and purpose of power.

One of the most striking and repeated aspects of discussion of international relations is the capriciousness which was seen to dominate them, the absence of system within the system. When asked to describe the greatest challenge that any British prime minister faced, Harold Macmillan, Prime Minister from 1957 until 1963, replied 'events, old boy, events'. Similar remarks have been made by many leaders.

However, the habit of seeing divine intervention at work in the affairs of mankind led many commentators to suggest that purpose underlay the apparent capriciousness of human affairs, that there was a morality, not an anarchy, in international relations. Commenting on the dramatic turns of fate that affected Peter the Great of Russia, defeated by the Turks at the river Pruth in 1711, and Charles XII of Sweden, shot dead in 1718 during a siege, George Tilson, a British under-secretary, wrote in 1722, 'a Pruth as well as a Frederickshall are the short ways Providence has to set bounds to ambitious and turbulent Princes'.[38] Nevertheless, although Providence might be seen to intend a moral order, it was far from clear that any predictable international system resulted. Indeed the very punishment of hubris that Providence might provide ensured that the only pattern could be cyclical, rise leading to fall.

Furthermore, it was apparent that religious systems could not prevent conflict, with all its unpredictabilities, between members, while they might actually encourage conflict with outsiders. This was the case with medieval and early-modern Christendom and Islam; and also with secular surrogates, such as the world of eighteenth-century European Enlightenment, or of twentieth-century aspirations towards a moral world order: the League of Nations and the United Nations. Thus, from the perspective of the prevention of war, religion was of limited value at the international level as an incorporating system, while divisions, both within and between societies, could be greatly exacerbated by religious differences.

The notion of capriciousness drew on the chance factors integral to dynastic politics, to military operations and, in a lesser degree, to the wealth of the community in the shape of the harvest. The unpredictability of the policy of individual states was, and is, a frequent theme in diplomatic correspondence, as was, and is, the rapidly altering nature of the 'system'.

Doubtless there were and are reasons why diplomats, unable to account for the activities of particular states, and rulers and ministers keen to avoid pressure to declare themselves, should refer to unpredictable change, but, nevertheless, the predominant impression is one of a perception of constant and kaleidoscopic change. In part, change can be seen as structural, a response to significant alterations in the international system. More common, in many cultures and contexts, was a sense not of structural change but of wilful unpredictability. William Fraser, a former British under-secretary, wrote in 1785 of 'these strange disjointed times. Where there is no system, but that of striving to . . . overreach'.[39]

Fraser was writing of Europe, but British commentators had similar views on Asia. In part, these were coloured by ignorance and a lack of sympathy, but many individuals had considerable experience of Indian politics. In 1787 John Shore, a senior official in Bengal, and later Governor-General, wrote that 'the motions of an Asiatic despot are not to be tied by the strictest rules of reason'.[40] The same theme of irrationality was echoed that year by William Kirkpatrick, British Resident with Mahadjī Shinde, one of the Maratha leaders. He wrote of a struggle involving Shinde:

> In the present case, when [the] conduct of either party is so little regulated by any fixed or steady principles of policy, and when so much depends upon a variety of contingencies which either do not occur or have not so much influence, in states further advanced in political and military knowledge, such conjectures are to be received with particular caution.[41]

This situation helped to produce an impression of an unstable, if not anarchic, international situation, with violence as an ever-present threat. This view, common in early-modern Europe, was central to one of the leading modern theoretical works on the causes of war, Kenneth Waltz's influential *Man, the State and War: A Theoretical Analysis* (New York, 1959). Waltz defined three levels of analysis – man, the state and the international system – and discerned a situation of anarchy in the last, which he regarded as a crucial level. A tense and uncertain international situation did not necessarily lead to war. On the other hand, it did encourage a constant anticipation of conflict. European ministers and diplomats frequently cited 'l'axiome des Romains SI VIS PACEM PARA BELLUM [if you want peace, prepare for war]'.[42] The attitudes this gave rise to were indicated in 1753 by a letter from the British envoy in The Hague to his brother:

> I think there can be no doubt, about declining the East India neutrality offered by France. She never would ask if it was for our advantage as much as her own, and I am clear that all treaties are useless with that power except those for a truce to be renewed from time to time; those of peace are merely nominal. She holds none of them, and whilst we act de bonne foi [in good faith], we are every hour the dupes of their double-dealing.[43]

This corrosive distrust helped lead to the vigorous pursuit both of alliance partners and of measures to retain their co-operation.[44] It also had an effect in encouraging the growth of armed forces in states that could afford them. Both, in turn, caused further insecurity on the part of other powers, producing a ratchet-like effect in which it was impossible to produce reassurance. In such a situation peace was maintained by fear, by the development of alliance systems and the deterrence they offered, but the same fear led to steps that encouraged the threat of war and made it difficult to view the moves of others with forbearance.[45]

Uncertainty, both in international relations and in their subsequent analysis, owed much to the problematic nature of the concept of national interest, for it was a concept that generally failed to place sufficient weight on the contingent and controversial nature of such interests. Nineteenth-century confidence in definitions of national interest, relating to territorial consolidation and expansion, domestic order and stability, and national strength, was of limited value, given disputes between politicians about the identity of such interests and about how best to pursue them. Such confidence is also of scant help for modern analysis of the situation in many countries where there was, and is, no constitutional, political or confessional consensus. In international terms, furthermore, even if there was agreement over national interests, it was far from clear whence the greatest opportunities and threats came, a situation more apparent today, after the end of the Cold War and the collapse of the American–Soviet bipolarity as a motor for structuring international relations.

The close involvement of foreign powers in domestic politics lent additional complexity to the situation over the last half-millennium. The intertwining of domestic politics and diplomatic developments was a characteristic feature of international and internal politics, was encouraged by the knowledge or suspicion that rival rulers were acting similarly, and made it even harder to define national interests. In the case of England, during the period from 1620 until 1672 she went to war with France once, Spain twice and the Dutch thrice. Volatility in English foreign policy was, in large part, a product of the volatility of English domestic politics, and hence encouraged foreign interventions in the latter: Spanish support for Catholics from the 1560s, a prominent Scottish role in the 1640s, Spanish intrigues with republicans in the early 1660s, and those of William III and the opposition in 1672–4, and of Louis XIV and the opposition in 1678.

The unpredictable nature of international relations, a systemic characteristic that owed much to the policies of individual states, encouraged war, although it also made the course of conflicts unstable because it was far from clear how other powers would respond; while this unpredictability ensured that the diplomatic consequences of wars were rarely lasting. This unpredictability of international relations both had to be accommodated to rationalist assessments of risk and opportunity and made such assessments suspect. The role of 'rationality', of the 'rational' calculation of interests and pursuit of objectives, is, indeed, contentious. It places a premium on the reasons for war as the explanation for their causes. Tim Blanning has argued that the reciprocal nature of war is crucial, that the victim of a predator has the option of submitting and avoiding war, and that both sides can exercise reason. In common with Geoffrey Blainey, whom he praises, Blanning has also claimed that the decision to prefer war to peace is taken by the two parties concerned because they have different assessments of their respective power.[46] Dismissing the notion of blame and the idea of attributing responsibility to one particular combatant, Blainey claimed that 'war is a dispute about the measurement of power'.[47] Such assessments can include a (mis)understanding of the international system, in particular the nature of alliances.

However, such a desiccated account of international relations and warfare is overly limited, not least because it underplays domestic pressures for war. As Quincy Wright pointed out, it is unlikely that war can be 'decided by highly intelligent generals without any bloodshed', [48] and in 1914, for example, the major powers had reasonably accurate information about the military capabilities and moves of the other powers.[49]

War was not a particularly effective way of testing the 'power relationship' between states. The problems of calculating power are matched by those of assessing what such calculations mean. The difficulty of ensuring victory, the rapidly altered nature of international alliances, and the potential role of domestic political considerations ensured that it was usually worthwhile for states, that felt themselves to be weaker, to fight or fight on. Although militarily outclassed by Germany, Poland fought in 1939, because the German demands were unacceptable to the government's sense of national integrity, honour and interest, in part because to accept all German demands would have discredited the government with its people, and, in part, because the international situation appeared not without hope. The relative emphasis that should be placed on these factors is difficult to evaluate and not open to mathematical formulation, and the very nature of an international crisis, the frequency of frenetic emotionalism, is such that a scholarly search for analytical precision may well be inappropriate. The German demands of October 1938 included the incorporation of Danzig in

Germany, a German-controlled corridor link with East Prussia and Polish accession to the anti-Soviet Anti-Comintern Pact. The German occupation of Bohemia and Moravia in March 1939 had led to British and French guarantees of Polish independence. The situation between France and Prussia in 1870 was not dissimilar, although it was Napoleon III who declared war.

Although it was, and is, possible to assess power in terms of the size of armed forces and the number of allies, such an assessment was, and is, both a poor guide to the results of a war and no reason why conflict should be avoided. It is possible to construct a general theory around this issue of different assessments, and to see the causes of war as resting on this point.[50] If a general theory is regarded as valuable, it is more appropriate, however, to draw attention to bellicist features of the culture, society and international system of particular periods, and to their impact on both 'risk preferences' and the action–reaction process of international disputes, in which one step provokes another, leading to, to employ the different images that have been used, a spiral, vortex or escalation, in which war results from this interaction.[51]

In addition, in many cultures, and, in what could be referred to as 'warfare societies', rulers and governing elites sought war, enjoyed conflict and felt they could profit from it. A French courtier referred in 1727 to 'le zele militaire [which] anime plus que jamais toute la nation'. [52] War has to be understood in terms of ideologies, elite roles, government and social purposes, sports and games. These explain how war was waged, why elites fought, and why wars began, and the latter three cannot be readily separated. This is a broader perspective than the argument that war arises from misperceptions, summarized in Blanning's view that 'it is the repeated inability of decision-makers to get their sums right which lead to repeated wars'.[53] Instead, Wright argued that 'false images depend not on misinformation about the immediate situation, but on prejudiced conceptions and attitudes rooted in distant history, in the national culture, or in the minds of important persons in the decision-making process'.[54] This prejudice can be seen in terms of the culture of the elite and the emphasis may even be seen as focusing Sigmund Freud's less specific argument that war was the violent reaction of the id to the repression of civilization.[55]

Furthermore, any emphasis on reciprocity, the notion of choice, and thus calculation, in the decision of both powers to fight – the claim that it takes 'two to tango' – is questionable. The history of imperialist wars suggests that violence was often a crucial aspect of the expropriatory character of imperialism; that, in short, the victims did not have a choice of submitting and avoiding war, because, whatever the legal definition, the process of war was seen as necessary and, frequently, desirable by the aggressor.

This was also true of wars designed to lead to the total overthrow of other powers within a particular international situation, as when a Dutch army under William III of Orange successfully invaded England in 1688 in order to drive William's uncle and father-in-law, James II, from the throne. Unpopular domestic policies had made intervention by William appear an option, at the same time as James's closer relations with Louis XIV seemed to make such intervention for William a desirable, even necessary, prelude to the resumption of Franco-Dutch hostilities. William's consideration of the situation was characterized by careful calculation. There was no failure to get the sums right; this was war for expropriation. In such a situation, a decision not to attack might be made on prudential grounds, as a result of an assessment of possible dangers, but the will to effect a major change will often lead to an interpretation of the situation in order to arrive at a more favourable assessment, or indeed to a determination to restrict the assessment to the question of planning 'when', not 'whether'. William himself had used force to seize power in the provinces of Holland and Zeeland in 1672 and to resist Louis XIV in the Dutch War of 1672–8. War was crucial to his purpose and *gloire*, and necessary to his ends. Thus, his calculations were predicated on the basis that war could be desirable.

Modern parallels to William's invasion can be seen in attempts to subvert or overthrow hostile governments, both during the Cold War and subsequently. This is true, for example, of the Middle East since World War Two.

A stress on bellicist practices and elements in culture and

society, Thomas Hobbes's 'will to contend by battle',[56] again risks the rejoinder that it might be an explanation of war, but not of wars. This can be countered, first, by suggesting that large-scale group fighting, a crucial feature of bellicist practices, is the definition of war, and, more specifically, that a dichotomy of hostility and war is not a helpful way of viewing relations between, and within, many states. To refer to bellicosity as a necessary condition for war is not, therefore, to confuse cause and effect, but to assert that in many circumstances the two are coterminous and that both are descriptive concepts.

Secondly, bellicist elements help explain why some disputes lead to war and others do not, and why, in particular, some rulers and governing elites accept, and even welcome, risk, which is important in establishing why particular situations lead to war.[57] The German decision to attack the Soviet Union in 1941 can be seen in this light, especially once attention is devoted to Hitler's views and psychology.

Similarly, the willingness to accept ambiguity and compromise varies greatly, and this willingness is of growing importance in disputes as the action–reaction process reveals incompatible goals. Bellicosity encourages a practice of hostility in which issues are treated as at once intractable and symbolic, and, thus, as encouraging bellicose attitudes as well as, more specifically, steps towards war. The transformation of disputes into crises, and of crises into war – indeed the very definition of crises as wars – depends not so much on the dispute in question as on how it is perceived. In short, bellicosity creates the severity of a crisis and then often ensures how it is handled. A tendency to resort to, or continue, violence is encouraged. In 1791 Earl Cornwallis, the British Governor-General and Commander-in-Chief in India, wrote to the prime minister, William Pitt the Younger, about the need to 'subdue' Tipu Sultan of Mysore:

> Perhaps the word subdue may appear too strong, but I have every reason to think that little short of absolute ruin will induce him to make such concessions and compensations to the confederate powers, as they could with the least regard to their honor or future safety accept.[58]

Six weeks earlier, Cornwallis had stated the necessity of the war:

I never entertained the smallest doubt of the absolute necessity of the war; we might perhaps have obtained a short respite from hostilities by abandoning our ally, and *soaping* our nose, but that would not long have secured us from being kicked . . . Being forced to have recourse to arms, without any alternative but the meanest and most contemptible submission to the insolent and unfounded claims of Tipu, I conceived it to be my duty to secure every advantage in my power.[59]

Thus, war seemed necessary, and, once began, it apparently had to be waged vigorously and to produce a clear-cut result, the last a victorious guarantee that conciliation would be difficult.

Bellicosity is crucial to the point that having a reason to fight does not necessarily entail action, and it is necessary to explain the latter as much as the former. Furthermore, the use of the concept of bellicosity, in part, overcomes the unhelpful distinction between rationality and irrationality in motivation and conduct. Bellicosity can be regarded as both, or either, a rational and an irrational response to circumstances. Such an argument, also, helps address the suggestion that while cultural factors act as an enabling force in allowing wars to happen, they do not cause them and that, instead, politicians have to want to go to war for some perceived benefit to the state.

Any explanation of war in a non-deterministic causal fashion depends on the reasoning of the participants. Such reasoning may well be deemed irrational by another view of rationality, as in the case of Hitler's racialism. However, the adequacy of explanation based on reasoning depends on the character of the evidence. This also involves interpretative issues, while, even if a particular episode can apparently be explained, it is difficult to translate either conclusion or method into an explanatory form which offers generalizations, predictions or universal concepts. The multiple nature of bellicosity – being an emotion, a system of, and approach to, reasoning, and an action (resort to violence) – not only makes for ambiguity but also ensures that the problem of evidence is especially acute. A considerable problem arises in distinguishing between the justification offered by participants for actions contemplated, or engaged in, and the 'real' reasons for the enterprise, in so far as the two are separable.

Declaratory policy, manipulative rhetoric, propaganda and appeals to popular sentiment are all used to conceal purpose. This is not an especially modern problem, although democracy and the media make it a particularly difficult one to unravel.

Rationality is citing and understanding the reasons for actions held by participants, but this is far from easy. Making these intelligible also entails engaging in some form of translation between times and cultures. The choice of ends for participants can only be understood in terms of their own values. The choice of means again depends on the participants' own rationale and on what they conceive as instrumental and appropriate.

The very use of the term 'rationality' may appear surprising, as miscalculations abound and enterprises using violence or its threat produce wholly unintended consequences. Without knowledge of the future, rationality can indeed be presented as irrationality, a rash and generally fruitless attempt to assess the future. However, there is a case for probability in limited forms of practical reasoning, and, while risk and change are inherent to the human condition, they do not preclude attempts to plan for the future. More specifically, although the success of participation in conflicts can be regarded as limited, for many rulers, elites and societies war itself is a role, a way of life, and thus a 'success'.

Bellicosity is also useful as an explanation of the continuation of wars once begun. If, for example, their outbreak is to be seen as arising from specific causes, or, indeed, as an accident, then it is pertinent to consider why so many have lasted for a long time and, indeed, spread. Many wars tend to have a life of their own, becoming a series or sequence of combats and changes of direction. This is especially true of world wars, but even more limited forms of war take place in a network of political action and reaction, often only loosely linked to, or even unconnected with, the initial clash. An explanation of the origin of a war, thus, should be an explanation not only of its outbreak but also of the subsequent conflict, and this requires an understanding both of socio-cultural structures and attitudes, and of the dynamic and processes of the subsequent developments. Consequences of action are other actions and decisions, and they depend for their meaning and significance on intentions and changes in these within the context of action. They are not external to this and cannot be treated as if they were. Thus, it is necessary to understand the view of the future that was the rationale of the actors, rather than to fit it into some linear continuum or conceptual framework.

An emphasis on bellicosity can also serve to highlight the degree to which warfulness and wars were as much the creators of states as their consequences. Much recent work has considered the relationship between war and state-building.[60] States, governmental systems and political practices, created or developed for, through and as a result of, warfare were likely to engage in war, and relationships between governmental activity, warfulness and military success can be suggested in many cultures.[61]

It is instructive to turn to *The History of the World-Conqueror*, an account of the career of the great Mongol leader Genghis Khan and his three successors, by Ata-Malik Juvaini, a Mongol official but also an orthodox Moslem, who explained Genghis Khan's invasion of Persia in 1218–19 as revenge for the execution of the Khan's envoys, but, also, as a scourge of God: 'He is the Avenger, and the glittering sword of the Tartar was the instrument of His severity'. The news of the execution 'had such an effect upon the Khan's mind that the control of repose and tranquillity was removed, and the whirlwind of anger cast dust into the eyes of patience and clemency while the fire of wrath flared up with such a flame that it drove the water from his eyes and could be quenched only by the shedding of blood'.[62] Juvaini was not present, but such an explanation appeared plausible to him and was the one he thought it appropriate to spread.

Reference to Genghis Khan might be regarded as anachronistic. He was a thirteenth-century conqueror and this book begins its coverage two centuries later, at the start of what is generally known as the 'early-modern period'. It is possible to see the Mongols as primitive or 'barbarian', the practitioners of a style of warfare and type of statecraft made redundant by the onset of modernity. The latter is often understood in terms of rationality, and, in the case of warfare, the implication is that an earlier chaos was replaced by a more ordered, if still violent, world, in which clear-cut sovereignty and the development of diplomacy brought regularity. Indeed, this development is commonly discerned, at least in Eurocentric accounts, in fifteenth-century Italy. The relations between states might still be very competitive, but practices of diplomacy and deterrence could bring a measure of order and stability, and it thus became possible to think of war as representing a breakdown of a system, caused by folly (hubris) or the failure of deterrence, but not as inherent to the system.

Such an approach, although comforting, faces a number of hurdles, not least the nature of European warfare over the last century. It also fails to note the degree to which the early-modern period saw not only European attempts to cope with the consequences of a multipolar state system without a hegemonic power, and to settle differences peacefully in such a context, but also the triumph of other military–political systems, for which war seemed necessary and a duty. Thus, the Ottoman Turks had a cult of holy war. When, in July 1997, I asked the Mughal specialist John Richards why the Mughal rulers of India went to war in the sixteenth and seventeenth centuries, he replied that they were at war all the time and used the analogy of a bicyclist to describe the Mughal empire and war: if it was not fighting it would collapse. Similarly, John Pemble wrote of the Gurkhas, who unified Nepal through warfare in the late eighteenth century, that 'their interests were almost exclusively martial, and they idealized conquest and valour in battle'.[63]

Such bellicosity did not mean that there was no element of choice of who and when to fight. Indeed, Turkish policy was entirely opportunistic within the context of the cult of holy war, while Gurkha opinion was divided over whether to fight the British in 1814.[64] Nevertheless, it was bellicosity that was crucial.

It is dangerous to assume that European states and state systems were necessarily different. Bismarck excused his wars by saying that he had to be true to the nature which God had implanted in him, just as the lion or tiger could do no other than behave according to their natures. He could, however, pursue peace with the same vigour that he applied to conquest, if he thought it *politique* to do so. To discuss an area not generally noted as particularly warlike, Italy contained a number of states after the 'Italian Wars' (i.e. after the Peace of Cateau Cambrésis of 1559) between the competing hegemonic rulers of western Europe, Henry II of France and the Spanish Habsburg Philip II. Of these, Venice generally only fought as a last resort, even against the threatening Turks; as opposed to the newly reorganized and aggressive state of Piedmont/Savoy, which appeared as the new Sparta and had strong, strategic imperatives in the early post-1559 period. In 1588 the Duke of Savoy successfully invaded the marquisate of Saluzzo. The factions within the Papal States continued to fight private wars, which often had the character of feuds and sometimes dragged in other parties. More generally, the rulers of early-modern Europe frequently eulogized conquerors of the past, holding them up as models. This was true, for example, of their treatment of Alexander the Great.

The combined role of domestic factors and cultural bellicosity in leading to war is particularly present in revolutionary situations. Then civil war often erupts into international war. Revolutionary states have often been bellicose because revolutions are frequently characterized by a paranoid sensibility in which there is little role for disagreement, debate and compromise. The steps taken by such states are also often seen as threatening by other powers that have no sympathy with revolutionary ideology.[65] In 1794 instructions were sent to Robert Liston, British envoy in Constantinople, asserting that barbarism within Europe had been reinvented in the French Revolution:

> In all your conferences with the Ottoman Ministers you cannot too strongly impress upon their minds the dangerous tendency of the avowed principles of the present French government if the most absolute anarchy can be so called, where the miserable people, deluded by the specious pretence of liberty, groan under the most despotic tyranny. Your Excellency will explain to them that those principles aim at nothing less than the subversion of all the established religions and forms of government in the whole world, by means the most atrocious which the mind of man will ever conceive ... without the shadow of justice, and in a manner unexampled in the history of the most barbarous and savage nations.[66]

In short, revolution was war – social and political war.

This paranoia affected attitudes both to Revolutionary France and to Communist states. However, hostile powers may indeed be correct. A determination to export revolution has been, and can be, important, and the definition of interests and methods by revolutionary states can, indeed, be threatening to others.

Conflict may also serve government interests on both sides of the revolutionary-established divide. It can serve to justify the monopolization of power, policy shifts and the mobilization of resources. Thus Mao Zedong was able to use confrontation with the USA in the Korean War (1950–53) in order to consolidate the position of the Communist Party within China and to push through land seizure.[67] As Cuba under Fidel Castro demonstrates, such confrontation does not have to take the form of war. Since 1960 Cuba and the USA have been bitterly divided, and this has led to subversion, economic warfare, propaganda offensives and hostile military interventions elsewhere – for example, the dispatch of Cuban forces to Angola. Yet, aside from the tacitly supported but rapidly disavowed 'Bay of Pigs' invasion, in which the CIA armed Cuban émigrés, there has been no American invasion of nearby Cuba. However, such confrontation contributes directly to a situation in which publicly demonstrated hostility is central to the ideology, rationale and practice of the state. Until the collapse of Soviet patronage, Castro's domestic and international position depended on American hostility.

It is clearly necessary to integrate an understanding of political culture with a study of particular conjunctures, to explain, for example, why the triumphal use of force in conferring greater acceptability on most rulers and bringing political success to ministers only leads to war in some circumstances. Such explanations need to encompass both endogamous and exogamous features, to explain both pressures and desires within particular states and aspects of their interaction. Thus, the military nature of the Argentinian government might have encouraged it to invade the Falkland Islands in 1982, but their sense that Britain would not respond, arising from the very small size of the garrison and the British failure to arrange deterrent naval patrols, was also important. The Argentinian government sought military success, not victory in battle.[68]

Similarly, the Iraqi regime of Saddam Hussein did not envisage much more than short operations when it invaded Iran in 1980 and Kuwait in 1990. Long-standing border disputes were important in both cases, as was the desire to improve Iraq's position in the oil industry, on which its economy was greatly dependent. Saddam needed more money to sustain his regime. However, such issues were by no means restricted to Iraq. Its warfulness was more important. The bellicosity of the regime was an element, as was a perception of the likely response of other powers.[69]

Saddam sought short and predictable wars, rather as Louis XIV and Hitler had done; but each was to find the conflicts he started difficult to contain. Equally, they were ready to use force against domestic opponents, or indeed elements of their population they thought hostile or unwelcome. This was true of Louis XIV and the Huguenots (French Protestants), Hitler and the Jews, and Saddam and the Kurds. The imposition of order in such cases reflects a sense that disobedience, or even difference, equates with disorder and, thus, danger. Violent regimes tend to have a low tolerance of disorder and anarchy, although their mode of operation creates both.

It is misleading to treat bellicosity and the response to foreign powers as separate. The very bellicosity of a government or society will encourage it to scapegoat foreign powers and peoples, and to emphasize reports of the international situation that favour a resort to force: 'warfulness' is a major cause of wars, aggressiveness of aggression. The question of whether bellicosity is a constant, at governmental, societal and systemic levels, is, therefore, crucial. Before turning, from a sketch of some of the main issues, to consider the chronological dimension in some detail, it is appropriate to begin with some general points. First, and most obviously, there is no easy measure of bellicosity. To assess it by counting the frequency and, in some way, measuring the intensity of warfare is only of limited value, most clearly because it does not consider bellicosity that does not lead to war.

Secondly, it is difficult to assess, certainly in any readily measurable fashion, the degree to which bellicosity and warfare are crucial, indeed integral, to particular governments, societies, states and international systems, and, in addition, to work out relationships between these particular categories. Nevertheless, it is possible to analyse both the composition and the culture of governing groups in order to ascertain their military interests and militaristic ethos. This can be seen as helping explain the resort to war. It has been argued, in the case of eighteenth-century Russia, and could be argued in many similar cases, that

> The high command was not merely an association of military leaders, it was also the political core of the ruling class. In preindustrial Russia, characterised by the enserfment of nearly half of the population and severe discrimination against the other half, the nobility . . . constituted a ruling class whose major goal was the distribution of responsible positions giving control over men and resources. The dynamism of that class was an important factor in the expansion toward the Black Sea, the Partition of Poland . . . the fraternity of officers and former officers was the unifying element of a ruling class . . . the high command, by virtue of its position as the political core of the ruling class, defined the options in foreign and domestic policy.[70]

Such a politics encourages a situation in which war is always an option, and this helps to increase the tension in any state of affairs. Furthermore, this socio-political context locates the role of economics. As military gain also connotes economic benefit in terms of territory and wealth, economics is, of course, a factor, but such benefit has to be considered more in terms of the interests of the governing elite than of any abstract consideration of national gain. These interests are as much psychological as financial.

Thirdly, the nature and causation of change in bellicosity are difficult to assess. One tempting analogy is that of sociability, the notion that individuals as they grow and mature become aware of the views and interests of others, accept self-discipline and become integrated into their community. This has classically been seen as crucial to childhood, although recent work on criminality in the West and its prevalence amongst young men has led to the suggestion that forming a stable relationship and acquiring employment in one's twenties is also important to this process. The wider social implications of this approach can be extended to include 'political' groups not otherwise integrated into the mainstream of social patterns and practices. This analysis was linked to the idea that settled peoples were inherently more pacific, and that, in contrast, those that were nomadic were more warlike – in short, that there was a relationship between social system and bellicosity, a sociology of violence that was linked to economics and environment, and a trajectory that was associated with social change. Such an interpretation places a premium on 'internal' rather than 'external' causes of war, on war as a product of domestic forces rather than the international system. Class theories of war, a prominent modern example of this approach, can thus be seen as a later example of a long-established view.

This view can be seen clearly in writers that have tackled global history. Thus, Edward Gibbon, in his *History of the Decline and Fall of the Roman Empire* (London, 1776–88), claimed that those he regarded as 'barbarians' were closer to the original state of man, and that this increased their military potency:

> In the state of nature every man has a right to defend, by force of arms, his person and his possessions; to repel, or even to prevent, the violence of his enemies, and to extend his hostilities to a reasonable measure of satisfaction and retaliation . . . The obvious causes of their freedom are inscribed on the character and country of the Arabs. Many ages before Mahomet, their intrepid valour had been severely felt by their neighbours in offensive and defensive war. The patient and active virtues of a soldier are insensibly nursed in the habits and discipline of a pastoral life . . . The arms and deserts of the Bedoweens are . . . the safeguards of their own freedom.

Similarly, in the seventh and eighth centuries, 'in Sardinia, the savage mountaineers preserved the liberty and religion of their ancestors; but the husbandmen of Sicily were chained to their rich and cultivated soil'.[71]

Given such a view, the processes of settlement, the development of an agrarian economy, and of specialization of function within society, can be seen as dissipating 'warriorism' – the cult of the warrior – and as creating a less bellicose culture and polity. To take the example of the Uzbeks of Central Asia, their nomadism was, increasingly, transformed in the sixteenth century into a dependence on agriculture and trade, this was linked to the growth of principalities, and the role of booty in Uzbek society and economy correspondingly diminished.[72]

This is very much a land-based account, although a maritime corollary is possible with fishing and piracy in the 'state of nature', and trade and less frequent warfare thereafter. As on land, the role of marginal communities and the often limited range of central authority were such that the notion of maritime war as a conflict between sovereign bodies is not helpful in a long-term perspective. Indeed, the sense of the sea as a separate sphere, in which hostilities could be tolerated without being seen as cause or aspect of formal war, generally remained the case across much of the world until the imposition of current European norms in a series of anti-'piracy' campaigns in the nineteenth century.

Settlement and civilization led to a loss of warlike virility. The theme was clear in Gibbon's work, and was related to his view that territorial expansion was dangerous not only for prudential reasons, namely that the state might become overextended as a force within the international system, but also because it posed a threat to the character and culture of the governing order. Gibbon presented conquest as weakening the Arabs:

> Had the impulse been less powerful, Arabia, free at home, and formidable abroad, might have flourished under a succession of her native monarchs. Her sovereignty was lost by the extent and rapidity of conquest. The colonies of the nation were scattered over the East and West, and their blood was mingled with the blood of their converts and captives.

The language used to describe the impact on the Mongols of their rule over China underlined his theme of the corruption of power:

. . . the Mogul army was dissolved in a vast and populous country . . . [Kublai Khan] displayed in his court the magnificence of the greatest monarch of Asia . . . His successors polluted the palace with a crowd of eunuchs, physicians and astrologers . . . One hundred and forty years after the death of Zingis, his degenerate race, the dynasty of the Yuen, was expelled by a revolt of the native Chinese; and the Mogul emperors were lost in the oblivion of the desert.[73]

Settlement in agrarian societies might, indeed, be linked to a diminution in bellicosity, but the history of the last two centuries scarcely suggests that 'developed' societies are necessarily pacific. William Robertson argued in 1769 that, from the turn of the fifteenth and sixteenth centuries, a systemic change in European society, namely the balance of power, had guarded against 'rapid and destructive conquests',[74] but such a benign view scarcely did justice to the role of European states in the following two centuries, both in attacking other polities elsewhere in the world and in causing bitter war within Europe. Social development did not lead to an end to war.

Possibly, therefore, it is appropriate to think in terms of a transformed bellicosity, of a situation in which societal and governmental pressures for violence and conflict are transformed so that they lead to more episodic warfare. In such an analysis, Germany in, say, 1890 would not be less bellicose than Central Asia in the fifteenth century, but this bellicosity would be differently expressed. Thus the question of the causes of war, in part, becomes that of the development of societies, states[75] and international systems.

ONE

1450–1650: An Age of Expansion

Leaving Cambray at four in the morning, which was
still and misty, I could not help contemplating the
then silent unoccupied battlements and solitary
ramparts, so often the theatre of bloody contentions
between people who could have no possible
inducement to cut one another's throats, but a
slavish adoption of the pride and caprice of their
own tyrants.

J. E. SMITH, *A Sketch of a Tour on the Continent*, I
(London, 1793), p. 62.

INTRODUCTION

Violence was endemic. It was a common means of settling disputes between individuals, groups, polities and peoples, and of
dealing with outsiders, including what has been estimated as
60,000 witches who were killed in Europe. This reliance on
force reflected the values of a group of societies that was more
prepared to accept violence than Western European society at
the close of the twentieth century. War appeared natural, necessary and inevitable, part of the divine order, the scourge of
divine wrath and the counterpart of violence in the elements,
as well as the correct, honourable and right way to adjudicate
disputes. War was the continuation of litigation by other means.
Rulers found less difficulty in getting people to fight for them
than would be the case now, although the terms of service they
offered might be rejected as unacceptable, leading to widespread desertion.

This was true not only of Europe. Modern attempts to argue
that the Europeans of the period had a unique propensity for

violence are misleading and should not serve to suggest a distinctive causation of war on that continent. War indeed appeared to be the norm. During his 42-year reign, Philip II of Spain was at peace for only six months. The situation was similar under his father, the Emperor Charles V, but it was not very different under the sixteenth- and seventeenth-century Mughal rulers of India, or in seventeenth-century China, or in West Africa.

A typology of war can be offered that distinguishes three main types of war: first, those between polities that derived from different cultures; secondly, those between polities that derived from the same culture; and thirdly, civil war. Thus, the first would include wars between the Ottoman Turks and Christian powers, while the second would address wars amongst the latter. The first type of war became far more common in this period as a result of European expansion, for that brought Europe into contact with North and South America and into direct contact with East Africa and South Asia.

This typology, however, hinges upon a workable concept of culture. One problem with concepts of culture is that they also change across time, and, consequently, there is no permanent concept of culture. Hence, a poor choice is offered: either to superimpose one particular concept upon any aspect of the past which happens to come under review, or to retain the changing concepts of culture that are to be found in the sources. The first fails to note differences in concepts of culture, the second reduces the communicability of what is being described.

Moreover, continuing distinctions between cultures may appear in different contexts and be used for different purposes. Cultural distinctions can be employed for purposes, and analyses, of integration or segregation. For the purposes of this study, with its emphasis on difference as a possible cause for conflict, although it is accepted that cultures can be variably defined, it is, nevertheless, apparent that contemporaries had a strong sense of such differences, and war played a major role in shaping cultural identities.

Human society was more disparate 500 years ago than is the case now, and to an extent that is greater than is readily conceivable today. The varied forces and mediums of global integration that have since become ever more powerful were absent. As a result, it was possible to imagine strange animals and humans and unusual social practices in different parts of the world. The discovery of difference, and what was defined as difference, were to be particularly intense as a result of the European voyages of exploration.[1] It was less marked on land because there was, generally, knowledge of neighbouring societies.

Wars across cultures did not arise as a simple consequence of difference, but it was far harder to solve difficulties in such cases. In explaining conflict it is possible to focus on difference, as, particularly, with the contrast between settled agrarian societies and their nomadic pastoral counterparts. This contrast can be seen as basic to conflict across Eurasia, whether the raids of Tatars on Muscovy or those of the Mongols on Ming China in the sixteenth century. This approach can be extended to consider comparable disputes in Africa and the New World.

Fear of the horseman, of the raiders from the steppe, played a major role in the consciousness of settled societies, especially those of Christian Europe, northern India and China. This fear looked back to over a millennium of repeated attacks and was a testimony to the military potency of, in particular, mounted archers. Indeed, it is possible to portray the period from 1450 until 1800 as the last, and by no means least, stage of the onslaught of the horse-people. In 1526 the Mughals from Afghanistan brought down the Lodi Sultanate of Delhi. Over the following 150 years they went on to conquer northern and central India. In 1571 Moscow was raided for the last time by the Crimean Tatars. In the 1640s the Manchus captured both Beijing and much of northern China, following with southern China in the 1650s. The horse-people acquired muskets and did not find that gunpowder weaponry required a developed system of central goverment or sedentary agriculture. In the 1720s the Afghans overthrew Safavid Persia and from 1752 until

1761 they successfully invaded northern India. Many Eurasian wars thus seem an inevitable product of clashing socio-political systems.

Yet such an analysis has been challenged by the recent work in frontier studies, not least that of relations between China and its neighbours. Analysis of raids on China by steppe people have emphasized their quest for politically useful luxury goods rather than subsistence, and have stressed that the steppe people raided to build alliances and to force the acceptance of commercial links. The relationship between the Russian princelings and the Tatars from the thirteenth to the late fifteenth century has also been presented in symbiotic terms.[2]

This work suggests that frontiers were generally zones of interaction and that conflict was only one part of the interaction. Trade and other aspects of symbiotic behaviour were, also, very important. Furthermore, nomadic attacks frequently arose because the commercial and other relationships had been disturbed or the terms were no longer acceptable to one party; in short, they were not the 'natural' characteristic of the relationship but a product of its failure, as with the Ming refusal to trade with the Mongols in the mid-sixteenth century, a refusal that has been traced to xenophobia and a determination to appear strong.

This is an important analytical shift, for it leads to the rehabilitation of the 'barbarian', no longer seen as product and part of the inchoate 'other', against which civilization must defend itself, but, instead, part of the world of civilization. If a rationality, other than that of the most basic, is ascribed to 'barbarians', this can be linked to a re-evaluation in which they enter into wars, rather than being in a permanent state of war.

A similar re-evaluation is possible in the case of cross-cultural conflict between, for example, Christendom and Islam,[3] or the Mughal empire and the Hindu polities of southern India. It is possible to complement an understanding of long-term antagonisms with a realization of the degree to which these did not preclude periods in which conflict was localized and, essentially, limited to frontier differences and groups.

That was not, of course, the ideological message of either side. In Islam the notion of *jihad*, war with the infidel, was

actively propagated and the shedding of Moslem blood was prohibited, while in Christendom there was a continual sense of an
Islamic threat, and a continuation of Crusading ideology and
practice.[4] In China, some officials opposed any conciliation of
Mongols and Manchus as capitulation to barbarians.

The perception of menace led not only to military and diplomatic measures but also to domestic counterparts, most obviously the Spanish expulsion, first, of Moslems and, later, of
converts to Christendom who were regarded as a potential fifth
column, culminating in the 1609 banishment of the Moriscoes.
The surveillance and persecution that the latter suffered, before
they were brutally expelled, was a form of 'internal war'. More
generally, identities were challenged by persecution and
forcible conversion. Sacred landscapes were seized, as mosques
and churches were expropriated and converted to rival purposes,
while shrines and graveyards were destroyed.

Yet, although neither Christendom nor Islam in this period
readily lent themselves to syncretic practices in their zone of
contact, it is also striking to see how it was possible to 'create'
international relations between their states and to reach a *modus
vivendi*, how the contested borderland of one year became the
long-established frontier of a half-century later. This was especially notable as the Ottoman advance in Europe ebbed, in
Hungary from the late 1560s and in the Mediterranean world
from 1574. The mercantile republic of Venice, which had long
experience of reaching accommodations with Islamic powers,
was only too ready to settle disputes with the Turks. Furthermore, the Turks ruled large numbers of Christians, especially,
but not only, in the Balkans, without embarking on genocidal
practices or 'ethnic cleansing'. Indeed, their system of autocratic,
but delegated, government could readily adapt to the rule of
non-Moslems.

Any sense of continual cross-cultural conflict had to be tem-
pered by the multiple commitments of different powers and
their consequent need to choose between different policy
options. Despite their ideal of world empire, and the belief that
a permanent state of war existed between Islam and the infidel,
there was nothing inevitable for the Ottomans about conflict
with Austria or Spain; instead, until 1639, Safavid Persia was

frequently a more pressing opponent. Selim I, 'the Grim', advanced on Tabriz, not Belgrade, in 1514; Suleiman the Magnificent took Iraq in 1534–5 rather than maintaining his pressure on the Habsburgs in Hungary. Selim's most extensive gains were obtained from an Islamic power, the Mamluk empire: Syria, Palestine and Egypt were conquered in 1516–17.

Ottoman Turkey was an expanding power, keen to obtain territory in order to provide fiefs, and with an ideology that glorified war. It, therefore, represented a very different polity, and military, from raiders who essentially sought booty, especially slaves. Some of the latter were linked to the Ottomans, for example the Crimean Tatars and the Barbary corsairs of North Africa, while their opponents could call on the Knights of St John, from Rhodes and, later, Malta, and, to a certain extent, on the Cossacks and, in the Adriatic, the piratical Uskoks of Senj. Such raiders tended to maintain a high level of violence; indeed, conflict was integral to their economy and *raison d'être*.[5] The economy of Senj was based almost entirely on plunder. To supply the town, the Uskoks needed regular and profitable booty – or regular payments from tributaries in exchange for not raiding. The Uskoks, who came from the Croatian–Ottoman border area, interpreted their circumstances in terms of the imperatives of holy war, the ideal of honour and the right to vengeance.

However, such warfare lacked the scale and, frequently, intensity of the operations of the Ottoman or Spanish forces, and the Uskoks could be seen as more akin to brigands than to competing states. There was a difference between *ghazi* warfare, the Moslem system of perpetual raiding of the infidel, and wars of imperial campaign,[6] as there was also, for example, between the raiding across the Anglo-Scottish border in the fourteenth and fifteenth centuries, and the campaigns of royal armies, such as James IV's invasion of England in 1512. Piracy, or robbery at sea, was possibly nearly as common between Christians in the Channel as in the Mediterranean and was, perhaps, more an unavoidable hazard of sea-borne trade than evidence of a state of war between nations, states or creeds.

The difference between *ghazi* and imperial warfare raises, anew, the question not only of the definition of war and warfare but also of their relation to state and social development. The fifth-century Church-father St Augustine's comparison, in his *City of God*, of Alexander the Great and a company of thieves – 'in the absence of justice there is no difference between Alexander's empire and a band [*societas*] of thieves' – was a moralist's vain attempt to argue that intentionality, not scale, was the crucial issue, and that sovereignty was not a legitimator of slaughter.[7] If a key issue with warfare is how it is possible to persuade people to kill, and run a strong risk of being killed, then there was not much difference, in the sixteenth century, between regular 'state-directed' warfare and its *ghazi*, indeed piratical, counterparts. The organized killing of humans was central to both, even if the objectives behind this killing were different. 'States' were inchoate, and not generally seen as enjoying the right to monopolize warfare and alone to legitimate conflict.

European expansion reflected a number of differing causes and purposes, and these had different consequences in terms of military activity and the degree and type of formal hostilities. One crucial difference was people. In areas where Europeans went in some numbers they sought land – land to cultivate, or at least control, and profit from the cultivation. This was true of North and South America, as well as of the Portuguese in Mozambique. Where the demographic and economic rationale was different, then the Europeans essentially sought a different type of control. The Portuguese sought to dominate the trade of the West African littoral and of the Indian Ocean, a policy that, in the latter, led them to destroy opposing fleets, especially those of Calicut, Egypt, Gujarat and the Ottoman Turks, and to seize bases, such as Goa and Malacca. They did not seek to conquer large areas of the mainland, and, once they had seized bases, there was no attempt to use them in order to overrun the hinterland. Thus, the acquisition of Mina or Ormuz was not followed by an expansionist policy in Guinea or southern Persia.

Such a model of imperial activity depended on force in order to establish bases and maintain a commercial monopoly, but, thereafter, war was undesirable, unless waged in order to enforce and maintain the monopoly. In other circumstances, war was the antithesis of trade and the enemy of profit. As a consequence, the Portuguese presence in the Indian Ocean was striking for the limited nature of the wars it gave rise to. Most were short-term and much of Portugal's military activity arose from its involvement with struggles amongst local rulers. By their nature, these commitments tended to be short-term and 'prudential', motivated by a sense of specific advantage rather than by an ideology of control or a practice of conquest – although that did not preclude a growing practice of territorialization nor projects for widespread conquest.[8]

A European emphasis on trade can be seen elsewhere, including on the west coast of Africa and around Hudson Bay in northern Canada. In each case, Europeans sought to exploit economic resources, such as slaves, gum arabic and furs, that could only be obtained if natives were willing to trade with them. There was no possibility of conquering large areas, and no purpose to it: territory without economic co-operation was of scant value. Indeed, in West Africa, the Europeans approximated to an African political model of political identity as a people, nation or tribe rather than a piece of territory. The European 'tribes' were restricted to their coastal positions, although, as in North America, their commercial exigencies and provision of firearms could greatly affect the situation in the interior.[9] This was particularly so with the slave trade.

The situation in Siberia was different. There, the pursuit of resources, in this case furs, led the Russians to abandon an interest in obtaining them through trade, and, instead, to seek to subjugate the native peoples and to force them to provide fur as tribute. In one respect, this economic rationale was similar to that of the Portuguese in the Indian Ocean – the use of force for the sake of profit – but, in Siberia, where the demographic and military balance was far more to the favour of the Europeans, it was accompanied by a degree of force and expropriation that can only be described as continual war. This continual war led the Russians to the Pacific and left them in control of much of Siberia by 1650.[10] Russian expansion was marked by great brutality and was characterized by a total contempt for the views of the indigenous population, who were treated as subhuman. Similarly, cruelty was also displayed in many other episodes of early-modern conquest, for example the actions of the Portuguese in Brazil.

Russian expansion in Siberia also entailed the assault of new diseases on the native population. This was an important aspect of European activity in the early-modern period, seen most obviously in North and South America. The indigenous population of both fell dramatically, as a result of diseases such as smallpox.[11] It is possible to use the term ecological war to describe the process, and, also, the destructive impact of disease on European expansion in tropical areas, such as the Zambezi valley, but such a description is of limited value in the present study which is concerned with war as a deliberate and organized form of violence amongst human beings.

Another major difference affecting European expansion, and offering the possibility of a tenuous typology, was the distinction between activities under state 'control' and those where governmental direction was far more limited. Initial Russian activity in Siberia was a good example of the latter. Merchants, particularly the Stroganovs of Novgorod, played a crucial role. An 800-strong Cossack force under Yermak Timofeyevich, in the service of the Stroganovs, advanced in 1581 and conquered the Tatar Khanate of Sibir in 1582, opening the way to further expansion. Similarly, in the New World, Spanish *conquistadores* were essentially adventurers seeking cities to plunder and bullion to loot. Once victorious, they established *encomiendas*, large estates. Their political thought was encapsulated in the expression 'Dios está en el cielo, el rey está lejos, y yo mando aquí' [God is in Heaven, the King is far away, and I give the orders here]. The Portuguese adventurers who established themselves in the interior of Mozambique were very similar. Short of European women, they also 'intermarried' with the local population, so that by 1650 to use the term Portuguese to describe the elites of such Portuguese colonies as Goa, Mozambique and Muscat is an unhelpful account of their ethnicity. Yet, it may describe their culture. This indicates the problem of defining relations in terms of different or overlapping cultures.

With adventurers, such as those in Mozambique, it is inappropriate to think in terms of declarations of war. These declarations might remain a prerogative of sovereign power, but the warfare of such groups did not require them, and was, instead, an aspect of their existence, a form of the seizure and control, of land, people, revenues and goods, that was their life.

Trans-cultural wars were not caused by differences in culture. Such differences might be responsible for hostility and for affecting the conduct of war, for example by encouraging or facilitating slaughter, enslavement or expropriation, as in Brazil or Siberia, but that was not the same as causing war, and, anyway, there were many examples of such differences being fruitful, as in patterns of economic specialization and exchange, both long-standing and more recent. Furthermore, within Spain, there was an academic debate on the extent of the right of conquest, with some scholars and theologians trying to limit this and denying Spain the right to enslave the Indian population. There was a distinction between European encounters with Asia and Africa, and those with the New World. In the former case, Europeans were aware of the existence of Asian and African peoples who could be classed as 'infidels' or 'pagans'. But the New World peoples were neither, since they had never had the opportunity to become Christian. Therefore they raised unprecedented moral and religious questions in the minds of Europeans. Europeans used violence against them, but in so doing provoked protests from the Catholic Church.[12]

Cultural differences could encourage conflict for a number of related reasons. Major cultural contrasts could be perceived as a serious violation of order, most usually divine order, that encouraged ideological pressure for war. In such a situation, the defiance of heavenly, or other, order could be seen as an act of violence that required correction. Thus, the very presence of infidels apparently necessitated purging them from the community and polity. The 'aggressor', therefore, was not the persecutor, but rather the individuals, groups or polities that defied order. These attitudes looked forward towards twentieth-century genocide, an aspect of internal conflict, if not war, that again raises the question of whether differences in war and its causes should primarily be related to changes in state and social 'development'.

Secondly, such cultural contrasts could make it more difficult to negotiate differences and to arrive at compromises, or even to define what might be meant by compromise – a problem, most obviously, demonstrated by difficulties in communication arising from different languages or different understandings of terms. Thirdly, such contrasts could lead powers to define their actions as if they were not dealing with comparable polities,[13] or even people with any rights. Thus, Europeans used Roman law notions of the right to take control of empty lands, and of the contrast between 'barbarians' and civilization, in order to justify the seizure of territory, as in North America.[14] Furthermore, it was possible to treat organized violence against 'barbarians' not as war but as policing actions that were not governed by the conventions or assumptions that affected the conduct of war. The availability and, at times, dramatic impact of gunpowder weaponry led to a sense of superiority that encouraged aggression. Enslavement can be seen as a form of war and, indeed, as one of the most important aspects, consequences and, sometimes, causes of trans-cultural conflict.

WARS WITHIN CULTURES

The distinction between trans- and intra-cultural conflicts is somewhat arbitrary, because so much depended on the perspective of participants. To Europeans, wars amongst Islamic powers were intra-cultural, and this was indeed the case with the Ottoman–Mamluk wars, such as that of 1485–91, which was essentially a struggle for hegemony in the Near East, or the struggle between the Mughals and the Lodi Sultanate of Delhi in the 1520s for control of northern India. However, the bitter struggles between Ottoman Turkey and Safavid Persia involved, in part, the conflict between two different conceptions of Islam: the Sunni and the Shiite. This divide, and the attendant conflicts, were continued by the successors of both regimes, whether Nadir Shah of Persia in the 1730s and 1740s[15] or the post-colonial regimes of Iran and Iraq, most recently in 1980–88. A similar point could be made about conflicts between Protestant and Catholic powers from the sixteenth century, and between both and Russian Orthodoxy. The language, hitherto, used by Europeans against Islam, especially against the Ottoman Turks, was turned, in part, instead, against Christian opponents.

Most typologies entail a measure of arbitrary differentiation. In the case of wars within cultures in this period, the defence is that, however serious the ideological differences, there was both a measure of understanding of differences in opinion and interest, and shared conventions and parameters of behaviour in diplomacy and war. Thus, in India, the process of aggregation and disaggregation by which alliances and armies expanded and collapsed was far easier in areas of similar culture, such as the Deccan or Rajputana, than across cultural divides, for example between the Mughals and the Ahom of the Brahmaputra.[16] The same was true of the Manchu conquest of China in the 1640s and 1650s. By then, the Manchu had incorporated sufficient Chinese governmental practices and allied with enough senior figures in the Ming system to qualify any clear-cut sense of distinction and contrast.[17]

In China and, to a lesser extent, India, there was a major power that dominated regional political and ideological culture. It was still necessary to adjust to other powers, as the Chinese had to do, for example, with Japan, Korea and the polities of Indo-China, but geopolitical dominance and a sense that invulnerability was normal were linked to assumptions about the proper operation of international relations. The nature of international relations and warfare was different in Christian Europe where there was no hegemonic power and where the theory and practice of a balance of power developed. Indeed, the multipolarity of the European states system (if indeed the term state can helpfully be used in this period), the anarchic nature of European power politics, and the kaleidoscopic character of alliances there, all help to account for the development of 'realist' paradigms of international behaviour, for European and European–American experiences and conceptions of international relations were to dominate subsequent writing on the subject.

The absence of such a hegemonic power in Europe was entrenched as a result of the Protestant Reformation of the sixteenth century. Thanks to the Reformation and the subsequent Catholic Counter-Reformation, the early-modern period in Europe can in part be defined as the age of religious wars. However, the expansion of the Ottoman Turks, and the conflicts between Abyssinia and Adal in the Horn of Africa, and between Portugal and Islamic powers, such as Egypt, Morocco, Aceh in Sumatra, and the Turks, emphasize the degree to which religious conflict should not only be discussed in terms of the Reformation. This was also true further afield. The unifier of Japan, Takeda Nobunaga, used particular brutality in the 1570s to extirpate the forces of religious confederacies, such as the Pure Land confederacy, seeing their opposition as more serious than that of other warlords. In the following century, the Tokugawa Shogunate set out to extirpate Christianity, leading to an unsuccessful Christian rebellion in Kyūshū in 1637–8.

Religious differences alone were not responsible for the high level of conflict in sixteenth-century Christian Europe, but they contributed to it, in struggles between and within 'states', and in both long-lasting and smaller-scale conflicts. Alongside well-known wars, such as those from 1585 until 1604 between Philip II of Spain and Elizabeth I of England and their successors, there were many others in which religious hostility played a role, such as the seizure in 1542 of the Duchy of Brunswick-Wolfenbüttel by the leading German Protestant rulers, the Elector of Saxony and the Landgrave of Hesse, and the resistance to growing English control in Ireland.

Wars were rarely fought for exclusively religious reasons, but religion was important in transforming local conflicts into either general European ones or, at least, into national conflicts. In the late fifteenth century, politics and warfare in, for example, northern Germany were only loosely connected to events in southern Germany. With growing confessional antagonism, at least from the 1530s, every local or regional conflict in which opponents were involved who subscribed to different confessional options, which was nearly always the case, assumed a far greater nationwide importance. Alliances were formed comprising many, if not all, members of a confessional group nationwide. Confessional antagonism created a national, as opposed to regional, framework for conflict in Germany and Scotland, and in France after 1560.

Doctrinal and ecclesiastical disputes, giving rise to tension and conflict between Christian powers, were not a novel product of the Reformation. Indeed, they had been central to relations between Byzantium and Western Christendom, although conflict had been episodic. Had the Protestant north-German princes been defeated by the Habsburg Emperor Charles V, as indeed seemed possible in 1547, then the Reformation would have been more clearly seen in a pattern of medieval politico-religious disorders, and Western Europe might well, even if only temporarily, have had a hegemonic power. Bullion from the New World could have been used to sustain the traditional universalist aspirations of the Holy Roman Emperors, a functional hegemony created by a long-standing ideology and new economic, or at least fiscal, resources.

However, the burden of pressures and commitments proved too great for Charles's *imperium*, in part because of divisions amongst the Catholic powers. The defeat of the German Protestants at Mühlberg in 1547 was reversed. French willingness to support the German Protestants in the early 1550s and to ally with the Turks set a pattern for the early-modern period in which warring blocs did not equate with religious divisions. Thus, in the Thirty Years' War (1618–48), although religious differences helped to cause and exacerbate disputes,[18] the French supported the Protestant Dutch against the Spanish Habsburgs and the Protestant Swedes against the Austrian Habsburgs, and, in the 1650s, they allied with the Protestant, republican, usurpatory regime of Oliver Cromwell against Catholic, monarchical and legitimist Spain.

The 'Rump' – the Protestant republican parliamentary regime that preceded that of Cromwell – had, itself, attacked the Protestant republican Dutch in the First Anglo-Dutch War of 1652–4. The latter has traditionally been explained as a mercantilist struggle largely due to commercial and colonial rivals. However, the most recent study, both of that conflict and of the Second Anglo-Dutch War of 1665–7, has offered a radical reinterpretation that emphasizes ideological issues. Prefiguring discussion of rifts between Communist regimes from 1949, first Tito's Yugoslavia and the Soviet Union, and later the Soviet Union and China, the First War is explained in terms of the hostility of one Protestant, republican regime towards a less rigorous counterpart.

Rump politicians and their supporters quickly concluded that the recent republican revolution in the United Provinces had not offset decades of political corruption promoted by the absolutist Princes of Orange. Until the Lord had shown them the rod, many in England reasoned, the Dutch people would follow the sinful Orangist policies of material self-interest and alliance with the Antichristian House of Stuart. The English were compelled to fight the Dutch in the 1650s to defend their own state against the assaults of monarchy and irreligion, against Orange and Mammon.[19]

A seventeenth-century Catholic counterpart was provided by Austria and Bavaria. That ideological divisions existed within cultural areas, but did not prevent alliances across them, ensured that there is a degree of similarity between trans- and intra-cultural wars. Again, in both cases, the bellicist nature of societies was important, as was the accentuated role of prominent individuals that was the consequence of dynastic monarchy. A habit of viewing international relations in terms of concepts such as glory and honour was a natural consequence of the dynastic commitments and personal direction that a monarchical society produced. It reflected traditional notions of kingship and was the most plausible and acceptable way to discuss foreign policy in a courtly context. Such notions also matched the heroic conceptions of royal, princely and aristocratic conduct in wartime, and this was true in different cultures, not least Christendom, Islam and Japan. Past warrior-leaders were held up as models for their successors. The example of Henry V of England was a powerful one at the court of Henry VIII, Edward III's victories over France were a touchstone, and Henry IV of France was represented as Hercules and was a model for his grandson, Louis XIV.

Similarly, aristocrats looked back to heroic members of their families who had won and defended nobility, and thus social existence, through glorious and honourable acts of valour. These traditions were sustained, both by service in war and by a personal culture of violence in the form of duels, feuds and displays of courage, the same socio-cultural imperative underlying both the international and the domestic sphere.[20] This imperative was far more powerful than the cultural resonances of the quest for peace: the peace-giver was generally seen as a success-ful warrior, not as a royal, aristocratic or clerical diplomat.

Most rulers sought to live up to dynastic models. To take the rulers of France, Charles VII (1422–61) ended the Hundred Years' War by driving the rulers of England from France; Louis XI (1461–83) defeated Charles the Bold of Burgundy; Charles VIII (1483–98) invaded Italy in 1494 in pursuit of the future goal of a crusade against the Turks; Louis XII (1498–1515) took part in the 1494 invasion, and campaigned extensively in Italy, defeating Ludovico Sforza at Novara (1500) and the Venetians at Agnadello (1509), only to be defeated by the Swiss at Novara (1513); Francis I (1515–47) invaded the Milanese anew, defeating the Swiss at Marignano (1515), only to be defeated and captured at Pavia (1525) and to attack the Habsburgs again in 1536 and 1542; and Henry II (1547–59) attacked the Habsburgs in 1552, and in 1557 broke a truce with them in order to invade Italy. The rulers of France were unwilling to accept the primacy of the Habsburgs. It challenged both their interests and their prestige.

Their great opponent, the Emperor Charles V (1519–56), campaigned not only against the French and the Turks but also captured Tunis (1535), unsuccessfully attacked Algiers (1541) and defeated the German Protestants in 1547. Charles was not a reluctant fighter. His son, Philip II, was brought up for a military role, and, in 1557, threw himself into organizing the campaign that led to victory over the French at St Quentin, a triumph given lasting form in the palace erected at the Escorial. He followed this up by leading the successful storming of Arras. Thereafter, however, he played no direct part in military opera-tions, leaving the invasion of Portugal (1580) and the suppres-sion of the Morisco (1568–70) and Aragonese (1591) revolts to others.[21]

In 1578, in contrast, Sebastian of Portugal was killed at the battle of al-Qasr al-Kabir, leading his army in a dangerous and disastrous invasion of Morocco. Much of the Portuguese aristocracy was also killed. Further east, Ivan III, Grand Prince of Moscow (1462–1505), spent much of his life at war. He conquered Novgorod and Tver, defeated Kazan, the Golden Horde and Lithuania. His son, Vasily III (1505–33), similarly fought the Crimean Tatars and Lithuania, while Ivan IV, the Terrible (1533–84), conquered the Khanates of Kazan (1552) and Astrakhan (1556), and fought Lithuania, Poland and Sweden in the long Livonian War (1558–83).

John Hale was inaccurate in claiming that by 1611 personal royal service in wartime in Europe 'was coming to be considered something of an eccentricity'.[22] This would have amazed subsequent monarchs and members of their families, both in the Thirty Years' War and later, for example Gustavus Adolphus of Sweden, Maximilian I of Bavaria and Louis XIV of France. It was also not true of the Ottoman, Mughal and Safavid dynasties.

The pursuit of land and heiresses linked the monarch to his peasants. As wealth was primarily held in land and transmitted through blood inheritance, it was natural at all levels of society for conflict to centre on succession disputes. Peasants resorted to litigation, a method that was lengthy and expensive, but to which the alternative was largely closed by state disapproval of private violence. Monarchs resorted to negotiation, but the absence of an adjudicating body, and the need for a speedy solution once a succession fell vacant, encouraged a decision to fight. Most of the royal and aristocratic dynasties ruling and wielding power in 1650 owed their position to the willingness of past members of the family to fight to secure their succession claims. The Tudors defeated the Yorkists to win England in 1485, the Bourbons had had to fight to gain France in the 1590s, the Austrian Habsburgs Bohemia in 1621, the Braganzas Portugal in the 1640s, William III to gain the British Isles in 1688–91, and the Romanovs to hold Russia in the 1610s. Battles such as Bosworth (1485) and White Mountain (1620) were crucial in this process. The Princes of Orange owed their position in the United Provinces to the success of the Dutch Revolt. The Vasas fought to gain Sweden in the 1520s and 70 years later to remove a Catholic Vasa: Sigismund was deposed in 1599, having been defeated the previous year at Stangebro by his uncle Charles, who eventually became Charles IX. The Portuguese invasion of Morocco in 1578 stemmed from a succession dispute within the Sa'di dynasty after the death of al-Ghalib. His successor, Muhammad al-Mutawakkil, defeated and driven out by his uncle, Abd al-Malik, fled to Portugal. Angola was convulsed in 1624–63 by what has been termed the War of the Ndongo Succession.[23]

The Ottoman, Safavid, Mughal and Ming 'states' were all based on violence. Such warfare was not restricted to the initial establishment of dynasties, before the rulers' households were supplemented by more bureaucratic institutions. In addition, several Mughal rulers had to fight to gain or retain their throne. Having acceded in 1556, Akbar defeated Hemu, a rival claimant, at the Second battle of Panipat, killing his captured opponent. Foreign wars were also pursued actively. Abbas I (1587–1629), ruler of Persia, fought the Uzbeks, Mughals, Portuguese and Turks.

Although peaceful successions of new dynasties did take place, as in England in 1603, war and inheritance were often two sides of the same coin; this was a problem exacerbated by varying and disputed succession laws, and by the need, in marital diplomacy, to avoid morganatic marriages. Royal dynasties increasingly rejected marriages with noble families in their own kingdoms, from about the 1550s considering only other royal or sovereign dynasties as equals. Furthermore, inter-dynastic marriages were a frequent means to give more stability to peace treaties; but, by giving rise to disputes over inheritances, they could also lay the foundations for future conflicts. The bellicist nature of court society and the fusion of dynasticism and *gloire* encouraged a resort to violence in the pursuit of such interests and claims.

More generally, warfare created 'states' and the rivalries between them were in some fashion inherent to their very existence. Examples include the importance of the *reconquista* of Iberia from Islam to Portugal, Castile and Aragon, of conflict with the Habsburgs for the Swiss Confederation and with England for Scotland, and the importance to the Dutch Republic of the threat from Spain and then France. 'State'-building generally required, and led to, war and also was based on medieval structures and practices that included a eulogization of violence. War was very important, not only in determining which dynasties controlled which lands, or where boundaries should be drawn, but in creating the sense of 'us' and 'them' which was, and is, so important to the growth of any kind of patriotism.[24]

For England, war with France forwarded the development of a 'national' state, encouraging xenophobia, royal war-propaganda, military service (and also resistance to it), national taxation and the expansion of the role of Parliament, a national representative body. The need for parliamentary consent for taxation was confirmed, and Parliament played a role in propagandizing policy and, thus, implicitly, in validating it. In 1344 parliamentary proceedings recorded Edward III's claim that Philip VI of France was 'firmly resolved . . . to destroy the English nation and occupy the land of England'.[25] War helped to confirm and convey identity. A soldier was either 'King Harry's man', or 'King Louis's man', their cry 'St George' or 'St Denis'.[26] The prehistory of the modern state, or maybe its very history, has to be considered, in part, in terms of these antagonistic identities, which were sustained through war and confrontation. A sense of identity was more crucial than political or constitutional structures, as now understood, although the latter could play a role in framing and sustaining the former.

These antagonistic tendencies were not static. In the thirteenth century, in both England and France, the idea of 'statehood' emerged, as opposed to the earlier *natio*, in its original meaning of people of a common descent. This territorialization was related to the development of a sense of political community separate from the monarch. An idea of political community, headed by the king, but to which he could be held accountable, lay behind the political and constitutional developments of the thirteenth century. The construction and territorialization of identity was not restricted to the political elite. These shifts were to serve as an alternative framework and ideology to those summarized by the term feudalism as a way to raise forces and to persuade people to fight. However, the martial configurations of these new political communities remained under monarchical control and direction. Indeed, the phenomenon of monarchical *gloire* was part of a code which served to integrate heterogeneous groups into the gradually emergent 'states', an element of social and political practice, articulation and even disciplining which served to integrate people into a state in a way which became visible in the title page to Thomas Hobbes's *Leviathan* (London, 1651).

Wars within cultures reflected not only the concerns of rulers but also the ambience and conventions within which they operated. The crucial role of the monarch in most societies across the world, and the dynastic perspective of monarchical ambitions, ensured a basic continuity in the conduct of international relations. Clearly, this perspective varied by individual. Dynastic concerns did not exclude other interests. They did, however, remain a central feature of early-modern international relations. If proprietary dynasticism[27] describes the attitude of most monarchs to their countries, it is not surprising that they were willing to use their resources for territorial accumulation. They did so in the context of court cultures that were predisposed to war, seeing it as a heroic endeavour.

Not all monarchs sought participation in war, but most engaged in it at some time, a tendency possibly increased by a demographic structure which often led to young men succeeding to thrones. Henry VIII of England and Suleiman the Magnificent were examples of young rulers who took aggressive steps that were not 'necessary' in terms of the diplomatic situation at the time. Born in 1491, Henry VIII came to the throne in 1509 and invaded France four years later. Born in 1494, Suleiman came to the throne in 1520 and invaded Rhodes in 1521 and Hungary in 1526. Born in 1542, Akbar invaded Malwa in 1561–2 and Rajputana in 1562–7. Correspondingly, Frederick the Great thought George II of Britain unlikely to want war in 1753 because of his advanced age and the absence of an adult successor.[28] This argument cannot be pushed too far. Some rulers were aggressive until their death, Suleiman dying in 1566 while on campaign in Hungary and Akbar extending Mughal dominions until 1601; equally, some young rulers were pacific.

The pursuit of dynastic claims can be regarded as an opportune sham. In 1741 Robert Vyner referred in the House of Commons to 'one of those imaginary titles, which ambition may always find to the dominions of another'.[29] The fraudulent manufacture of some pretensions and the willingness of rulers to barter claims for 'equivalents', other benefits to which they did not have a legal right, lends some substance to this charge. The allocation of Italian principalities during the Italian Wars of 1494–1559 was motivated by much besides dynastic legitimacy. It is possible to present monarchs and ministers as adopting pretensions to serve their long-term plans – in short, of using dynasticism for the sake of *staatspolitik* – and much of the debate surrounding the policy of particular monarchs revolves around this analytical device. However, it is more reasonable to assume that when monarchs said they were pursuing dynastic claims they were not all being disingenuous, accepting, of course, that prudential considerations could affect the extent to which these claims were pushed.

Dynasticism, understood in terms of the pursuit of inheritance claims that had at least some possible basis in legality, was more appropriate in some parts of the world than others. Understood as a situation in which rulers saw territories primarily as extensions of their own and their families' rights, interests and will, and were determined to maintain and enhance this inheritance, dynasticism was far more common.

There was also a more functional aspect of rulership. The ruler was the war-leader, the leader of a socio-political hierarchy and a related economic system based on property rights that were in large part predicated on war or, at least, on military prowess. Warrior lineages, such as the *zamindars* of India, ruled the peasantry across much of the world, helping to ensure that local disputes were often conducted as feuds. The importance of military prowess for honour, status and wealth helps to explain the way in which many societies fought and the pressure to acquire such prowess. An emphasis on the prowess of particular individuals was important in many societies, for example those of South-East Asia[30] and Mamluk Egypt.[31]

The resulting practices were vulnerable to the anonymous potency of the collective mass, especially, but not only, if it used gunpowder weaponry. Thus, Swiss pikemen helped to defeat Burgundian cavalry in the 1470s, and Ottoman firepower brought low Mamluk cavalry in the 1510s and its Hungarian counterpart in 1526. Japanese warfare was affected from the 1540s. Nevertheless, traditional expectations and patterns of behaviour adapted to the new emphasis on gunpowder weaponry. Aristocracies did not give up war because of the gun. Instead, they retained their desire for mounted prominence, both in the cavalry and in positions of control over the infantry. In Japan, glory was gained by individual heroism in battle, producing a cult of the warrior. Heroism was assessed by an inspection of heads after battles, for warriors decapitated their fallen opponents and were rewarded accordingly. Past achievements were recorded in war tales.[32] Promotion to boyar rank in sixteenth-century Russia was dependent on prowess in battle.

The highly bellicist nature of the societies of the period helps to explain why great-power wars were more frequent in the early-modern period than subsequently.[33] It does not necessarily explain why particular wars began. The best explanation is that this nature encouraged the vigorous and violent pursuit of interests, claims and disputes, whatever their origin and nature. Such an explanation concentrates on the culture of power, politics, diplomacy and warfare, and treats it as central to its content. It is, of course, difficult to arrive at more than a suggestive psychological profile of particular ruling groups. An instructive attempt to use the psychological approach is offered by E. H. Dickerman's work, based in part on medical records, on Henry IV of France's personal, especially sexual, problems and perceived inadequacies in the late 1600s, and how these led him to take an aggressive stance in the Jülich-Clèves succession dispute.[34] This led in 1610 to preparations for a major war with Spain that were only stopped by Henry's assassination.

One of the biggest wars of the period, the Japanese invasion of Korea in 1592, can, again, be traced to the character and views of a leader, Toyotomi Hideyoshi, the unifier of Japan through violence. A recent account makes clear the uncertainty over his motives:

> Even before subduing the Shimazu back in 1587, he had dreamed of conquering China and standing astride the known world. No one knows whether he was inspired by conquest legends of the *Kojiki*, the past exploits of Mongols, the example of globe-girdling Europeans, some inner messenger whom he alone could hear, or by a wish to exhaust daimyō armies in further warfare.[35]

There was certainly no danger of a Chinese attack on Japan, but Hideyoshi planned to invade via Korea, a Chinese client state, and to rule the world from the Chinese maritime city of Ningpo. From there, he intended to conquer India. Hideyoshi also demanded that Taiwan and the Philippines submit to him. Given his violent background, as a general who had fought his way into dominance over other *daimyō* (major warriors), Hideyoshi's role and self-regard can be seen as dependent on continued warfare: the invasion of Korea can be seen as the necessary next stage after the conquest of Kyūshū in 1587 and the defeat of the Hōjō in 1590. The invasion would provide new lands for his warriors and enable Hideyoshi to keep his control over them. Furthermore, continual success had led him to lose a sense of limits, while, anyway, the cult of the warrior discouraged an interest in limits. It was not so much a case of misperception as of no perception: an assessment of the capability of others was less relevant than a decision that such perception was not appropriate. Hideyoshi, however, had exceeded his grasp. The invasion was initially successful, but Korean naval and military resistance altered the situation, and in 1593 the Chinese committed large forces that drove back the Japanese.

A century earlier, Sonni Ali (1464–92), ruler of the West African Songhay empire on the middle Niger, fought every year of his reign. Motives varied, and some of his campaigns, most obviously against the Tuaregs, can be characterized as defensive rather than aggressive; but war was central to the Songhay state, as Sonni expanded at the expense of Jenne, the Fulani of Dendi and the Mossi. These wars of expansion were continued by Askia Muhammad (1493–1528). Similarly, Bayin-naung (1551–81) and Nan-da Bayin (1581–99) of the Burmese Taung-ngu dynasty fought almost continous campaigns in order to control and expand their far-flung state.[36]

The emphasis on monarchs, glory and dynasticism has the advantage that it matches contemporary views. Such an emphasis did and does not lend itself to reifications of the state. Furthermore, the argument that the early-modern period witnessed the origins and growth of the modern impersonal state can be queried on the grounds that insufficient evidence has been advanced to support the theory, that much of it relates to the writings of a small group of, arguably, unrepresentative thinkers, and that the political *practice* of the age was still essentially monarchical in a traditional fashion across most of Europe. As a result, both the goals and the practices of rulership and foreign policy contributed to the frequency of confrontation and war. The role of ministers might seem an important qualification of any argument centred on monarchs, but the position of ministers depended on their favour. Dynastic considerations clearly played an important part in ministerial discussions.[37]

CIVIL WAR

As a specialized form of organized mass violence, war is, and was, commonly defined as a conflict between two sovereign states. Aside from the range of conflict that that definition comprehends, in terms of the number and intention of the combatants and the type and duration of the conflict, sovereignty itself entails too exclusive a definition. The position of major rebellions, such as the Dutch revolt against Philip II of Spain from the 1560s – Dutch Revolt or the Eighty Years' War – Portuguese and Catalan rebellions against Philip IV from 1640, the Cossack rebellion against the Poles from 1648, the rebellions against Akbar, for example in Bengal in 1574 and 1579, and that of the Marathas against the Mughals in the following century, is particularly difficult. So also is the position of wars of unification and consolidation, such as those in northern India in the mid-sixteenth century, in Japan in the 1580s and 1590s, and the war against Yang Yinglong in Southwest China from 1587 until 1600. Such wars of unification involved the suppression of opposition that was defined as rebellion, but that could be regarded as displaying inchoate statehood, or that might lay claim to it. In 1574 Daud Karrani, the Sultan of Bengal, repudiated Akbar's nominal sovereignty before attacking Mughal territory, leading to a war that continued until the late 1580s, although Daud was defeated and killed in 1575. In addition, a group of imperial officers in Bengal rebelled in 1579.[38] The latter was clearly rebellion, but the former is harder to define. Yang Yinglong's family had long controlled part of Southwest China, but this autonomy was crushed. As the control had not been that of a sovereign power, this could be regarded as the suppression of a rebellion, but that does not describe the reality of a war of expansion, as much as consolidation.

'State building', a major cause of war, could lead to conflict, both with domestic and with foreign opponents. The same elite, interests, rationale and dynamism drove both, and it was not always clear how readily they could be distinguished. Thus Louis XI of France fought Charles the Bold of Burgundy in the 1470s, defeating a ruler who was, thanks to his possessions and status, at once a domestic and a foreign threat.

Furthermore, the sovereignty of the ruler in individual polities did not preclude traditions that bad kingship could be redressed by rebellion, and, if necessary, 'foreign' assistance could be summoned. In 1618 the Bohemians rejected the traditional authority of the Austrian Habsburgs and followed this up by electing a different monarch. This led to an armed conflict, beginning the Thirty Years' War. Whether the outbreak of hostilities should be seen as rebellion, war or both, is unclear. Bohemia was an elective monarchy, but successive Habsburgs had held the crown for nearly a century. The Bohemians, instead, elected a Calvinist, Frederick V of the Palatinate, while the Habsburg claimant, the Emperor Ferdinand II, sought, and received, Bavarian, Spanish and Saxon military assistance.

Some uprisings, such as those in Scotland in 1560 and 1566, involved organized struggle between armies and were a significant feature in the international relations of the period. Many domestic campaigns, such as those of the French against the Huguenots in the 1620s, entailed a military commitment that was equal to that of a foreign conflict. The lengthy siege of La Rochelle in 1627–8 required the military resources of the French state.

Rebellion leading to an acknowledged and independent state with a sovereign right to wage war was rarely successful, although the Swiss Confederation, United Provinces (Dutch) and Portugal gained such a status. It is, therefore, difficult to decide when it is reasonable to cease talking of rebellion, as in the Dutch Revolt, and, instead, begin considering it as a war. Early-modern European history is littered with instances of polities that failed to become independent states: Wales in the 1400s, Corsica in 1559–69, Bohemia in 1618–21, Scotland from 1638, Catalonia in 1640–52, Hungary in 1704–11, the Ukraine in 1708–9, Ireland in both the sixteenth and seventeenth centuries. The crisis of monarchical authority in Scotland helped to precipitate the English Civil War of 1642–6. It is difficult to determine which of these struggles can be regarded as wars.[39]

Yet this issue is, more generally, important to that of the causes and dating of war, because so many wars were not classic dynastic conflicts in which two dynasties claimed the same principality, basing their claims on rights of inheritance, but were, instead, linked to a domestic crisis affecting at least one of the participants. Thus, the Dutch Revolt helped to lead to Anglo-Spanish conflict, and also to war between France and Spain. This had been, further, provoked by the French Wars of Religion which provided Spain with an opportunity to intervene. The myriad conflicts of the Thirty Years' War were triggered and, in part, caused by the consequences of the rebellion in Bohemia and the constitutional crisis of the Empire.

It is similarly difficult to assess conflicts that were clearly civil wars, in which domestic violence reflected not pressure for the lessening of tax demands, as in so many peasant uprisings,[40] but, rather, a struggle with more distinctive political objectives. In several, such as the French civil war of the 1590s, the conflict within China in the early 1640s (the rebellions, not the Manchu invasion, of the period), or that within the Mughal empire in the 1650s, the source of the conflict was the identity of the sovereign. Some of these civil wars based on disputed successions were subsumed within larger conflicts, thanks to foreign intervention, as in Scotland in the mid-sixteenth century and France in the 1590s,[41] but that does not ease the question of deciding how best to define them, or to discuss their causation, within a general typology of war. It also greatly complicates the classification and, thus, quantification of wars.

The significance of domestic struggles, their sometimes close relationship with international conflicts, and the ambivalence of the concept of sovereignty, particularly in the case of disputed successions, makes it difficult to accept the definition of war adopted by writers whose empirical consideration has been devoted to modern conflicts defined as a struggle between two sovereign powers. In the twentieth century, this interpretation has been subverted by the frequency and importance of insurrectionary struggles. It is also inappropriate for much of the early-modern period. The interpretation is especially problematic for central Europe. In the Holy Roman Empire (essentially Germany) and the *Erblände* (the possessions of the Austrian Habsburgs) there was not a clear fusion of political power and sovereign authority. In addition, it is unclear how to categorize conflicts between powerful territories within the Empire that possessed armies, such as Bavaria, Hesse and Saxony, and the ambiguities in the constitutional position of the Emperor, in particular, help to explain the difficulties of determining when the Thirty Years' War became a war. Furthermore, there was a lack of agreement as to whether princes of the Empire had a right to wage war and could enter into alliances with foreign powers. There was a long history within the Empire of military alliances between territories, such as the Swabian League of the early sixteenth century. The evolution of individual 'Estates' of the Empire, such as Bavaria, into 'States' intrigued contemporary theorists, for example Abraham de Wicquefort. In Ireland, the Dublin Parliament of 1541 recognized Henry VIII and his successors as kings, but the violent response to Protestantism, Anglicization and royal policy in 1595–1603 was referred to as the Nine Years' War rather than being seen as a rebellion.

Disagreements between contemporaries, both in this and in other struggles, the same conflict being termed war and rebellion, was not due to insincerity and was not, solely, a consequence of polemic. There were fundamental differences in opinion, frequently directly related to the cause of the conflict, and these pose problems for historians today, just as at the time they caused jurists to quarrel. Furthermore, historians' disagreements about the nature of wars are not restricted to the issue of their legal status. Thus, the Thirty Years' War has been interpreted within the Marxist tradition as owing much to class tension and being an aspect of class control over the peasantry,[42] while other scholars have taken seriously contemporary presentation of motives, for example, accepting that Christian IV of Denmark became involved due to a *Reichsfürst* mentality, specifically his concern for princely liberties in the face of what he saw as an inexorable Habsburg advance, as opposed to treating his claims as a cover for selfish territorial ambitions.[43]

To restrict the definition of war to a conflict between sovereign states fails to take note of many major military commitments and much large-scale fighting. In contrast, the argument that all major conflicts were functionally wars, and should be treated as such, represents a major qualification of this definition of war, but, as it leads to a massive expansion in the number and type of conflicts that have to be considered, to include, for example, all significant policing operations involving troops, this creates major problems for the study of the causes of war.

Military operations took place along a continuum stretching from formal war to actions against smugglers. Formal war did not necessarily entail greater commitments or problems than domestic action, although it generally did so. There was much in common between domestic and international conflicts, as the warfare of Mughal India in the seventeenth century made clear. Indeed, the notion of 'internal', as well as foreign, boundaries and wars has been advanced in discussion of Mughal policy and warfare. More generally, in both domestic and international conflicts, it was not necessary for 'war' to begin with a specific move, and, in both, sustained hostilities were often not sought. Negotiations could precede and, indeed, accompany conflict, and the latter was often ended by an explicit or implicit settlement that was essentially a compromise, reflecting the manner in which the struggle had revealed the strength and determination of the combatants. Frequently, part of the opposing coalition was bought off, only to begin hostilities on a future occasion. This was true not only of India but also of such European conflicts as the Thirty Years' War and the coalition struggles against Louis XIV.

The functional definition of war in terms of the use of military force is not without its problems. European commentators were generally able to differentiate between the policing and war functions of the armed forces. There was also a relatively clear distinction in the *mentalités* of courtly society. Glory and honour could be gained through suppressing domestic discord, but it was, primarily, a function of defeated foreign rivals, and certainly not peasants. Domestic conflict could be a serious problem, but, in the views of the rulers concerned, and in that of most other monarchs, it was a matter of rebellion, not war. However, in the case of large land empires with universalist pretensions, most obviously China, not only was there scant clear understanding of the sovereignty of foreign polities but also little clear distinction between war and rebellion. China, the Middle Kingdom, expected other rulers to accept a tributary relationship. In 1597 the Chinese thought that the end of the conflict in Korea should involve the Chinese bestowal of the title of 'king' on Toyotomi Hideyoshi. He sought a more equal relationship.

With the exception of the Korean invasions, warfare in Japan during the period was entirely civil. Japan was controlled by a thoroughly militarized class, the samurai, who, in part, derived their importance from conflict. The limited authority of the Shogun ensured that disputes between samurai were difficult to control. The leading samurai were autonomous provincial *shugos* (constables). Disputes between and within samurai families led to conflict and, in the mid-fifteenth century, disputes over the succession to several leading constables culminated in the Onin War of 1467–77, when the shogunal succession itself was disputed.[44] This war became intertwined with local conflicts. The *daimyōs* who came to replace *shugos* headed groups of vassals who expected to fight both for 'rational' or 'prudential' reasons – to gain land – and because that was their way of life and source of self-esteem and value. Thus, sixteenth-century warfare in Japan was driven by a militaristic elite society that was unconstrained by central authority. This was an 'anarchy' that was constantly unsettled by treachery and rebellion.

It was through force and treachery that Japan was unified in the late sixteenth century. The unwillingness of Takeda Nobunaga and Hideyoshi to accept lasting compromise ensured that any limits to their power led to conflict, as when Hideyoshi invaded Shikoku in 1585, Kyūshū in 1587 and the Hōjō lands in 1590. The cruelty displayed towards the defeated, including the slaughtering of women and children, underlined the degree that this was warfare, not political calculation with some added fighting. Still controlled by the samurai, although now with a stronger central government, Japan then began an extraordinary period of two and a half centuries of almost uninterrupted peace. This included a restriction on the ownership and availability of weapons greater than that practiced in Europe.

To extend a discussion of the causes of war to include all rebellions is inappropriate in any single-volume study, especially a short one. It would be to provide a political history of the world. However, it is worth underlining the disadvantages of abstracting 'war' from those wider contexts of political concerns and military action.

What civil and international conflict have in common is that the scholarly tendency to treat them as a breakdown in a political system, a 'mistake' caused by a failure to negotiate difference, needs to be complemented by, and, at times, heavily qualified by, a cultural stress on factors encouraging conflict. In the widest sense, these can be referred to as a bellicist culture, but such an analysis has to take note of specific military and political characteristics and circumstances. In the case of early-modern civil wars, these included the widespread distribution of weapons; the possibility of inflicting defeat on regular forces whose military superiority was limited, not least because of logistical, manpower and financial problems; ideological traditions justifying, but, in turn, constraining, rebellion, not least the contractual nature of authority; the employment of violence as part of a form of mass demonstration; and the degree to which 'states' had only a limited ability to integrate, or interest in integrating, the often disparate communities, groups and territories that composed them. The consequent limitations on the ability of 'states' to unite, and to assimilate, increased the possibilities of rebellion and make it less accurate to see it in terms of civil war. Hobbes understood his own time: violence and warfare were endemic to society.

As with international conflict, issues of honour and reputation played a major role in encouraging civil conflict. At the level of the locality, status was frequently threatened, not least by insults which challenged esteem, both self-esteem, and esteem in the eyes of the community. This was the background to much lawlessness, to aristocratic and other feuds, and to the public use of violence.[45] In the late Middle Ages, warfare was the continuation of litigation by other means. Litigation and warfare were not yet an either/or, but were seen as naturally complementing each other. This was less the case in the seventeenth century. At that time, those who pursued their cause in court were seen as having no right to wage war, while those who waged war were seen as not accepting the jurisdiction of any court of law. In the Holy Roman Empire the *ewige Landfriede* of 1495, part of the *Reichsreform*, outlawed all feuds. It was not immediately successful, but in the long run there was a decline in feuding. The last knight to organize a traditional feud was Grumbach in the 1560s. He was executed, and the prince who acted as his patron, the Duke of Weimar, became the Emperor's prisoner. However, in Italy, for example in the Veneto and Lombardy, there was a rise in violence and a revival of feuds at the close of the sixteenth century. Brigandage, often associated, like much lawlessness, with the social elite, remained a marked feature of Sicilian society. Throughout Europe, aristocratic power and attitudes were persistent.[46]

While many nobilities and nobles derived their importance and sense of identity in large part from warfare, that did not ensure that conflict was incessant. Many disputes between nobles which had the potential to become wars did not escalate into warfare. This owed much to the role of central authorities. Thus, civil warfare had much to do with the balance of power and authority between larger political entities, states and kingdoms, and smaller entities, such as nobles, war bands and cities. This situation prefigured that of weak modern states, such as Sierra Leone, where central government is unable to control highly armed smaller groups, leading to a situation of incessant warfare.

However, in the early modern period, unlike today, it was easier to sustain both war and a viable society. War, generally, was less destructive. Peasants knew how to move the movable wealth of a village away when an army was passing through. The use of relatively inefficient guns was such that the serious killing effects of guns had not yet been realized. This is not intended as a functional explanation of civil (or international) war, but it helps to explain its frequency.

CONCLUSIONS

Warfare defined and reflected the respective strength of 'states', but it did far more than that. It provided and fulfilled objectives and roles and served to define identities and to propagate ideologies. As a definition of the strength of 'states', war can be treated as part of the operation of a states system. However, this approach is of limited value, because warfare was called upon to discharge a greater range of functions, and these functions affected the 'rationality' of the pursuit of objectives within the states system – indeed, created objectives, such as the acquisition and accomplishment of glory and unity through war.[47]

Moreover, war helped create an unstable context for both domestic and international developments, and, in turn, partook in these instabilities. A scholar of Russian expansion noted, ' "When to stop" can be a very delicate judgement to make, for it implies a clear understanding of the country's goals, resources and structural strength. Few governing elites possess this amount of knowledge or insight'.[48] In addition, first , there may be no obvious goals to understand clearly, and, secondly, goals are transformed by warfare, especially by success in war and by shifts in alliance patterns.

Aside from those directly affected by death and devastation, it was taxation, currency debasement, trade interruptions, food shortages and recruitment that brought the effects of war home to most. The monarchs, ministers, diplomats and generals of the period faced a hazardous and complex international and domestic situation. Information was difficult to obtain, and often unreliable. Rulers were short of money, generals of men. Activities, whether military operations or the journeys of couriers, were dependent on weather and climate, the condition of the roads, the crops and the countryside. Chance factors of birth, ill health and death played a major role in creating and affecting the diplomatic agenda. The unpredictability of developments cannot be disguised by terms, such as the balance of power and natural interests, which imply that a hypothetical international system operated according to some rules.

TWO

1650–1775: An Age of Limited War?

That impotence of mind in the great ones of the
Earth, vulgarly called ambition, may well be cursed
by the inferior part of mankind; since it is the cause
why so many thousands of lives are sacrificed, for the
worthless acquisition of a small extent of territory, or
perhaps (what is still less) an empty name.

Anon., *War, An Epic-Satyr* (London, 1747), p. 67.

INTRODUCTION

The standard interpretation of warfare in this period is that it
was an age of limited war. This is a Eurocentric model and one
that reflects an interpretation of European international relations and warfare in this period. It is also an interpretation that
involves a particular view on the causes and origins of war. The
period is seen as a secular, non-ideological age, and the method-
ology that has been used to describe it is one that is essentially
derived from the late nineteenth century, when states appeared
to operate their foreign policies in a cool and dispassionate
fashion, unaffected by ideology.

This view was an inaccurate assessment of the international
relations, both of the late nineteenth century and of the earlier
period. It was an assessment that throws light on how the intellectuals of the age wished to believe that diplomacy operated.
Because all the European great powers of the nineteenth
century – Austria, Britain, France, Prussia and Russia – were
already distinct and important actors on the international stage
in the period from 1650 until 1775, it was understandable that
the diplomatic relations of the earlier age should be treated in

79

terms of the analyses and attitudes that appeared to be most appropriate for the later period.

The resulting treatments varied with the skills and interests of particular historians, but the general stress was on policy and long-term planning, carried out rationally and in accordance with an unemotional *raison d'état*, by monarchs without illusions, pre-eminently Frederick II 'the Great' of Prussia (1740–86), and by European chancelleries that were bureaucratically distinct and independent, and capable of generating informed policies. Leading ministers, such as the Austrian Chancellor Wenzel, Prince Kaunitz, were seen to prefigure nineteenth-century counterparts.

Thus, historians of the foreign policy of Louis XIV of France (1643–1715), the principal late-seventeenth-century topic that engaged the interest of diplomatic historians two centuries later, searched for some policy, such as the quest for 'natural frontiers' or for the Spanish succession, that would reduce the varied themes and episodes of their subject to some order by which his moves could be explained, judged, and, also, linked to subsequent episodes in French foreign policy.[1] Similarly, the response of other rulers was seen in terms of a coherent counterpointing of French moves, to be understood and assessed in terms of the reply to the intentionality and systematic planning of Louis's policy. An inherent competitiveness was stressed and presented as both product and motor of international relations.

In such a form of analysis, the so-called 'realist' paradigm was adopted, and war tended to be regarded as a device of deliberate policy, the decision to resort to it based either on a rational consideration of national advantage, or, in the case of rulers or ministers who were to be condemned for folly, on a failure to make such an assessment. Ideological demands for war were seen as limited, and domestic pressures for conflict were generally ignored, with the exception of states possessing a representative assembly, such as Britain and the United Provinces, the systems of government of which led them to be regarded as conspicuously different from those described as absolutisms. This led them to offer a field for research prefiguring modern scholarly interest in the degree of propensity of democratic states for engaging in war.[2] The Dutch Republic was seen as particularly pacific.[3]

The *mentalités* that affected the conduct of foreign policy in Europe were rarely discussed, but, when they were, they were judged to be – what was implicit in the vast bulk of the scholarship – a matter of *raison d'état*, a prudential, at times machiavellian, assessment of opportunities and interests. This was illustrated by the publication of documentary series, most prominently Frederick the Great's *Politische Correspondenz* from 1879[4] and the *Recueil des Instructions données aux Ambassadeurs et Ministres de France depuis les Traités de Westphalie jusqu'à la Revolution Française* from 1884.

The limitations of this account as an explanation of the causes of war and, indeed, international relations in this period will be dealt with in the section on wars within cultures, but first it is necessary to turn to conflicts that were, and are, completely ignored in this account – those across cultures.

WARS ACROSS CULTURES

It is terribly easy, again, to adopt a Eurocentric perspective and to discuss this period, first, in terms of the driving back of the Turks on the Euro-Asian frontier with, for example, specific outbreaks of war between Austria and Turkey, as in 1664, 1682, 1716 and 1737, and Russia and Turkey, as in 1735 and 1768, and, secondly, to consider transoceanic European expansion and attendant warfare, both with other European powers, most obviously in North America, and with non-Europeans, most prominently in India. However, it is necessary to place due weight on conflicts that did not involve European powers, not least because the vast majority of wars in Africa and Asia were in this category.

In practice, in terms of wars across cultures, the most important were arguably those involving China. However, Manchu China was a hybrid, like Mughal India, the leading regime in South Asia in the seventeenth century, Safavid Persia and Ottoman Turkey. Their culture, political system, ideology, and military arrangements and methods reflected the traditions of conquerors and conquered. In part, this was a matter of assimilation, in part of the maintenance of separate practices, which was itself crucial to successful political and military incorporation. When the Mughals campaigned against the Uzbeks across the Hindu Kush in the 1640s or the Manchu Chinese conquered Mongolia in the 1690s, it is difficult to see such campaigns in terms of the clash of totally different cultures. Nevertheless, there had been a process of assimilation on the part of conquering Manchus, Mughals, Safavids and Ottomans, and, partly as a result, the element of cultural clash was apparent. This can be seen in the Manchu Chinese campaigns in Tibet and Xinjiang in the first half of the eighteenth century, and in the Afghan overthrow of Safavid Persia in the 1720s.

The Manchu fought to expand. Their expansionism was mostly imperialistic, for glory and possessions rather than for resources and trade. In contrast, the earlier Ming dynasty had fought mostly to preserve itself and its dependents, such as Korea. Manchu warfare was certainly not limited, no more than that of the Europeans against Native opponents in North America or the Russians against opponents in Siberia, such as the Chukchi.

The issue of cultural clash raises similar points to those pertinent in the period from 1450 until 1650, namely the problems of classification, as with the difficulty of deciding how best to assess *jihads*,[5] the targets of which could include insufficiently zealous Moslems; the relationships between difference and conflict; and those between frequent, even continual, conflict of a certain level, and particular episodes of major war. As suggested earlier, difference was not incompatible with reasonable relations. They could be mutually beneficial in an economic sense or, indeed, in a political one. Thus, for example, it was possible for a settled society to ally with a pastoral neighbour in order to obtain its military support against other nomadic neighbours. Such a relationship could involve payment, in the form of beneficial trade and presents, as well as marital alliances and the provision of arms. This was certainly the case for China's relationship with its steppe neighbours for much of the early-modern period: great care was taken to secure the support of particular Mongol tribes, and, thus, to lessen the Mongol threat.

It was also the case with European relations with Native Americans in North America. The fur trade led to the creation of political-economic networks and to the involvement of Europeans in Native wars, and vice versa, a process facilitated by and in part due to the increasing provision of European arms and ammunition. However, this involvement was not a case of more of the same. In North America, as elsewhere, European intrusion intensified war amongst non-state peoples.[6]

Furthermore, the notion of hostility across cultures has to be qualified by a realization of the degree to which intra-cultural wars were as important, or took precedence. In Eurasia, the Russians devoted more effort to fighting Christian European neighbours, especially a life-and-death struggle with Charles XII of Sweden in the first half of the eighteenth century, than to fighting other polities, although they did devote much effort to war with the Turks, especially in 1711 and 1736–9. In North America, the British, French and Spaniards devoted much effort to conflict with each other rather than with Native Americans, and this is even more apparent if expenditure on fortifications and naval support is also considered.

In India, the British were more concerned about France in mid-century than about native states, especially in the Carnatic. The situation changed only after the defeat of the French in 1760–61: the Battle of Wandewash and the fall of Pondicherry were crucial preludes to more assertive British policies towards native rulers. The destruction of an Anglo-French balance and of a French threat were followed not by peaceful hegemony in regions where the British were strong but by bouts of expansionist activity that were aggressive in impact, if not always in intent.

So there was no necessary pattern of continual warfare. Instead, it is more helpful to consider peace, wars and the cause of the move from one to the other. As with intra-cultural wars, this was largely a matter of the complex relationship of fear and opportunity. Native Americans could attack European settlers because they feared their advance and despaired at the inability or unwillingness of colonial authorities to control it. This happened in the Carolinas in 1715, in what was to be Vermont in the 1720s, and in Pontiac's war in 1763–4, a war presented by European-Americans as a rebellion or rising.

Fear also played a role in Asia. The Chinese feared the creation of a hostile Mongol confederation from the 1690s. The newly acceded Nawab of Bengal was concerned about British activity and saw an opportunity to attack in 1756. Burmese conquest in 1767 made later Siamese rulers fearful, encouraging them to take an aggressive stance and, also, to dominate the lands, especially the Laotian principalities, through which the Burmese had advanced, and might do so again.

In other circumstances opportunity, rather than fear or anxiety, played a greater role. A perception of weakness providing the chance for gain encouraged the Afghans to attack Persia in 1722 and Nadir Shah of Persia to invade Mughal India in 1739. Both attacks were successful. The latter was more in the nature of a raid than a war, but the size of the force involved would have led it to have been accounted a war in most cultures. The weakness, first, of Persia and, then, of Mughal India, spurred other 'regional powers' to act, either by attacking from outside or by emerging from within, gaining autonomy and *de facto* independence, as the Nizam of Hyderabad did in central India in the first half of the eighteenth century. This volatility, in turn, encouraged conflict, as powers sought to define their position and understand and defend their interests in a situation made uncertain and threatening by fear and opportunity. Thus, for example, the Nizam fought the Marathas, who also benefited greatly from Mughal decline. From the 1760s, both came to compete with Haidar Ali of Mysore.

Haidar Ali, like Nadir Shah, was a military leader who seized power through violence and then spent much of his reign at war or preparing for war. Violence was normal to both men, and they fought not only other expanding powers but also more vulnerable states. Thus, Nadir Shah intervened in Oman, while Haidar Ali invaded the independent kingdoms of Malabar in 1766 and occupied them in 1773. Taksin and Rama I, military leaders who revived Siam after the devastating Burmese conquest of 1767, can be seen as similar.

Weakness could also be shown, at least apparently, by Europeans. The causes of the Austro-Turkish War of 1682–99 were varied, but it is symptomatic of the threat that the Turks posed that the war began with a Turkish act of aggression, despite Leopold I's wish to maintain the peace. Leopold faced opposition in the section of Hungary he ruled, in large part because of his autocratic and Catholicizing policies, and this was seen as an opportunity by both Louis XIV and the Turks, the leading opponents of the Austrian Habsburgs. Weight must also be placed on the bellicose nature of the Turkish state and society, on governmental military adventurism, and on the Grand Vizier Kara Mustafa's need for money and prestige in order to maintain his power.[7]

In 1682 the Turks decided to help Imre Thököly, the Hungarian leader, and Thököly agreed to be a vassal of the sultan. The Turks were defeated in this war, but other episodes of adventurism were more successful. An attack on Poland in 1671 led to a war in which they gained Podolia in the Peace of Zuravno (1676). Having declared war on Venice in 1714, the Turks easily overran the Peloponnese the following year.

Further afield, vulnerable European positions were also attacked by bellicose peoples seeking to expand their territorial sway. In the second half of the seventeenth century, the Omani Arabs attacked Portuguese positions on the East African coast, such as Mombasa, which fell in 1698. The Marathas attacked Portuguese India in the 1730s.

It was, in part, in this opportunistic context that the Europeans operated, as an aspect of uncertainty rather than as an alien force pressing against stable societies. The widespread hiring of Europeans in South Asia from the sixteenth century was a testimony not only to their skill with gunpowder weaponry but also to the porosity of cultural divides. Clearly this varied, and was greater in areas of active trade, religious heterogeneity and political multipolarity, such as the South Asian littoral, rather than in East Asia. However, this recruitment ensured that the Europeans could, often, be viewed as yet another stage in a historical process, akin to the earlier, and contemporaneous, role of Turks and other Central Asian Moslems rather than as a force that could not be accommodated. The extent to which Europeans pursued trade, rather than territory, in Asia and Africa encouraged this attitude. Furthermore, the Europeans were increasingly less of a novelty and, with time, their local agents became more attuned to the nature and mores of non-European international relations and warfare.

By 1750 the Europeans had been in India or West Africa for a quarter-millennium. They scarcely counted as 'aliens' and, indeed, many had acculturated. This was equally true of the Portuguese in Mozambique. Portuguese power there and on the West Indian littoral was longer established than Mughal power in the Deccan.

However, this argument should not be pushed too far, as there were new officials and settlers in the colonies, especially when new or newly energetic European powers arrived or expanded the pace, range and demands of their activities. This was true of the Dutch in the early seventeenth century, both in areas where they supplanted other Europeans, such as Sri Lanka, Formosa, Malacca and, eventually, the Malabar coast of India, and where they established European power, as in Java. The novelty of European demands was also true of the territorial role of the British in Bengal in the mid-eighteenth century. New officials and settlers could seek to introduce alien concepts and practices, for example of property rights and boundaries or of more regular taxation. Such novelty became more common and insistent as respect for, and fear of, non-European attitudes and societies decreased, and as the pace of settlement grew. Control over land entailed less consensual practices than trade, and led to low-level conflict in terms of taxation, rent collection, poaching and labour control.

Wars can be understood in terms of specific causes, but within contexts that encouraged a predisposition for conflict. Although hostility might be directed towards those deemed outsiders and alien, it is frequently difficult to show that the causes of conflict were in any way different to those of wars within cultures.

WARS WITHIN CULTURES

The interpretation of European international relations and warfare outlined in the introduction to this chapter can be challenged. Rulers and politicians, and ministers and diplomats, far from recognizing their position in an international system, from assessing clearly the interests of others and, therefore, from discerning structural tensions and rivalries, operated in a context of opacity and controversy. There was a lack of clarity and agreement about 'national interests', about the views of others and other resulting relationships. Contemporary conceptualization, classically in terms of the balance of power, or of related or similar terminology, served to disguise this confusion and division, frequently for political or polemical purposes. However, the concept of the balance reflected concern for stability and, in general, the conduct of policies as a zero sum game.

In analytical terms, the balance of power and the related concept of natural interests can be criticized as ambiguous and misleading, but, in practice, their very flexibility ensured their value, both because they could be applied widely and because they could readily serve political and polemic purposes. To a certain extent, systemic theory is the modern counterpart, and descendant, of the balance of power. It has a similar apparent – a critic would say spurious – precision, and a similar openness to quantification and consequent analysis. The great use of the balance of power in the eighteenth century reflected the fascination with Newtonian physics and its mechanistic structures and forces, and, more generally, with reason, understood in terms of secular cause and effect, that characterized the age or, at least, its intellectuals.

There was an awareness of change and of the danger that, in international relations, vicissitudes of dynastic arrangements, the conduct of battle and all sorts of contingent factors existed that made international relations less calculable. Theorists tried to reduce those factors to the extent that such relations could be perceived as calculable. Power was to be understood and conserved, not driven or changed by forces outside the system, such as Providence. Similarly, modern systemic theory can in part be traced not only to contemporary concerns but also to the determination to try to make rational, analysable and readily comprehensible the inchoate nature of our world – a laudable goal, but one that can lead to serious error, not least through misplaced precision in the analysis of interests, structures, changes and processes of causality.

In essence, both sets of theories suffer from a propensity to emphasize reason, or, rather, a conception of reason, at the expense of passion, greed and inertia. It is instructive to consider the eighteenth-century debate. The essentially mechanistic argument that every state had innate interests which, properly understood, dictated a course of policy to which other states could respond by alliance or enmity was at the heart of most discussions of the balance of power and the international system. To adopt eighteenth-century British classifications, this argument can be described as the Whig view. It has dominated our assessment of the period. However, there was a conflict between an optimistic Whig assessment of the possibility of establishing consistent policies and creating a world order that was predictable and stable, and a pessimistic Tory realization of the fallibility of human ambitions and schemes. The Whigs placed insufficient weight on the personal role of rulers and the unpredictable nature of most policies. In 1711, during the War of the Spanish Succession, in which Britain was taking a prominent role against Louis XIV, the leading Tory writer and polemicist, Jonathan Swift, wrote:

> ... great Events often turn upon very small Circumstances...
> How to insure Peace for any Term of Years, is difficult
> enough to apprehend. Will Human Nature ever cease to
> have the same Passions? Princes to entertain Designs of
> Interest or Ambition, and Occasions of Quarrel to arise? May
> not we Ourselves, by the variety of Events and Incidents
> which happen in the World, be under a necessity of recover-
> ing Towns out of the very Hands of those, for whom we are
> now ruining our country to Take them?

When he wrote of Britain's ally, the Emperor Joseph I (1705–11), ruler of Austria, sacrificing 'the whole Alliance to his private Passion'[8] to subdue rebellious Protestant Hungary rather than fighting Louis XIV, Swift was showing his support for a pessimistic, or perhaps realistic, assessment of the extent to which Europe was an international system, and thus of the chances that British ministers could devise a consistent policy through alliance diplomacy.

Another leading Tory writer, Samuel Johnson, in his *Thoughts on the Late Transactions Respecting Falkland's Islands* (London, 1771), stressed the unpredictability and volatility of human affairs:

> It seems to be almost the universal error of historians to suppose it politically, as it is physically true, that every effect has a proportionate cause. In the inanimate action of matter upon matter, the motion produced can be but equal to the force of the moving power; but the operations of life, whether private or public, admit no such laws. The caprices of voluntary agents laugh at calculation . . . Obstinacy and flexibility, malignity and kindness, give place alternately to each other, and the reason of these vicissitudes . . . often escapes the mind in which the change is made.[9]

The pessimistic sense that developments, both in individuals and more generally, could not be predicted because they were 'irrational' constituted a major strain in Tory thought. The stress on the uncertainty of human affairs reflected a distinct religious, moral and intellectual position. Thus, foreign policy and its analysis both risked upset if they sought to create a system based on the views and interests of others and on apparently rational action, the basis of 'Enlightenment' attitudes.

Swift and Johnson were writing about the world they observed. To both, passion played a major role in human calculation, although each also had specific reasons for writing. Swift was trying to rally support, and provide arguments, for disengagement from Britain's alliance system and the war. In 1771 Johnson was concerned to defend the government of Lord North from passion, specifically from popular pressure for war with Spain. He dismissed such agitation with the sentence, 'To fancy that our government can be subverted by the rabble, whom its lenity has pampered into impudence, is to fear that a city may be drowned by the overflowing of its Kennels'.[10]

In 1770–71 Lord North's government was to resist such pressure, just as Louis XV then resisted the different pressure to come to the aid of his ally Spain. Without French backing, the Spanish government backed down from the prospect of war. This was a war avoided, in large part because bellicose pressures were faced down. It would, however, be misleading to see this in simplistic terms of rational governments preferring the politics of calculation to those of passion. Indeed, by failing to support Spain, Louis XV denied the exigencies of alliance politics.

Aside from the dangers of adopting an overly 'rational' approach to international relations, both Swift and Johnson more specifically alert us to the need to assess the attitudes that influenced the formulation and execution of policy. Even if a systemic analysis is to be adopted, and, for example, certain conflicts are seen as resulting from attempts to change position in the system, or to resist such change, then it is necessary to consider the contemporary perception of such attempts, and of the system itself, and the confusions and complexities of intentionality.

Here again, we move from the apparent clarity and precision of systemic theory, and from its openness, to quantification, into a world that is more tentative, problematic and opaque. This can be seen when attempting to assess domestic factors in the origins of war, or, more generally, in shifts in foreign policy. It is clearly a particular problem in the case of Britain, as the Westminster Parliament, a developed and powerful representative assembly, came to play an important role earlier than in most other states. Here again, one encounters problems with a systemic analysis that centres on relationships between states, especially their ranking in respective power, and on geopolitical considerations. It is necessary to consider both the porosity of the decision-making process to domestic political attitudes and pressures, and the extent to which many decision-makers only retained their ability to act so if they followed certain policies. Again, analytical problems are encountered, because there are major conceptual difficulties in addressing such questions and an absence of a body of documentation even remotely comparable to the diplomatic records to aid such an analysis.

There are also problems with exaggerating the modernity of the period. Just as it is too easy to interpret changes in artistic fashion, religious practice and the style of kingship as fundamental alterations, so it is necessary to be cautious in assessing signs of 'modern' behaviour in the international relations of the period. Two major elements of international relations that were far from novel and that suggest that the years from 1648 until

1775 should be seen as part of the early-modern period, rather than a precursor of nineteenth-century diplomacy, were the role of dynastic concerns and the continued habit of discussing relations in religious terms. The latter has received relatively little attention, but religious considerations engendered and reinforced hostility, and also played an important role in explaining action for contemporaries.

It was, of course, true that the alliances of the period rarely conformed to confessional lines. Count Osterman, the Russian foreign minister, himself of German Protestant origin, observed in 1740 with reference to the Jülich-Berg succession dispute, in which a Protestant claimant, Frederick II, clashed with a Catholic, that 'religion is more talked of, than really minded in transactions of this kind'.[11] Religious animosity was more important both in creating or exacerbating distrust, and in encouraging support for and explaining a conflict that had already begun, than in leading to a breakdown in peace.

This, however, was not too dissimilar to the period prior to 1650. It both suggests the danger of differentiating too starkly between periods, whether in Europe or elsewhere, and also helps to account for the generally uncritical response of the clergy to warfare and to killing. This was important, as religion was the source, context and agency of moral teaching.

A guide to the dominant ideology of the age can be found in religious ceremonies held to secure divine intercession, for example fast-day sermons, and in the pageantry of victory: *Te Deums*, processions, fireworks, addresses. Defeats in the early stages of the Seven Years' War (1756–63) led Edward Weston, a British career bureaucrat experienced in diplomatic negotiations, to write an anonymous pamphlet, *The Fast* (London, 1756), in which he called for a national fast day to win divine support for a country enervated by immorality and irreligion. British newspapers, such as the influential *Monitor*, frequently saw Providence at work in the war. National fast days were held in Britain in all but one of the years of the American War of Independence (1775–83).[12] George III of Britain declared 13 December 1776 a day of 'General Fast and Humiliation' because of 'the just and necessary measure of force which we are obliged to use against our rebellious subjects'.

Some of the religious ceremonies and language was doubt-less a matter of convention, but, in searching for any supposed changes in attitudes to war, it is necessary to remember that Europe was still fundamentally a religious society and that most ethical problems were expressed in religious terms. The notion of a just war was well entrenched in Christian thought and teaching.[13] Attempts to lessen religious antagonism had, at best, limited success. The Chinese Rites controversy – the dispute within the Catholic Church over how far the attempt to convert China should entail accommodation of its practices, particularly ancestor worship – ended with a defeat for the Jesuit accommodators.

Edward Weston was an Under-Secretary of State when George Frederick Handel wrote the *Dettingen Te Deum*, first performed at the Chapel Royal in London on 27 November 1743. His celebration of George II, as the royal hero as victor after the French defeat at Dettingen, was part of a long tradition of exalting majesty in its most impressive function, the display of power. This display ranged in style and form, from medals to the foundation of chivalric orders for the nobility under royal patronage, but it was a constant feature of the period. War was not the sole sphere in which such display could occur, but it was one that best served the aggressive dynastic purpose that illuminated so many of the polities of the period. Handel's triumphal piece looked back to such works as Philippe Quinault's libretto for Jean-Baptiste Lully's opera *Issus* (1677), which presented Louis XIV as Neptune and referred to a recent French naval engagement off the coast of Sicily and to the seizure of Messina. Louis was presented as near superhuman in the decorative pro-gramme presented in the Galerie des Glaces in his new palace at Versailles. Such triumphalism both set the atmosphere in royal courts and affected the way in which the views of others were seen. Sir William Trumbull, the unsympathetic English envoy in Paris, reported in April 1686,

The Emperor's envoy was yesterday at Versailles to press Monsr. de Croissy [French foreign minister] for some favourable answer to the memorial he gave in of several damages done by the French troops in the domains of the

Emperor, signifying the ill consequences that might happen, if the Emperor should be obliged to take satisfaction upon the new conquests of the French adjoining [the *réunions*]: Adding that the Emperor was not in the condition of a slave with his hands tied in chains, otherwise than in the fancy of Monsr. de la Feuillade. (This he thought fit to take notice of, upon occasion of one of the figures under the new statue, representing a slave in chains, with the arms of the Empire, the spread-eagle, by him.)[14]

His reference to the statue of Louis XIV on the Place des Victoires, commissioned by Marshal Feuillade and recently erected,[15] was unusual in diplomatic discussions. However, it is probable that the iconography of kingship and triumph was indeed potent in creating the context for such discussions, in some cases literally so, as meetings were held in palaces, such as Versailles or the Hofburg in Vienna, where such iconography was deliberately and lavishly displayed.

The dynastic theme in the diplomacy of the period, and in the attitudes that conditioned its formulation and execution and the consequent causes of conflict, serves, like its religious counterpart, to link the pre- and post-1650 period. This continuity limits the mid-century changes commonly seen as stemming from the Peace of Westphalia (1648), which ended the Thirty Years' War in Europe, and from the Manchu seizure of China. As monarchs owed their position to dynastic inheritance, it is scarcely surprising that dynasticism provided the theme and the idiom for the policies of most of them. In the context of the age, dynasticism tended to mean dynastic aggrandizement by advantageous marriages and territorial accumulation through war. This accumulation, however, was often clearly for the benefit of dynasty rather than state. Thus, for most of the War of the Spanish Succession the Austrians fought to gain the Spanish inheritance for an Austrian cadet branch: Archduke Charles, 'Charles III' of Spain, was the younger son of Leopold I and only became the Emperor Charles VI after the death, without sons, of his elder brother, Joseph I (1705–11). This ensured that his eventual gains from the Spanish inheritance – Lombardy, Naples, Sardinia, and what are now termed Belgium and Luxembourg – were added to the Austrian patrimony. Dynastic fortune took a different course in the case of the Bourbons, so that the French ended up fighting to place a cadet branch, in the shape of Louis XIV's younger grandson, on the throne of Spain. This process was repeated when this grandson, Philip V, used Spanish resources to establish in Italian principalities his two sons by his second marriage.

Frederick the Great might describe the rulers of Prussia as the 'first servants of the state', but he had no children. For most monarchs their subjects were the servants of the ruler, albeit theirs was a service defined by traditional and legal limitations. Most republican regimes had monarchical elements, either from the outset or soon after. This was the case, for example, with the Princes of Orange in the United Provinces, and with Oliver and Richard Cromwell in the British Interregnum in the 1650s.

Imbued with bellicist values, monarchs faced an international situation made unpredictable and turbulent by the vagaries of dynastic chance. It was no accident that many of the major European wars of the period, and, also, of the quarrels that did not lead to war, took their name from succession disputes, ranging from the relatively minor, for example over the Jülich-Berg inheritance, to that over the Spanish succession which involved the largest empire in the world. In the last, it was not only the Spanish succession that was at stake. Louis XIV's recognition in 1701 of the claims of 'James III', the son of the expelled James II, made any last-minute attempt to prevent Anglo-French hostilities appear redundant.[16] The English Ambassador at Paris, the Duke of Manchester, observed, 'It shows at least this court does not intend to keep any measures with His Majesty [William III]'.[17] Dynastic claims were not by their nature readily subject to compromise, as the failure of the Partition Treaties of 1698 and 1700 to prevent war over the Spanish succession indicated. Many other conflicts arose as a result of these succession disputes. The European element of the Seven Years' War was essentially another round of the conflict caused by Frederick the Great's conquest of Silesia in 1740–41, during the War of the Austrian Succession.

A disputed succession posed a particular problem for the policies of brinkmanship followed by most powers – the attempt to obtain benefits by military preparations and the threat of force. A vacant succession lasted only for a certain period before being filled by a coronation and, in some cases, the election, or, in some other fashion, selection, of a new monarch. This forced interested parties, such as Austria in 1701, Turkey and Russia in the mid-1720s, Russia in 1733 and Bavaria in 1741, in the case of the Spanish, Persian, Polish and Austrian successions, to act speedily. It was necessary to threaten more obviously and to intervene, if intervention was judged necessary, before a certain date. The need for speed exacerbated the usual problems of brinkmanship, such as rumour and the obligation to begin military preparations early if they were to have any impact. The advance in 1701 of an Austrian force, sent to seize Milan, led to the beginning of hostilities in the War of the Spanish Succession. In 1733 the Russians could not delay moving their troops for too long if they were to reach Warsaw by the date of the royal election and thus block the election of a hostile candidate, Stanislaus Leszczynski, a former king of Poland, now father-in-law of Louis XV of France. In 1740 Frederick the Great felt it necessary to force concessions from Maria Theresa of Austria while the Habsburg succession was weak. He therefore invaded Silesia. In the summer of 1741 the French had to move troops into the Empire (Germany), and prepare diplomatically for such action, in enough time for them to be able to contribute to the invasion of Austria that campaign. The Lao dynastic schism of the 1700s led to the division of the kingdom of Lan Chang, encouraging both Burma and Siam to intervene.[18]

Whether or not the dispute involved a succession, once threats were uttered or moves were made it was difficult both to retract them, lest that was interpreted as a sign of weakness, and to control their consequences. Force was habitually used in the pursuit of interests, and not simply by notorious rulers such as Louis XIV. Danish conduct towards weaker neighbours, such as Hamburg, Holstein-Gottorp and Lübeck, was characterized by violence and the threat of violence, including blockades of Hamburg. The Danes did have a legal claim to Hamburg, which had not been an Imperial Free City in the sixteenth century. A situation which was open and, in legal terms, poorly ill-defined in the sixteenth century, with the absence of a clear notion of sovereignty – Hamburg claimed to be a Free City when the King of Denmark demanded taxes and a *Landstadt* when the Emperor did so – gave rise to conflict, once the need was felt by both sides to clarify the position in strict legal terms.

The Dutch proved singularly unwilling to withdraw their garrisons from a number of nearby towns, such as Wesel, occupied in the first half of the seventeenth century. In addition, immediately after the death of the childless William III in 1702, the Dutch seized the Orange counties of Moers and Lingen, in north-west Germany, ostensibly on behalf of a claimant, the prince of Nassau-Dietz, but, in reality, to prevent the claims of Frederick I of Prussia, who was seen as an unwelcome neighbour. Despite protests by Frederick and the Westphalian Circle, and a judgement by the Imperial Court, the Dutch refused to withdraw. Such actions add an interesting historical perspective to the modern debate about the aggressiveness and warfulness, or otherwise, of democracies. So also do Swedish attacks on Russia (1741) and Prussia (1757) during the Swedish 'Age of Liberty', when the monarchy was constrained by a powerful representative assembly and strong political parties. By modern standards, however, neither Sweden nor the Netherlands were democracies, as they were dominated by aristocratic or oligarchic factions.

Nevertheless, it was also the case that many crises did not lead to war. In 1679–81, in the *réunions*, Louis XIV occupied much of the Spanish Netherlands, as well as neighbouring parts of Germany, advancing often fanciful claims to the dependencies of territories earlier ceded to him. Despite the construction of an opposing alliance system in 1681–2, the unwillingness of the powers to fight France ensured there was no war. At the beginning of 1685, the Spanish envoy in London thought war inevitable, over the French intimidation of Genoa, and Charles II of England wanted the dispute settled, as he feared that if war broke out, it would become general.[19] And yet the issue did not lead to war. The same was true of the Baltic crisis of 1683, and again in 1686–9, as war between Denmark and its neighbours was averted.[20] War was also feared when the English and the Dutch clashed over trade in the East Indies, the English being driven out of Bantam in 1682, but it was avoided.

However, the fact that some crises did not develop into war, as threats and other moves were handled without a serious breakdown, does not mean that such threats and moves could not be crucial in leading to war. Equally, the pressure for action made it difficult to avoid moves that would serve to provoke others or to vindicate claims about the malevolence of a state's intentions. As Marshal Noailles pointed out in 1744, a long war had not been anticipated, but, once the War of the Austrian Succession had broken out, other powers had felt it necessary to intervene.[21]

That year the French foreign minister, the Marquis d'Argenson, wrote to the veteran diplomat Anne-Théodore Chevignard de Chavigny, then accredited to the court of France's exiled ally, the Emperor Charles VII, criticizing him for his continued support of aggressive schemes. He condemned Chavigny's belief that the best way to bring Austria to peace was to force her to it, claiming that this policy in the early seventeenth century had led to a war of 30 years.[22] However, three years earlier, French generals and diplomats had not yet learned the danger of leaping into the unknown and of exchanging diplomacy for war. Cardinal Fleury, the temperamentally pacific first minister at the beginning of the conflict, and a very old man who could remember the problems of the War of the Spanish Succession when his bishopric of Fréjus had been temporarily overrun in 1707, had been pushed into war by bellicose nobles at court.

An emphasis on the problems of brinkmanship in a fast-altering situation, indeed on the 'failings' of the diplomatic system, is not intended to displace the suggestion that the wars of the period cannot be simply explained with reference to 'rational factors'. It is all too easy to account for developments by suggesting the constraints and limitations of a system, to 'rationalize' and systematize both the actions of individuals and the rapidly altering flux of events in order to make wars appear obvious in hindsight and predictable to contemporaries. Such an account takes little note of the uncertainties of the past and, indeed, of the factors advanced by contemporaries: considerations of glory, honour and opportunity.

As already suggested, these linked the period to the preceding age. France went to war in 1733 more to support royal honour and to prevent humiliation and isolation than from a wish to establish her power in eastern Europe. In 1750 the Abbé de La Ville, French envoy in The Hague, informed the States General of the United Provinces, when he sent them his letters of recall, that Louis XV would not hesitate to go to war if forced by considerations of glory or in order to help his allies and maintain his engagements.[23] 'La Gloire du Roy' could be regarded as a pretext, as one British Secretary of State suggested during a breakdown in Anglo-French relations in 1755,[24] but such an argument has to be handled with care, lest it become akin to the reductionist approach employed to explain away the significance of religion in early-modern history.

It is necessary to discard the notion that glory, honour and prestige were somehow 'irrational' pursuits, and that opportunism and the absence of consistent policies were somehow less intelligent than long-term plans. Even if the argument of pretext is to be adopted, it is still necessary to assess the way in which *gloire* or national dignity could serve to win support for a policy and provide the emotional impetus that might lead to war being risked. Prestige and glory were the basis of the power of early-modern monarchs, both domestically and in international relations. They conferred a mantle of success and magnificence that was the most effective lubricant of obedience in societies that had poorly developed systems of administration and that essentially rested on willing obedience.

Most monarchs had only a limited personal interest in domestic 'reforms' or administrative change, and that which took place is often correctly linked to important ministers, such as the Köprüli Grand Viziers of the Ottoman Turks, rather than to their monarchs. Far from being a diversion from intractable domestic problems, or a means of solving these problems, war was regarded as the natural activity, indeed 'sport', of monarchs. Their upbringing conditioned them to accept such a notion, and most male monarchs spent their years of peace in activities that were substitutes for war and which served to keep their minds on military matters: manoeuvres, reviews, and the royal cavalry exercises for the court aristocracy known as hunts. Peter the Great's war games were matched by those of other young princes.

At times of war, most monarchs took seriously their role as warriors, leading their armies towards, if not always into, battle. Jan Sobieski, king of Poland, led his army to the relief of Vienna in 1683; Peter the Great led his to the sieges of Azov in 1695 and 1696, at the battle of Poltava in 1709, on the Pruth expedition in 1711, and on the advance down the western shore of the Caspian Sea in 1722; Augustus II of Saxony-Poland commanded the invasion of Livonia in 1700, and Frederick IV that of Holstein-Gottorp the same year; while Charles XII led the Swedes throughout the Great Northern War until his defeat at Poltava. Eighteenth-century European monarchs dressed increasingly in military uniform.

The situation was no different in Asia. Manipur forces under their ruler, Gharib Newaz, attacked Burma between 1723 and 1740. The Chinese Emperor commanded the army that defeated the Dsungars in 1695. Karim Khan Zand of Persia captured Basra from the Turks in 1776. Young princes were placed in the command of armies at an early age. Aurangzeb, one of the sons of the Mughal Emperor, led the expedition against the Uzbeks in 1646–7. Yün-t-'i, one of the Emperor's sons, commanded the Chinese invasion of Tibet in 1720.

The iconography of kingship, the theatre of display and cere-monial, within which monarchs lived, and through which they sought to have their role perceived, stressed martial achieve-ments, as it had done from the outset. Louis XIV had Versailles decorated with frescoes and paintings of his triumphs, such as the crossing of the Rhine in 1672. In Jacques Dumont 'le Romain's' *Allegory of the Peace of Aix-la-Chapelle*, exhibited in the Paris Salon of 1761, Louis XV, portrayed as the peace-giver, was dressed in armour as Alexander the Great.[25] In the War of the Austrian Succession, Louis, who was not an obvious candidate for warrior-kingship, had indeed been present at the battles of Fontenoy (1745) and Lawfeldt (1747) and at the siege of Freiburg (1744).

In the culture of the age, it was necessary to be a warrior to bring peace; peace was caused by war. The glory of waging war was thus also the glory of imposing peace: it was victory, not negotiation, that was glorious. On tapestries and in eques-trian statues, monarchs were depicted in military poses. Victor

Amadeus II was depicted in such a statue in the royal palace at Turin. The magnificence of ambassadorial entries was intended to reflect royal dignity and power. The emphasis on military success helped to ensure that, as far as possible, failures were presented as successes. An elaborate 'cover-up' campaign of receptions, prayers, rewards and eulogies greeted the return of Prince Golitsyn, the leading minister, and lover of Sophia, Regent of Russia, from his unsuccessful campaign against the Crimean Tatars in 1689. His failure, however, weakened his position and helped to lead to his fall from power.

Louis XIV saw victory as a crucial source of *gloire*, and this led him to favour war. This was particularly so in his early years. He clearly favoured war with the Dutch in 1672 and adopted an aggressive approach, but Louis was also willing to heed ministerial arguments for delay, although these arguments had to be couched in terms he found acceptable; in other words, they had to accept the value of war. Fluctuations in French policy in the build-up to the conflict can be attributed to Louis and to particular advisors. The finance minister, Colbert, who attempted to subject warfare (both the decision to go to war, and its conduct) to economic and fiscal criteria, was outmanoeuvred by Louvois, the army minister, and forced to find the funds for the war in order to avoid dismissal. Louvois' reiterated pressure for action appealed to Louis: he disliked quietism. Turenne, the general with Louis' ear, offered the prospect of easy alliances and quick victories, and although in 1669–70 he was initially thwarted by other advisors, his ideas gained currency, especially because they appealed to Louis and were known to do so.

However, there was little sense of how any war would develop diplomatically or militarily. Rather than planning to take Amsterdam, Louis, who closely controlled foreign policy, hoped that Spain would come to the aid of the Dutch and that he could, therefore, resume the conquest of the Spanish Netherlands, broken off when peace had been negotiated in 1668. The actual outbreak of war was delayed until the diplomatic situation was favourable, with the Dutch isolated and Louis sure of the support or neutrality of most of western Europe. That might appear an argument in favour of a prudential assessment of the decision to fight and of relative risks, but such an assessment was made within a context overwhelmingly shaped by Louis and Louvois' desire for a series of gratifying acts of valorous seizure. As so often in Louis' reign, and those of other rulers, this was a case of reason in the service of passion – if such a questionable dichotomy can be advanced. Once the war had broken out, Louis failed to use the opportunity of early successes to negotiate peace, and he lost control of the international situation.[26]

Military success was crucial to the reputation of monarchs, especially to their personal and dynastic honour.[27] War brought gains and *gloire*, both to monarchs and to their aristocracies. The latter were often eager for war, for a variety of reasons that included personal profit and prestige, a hope for advancement, and a sense that conflict was their proper role in a society in which derogation of rank for participating in a range of economic activities epitomized aristocratic notions of behaviour. Thus, the French court nobility pressed for military glory, not least in 1667 and 1741 when decisions were made for war. In 1672, when the French army crossed the Rhine, a group of young nobles shouting 'kill, kill' charged a Dutch force that was ready to surrender, only for some of them to be killed.[28]

There was a marked preference for aristocrats in command positions, especially senior command positions. This was true of the appointment and promotion policies of rulers, from Louis XIV to Frederick II. In Russia, the duty of the nobility to serve the ruler was stated and employed to rank society in Peter the Great's Table of Ranks of 1722. The prestige of military service in Europe was not undermined by the fact that many aristocrats did not serve.

'The rash measures and false steps which men are apt to be hurried into by their passions and delusive prospects of success',[29] were a frequent theme of eighteenth-century writers, both political commentators and historians. They suited the personal and moral exposition and analysis of action, the principal approach of the period. The Princess of Orange suggested in 1750 that Russian hostility towards Sweden, which nearly led to war in 1749–51, could be 'attributed in some measure to the personal dislike Chancellor Bestuchef has to Count Tessin'.[30] The same year, the Duke of Newcastle, the leading British

Secretary of State, feared that the French foreign minister, Puysieulx, would propose 'un coup éclatant' in order to maintain his tottering position at court.[31] In December 1761 Henry Fox, a former Secretary of State, wrote 'War with Spain . . . is certain', and the Spanish envoy's memorial 'imputes the war entirely to Mr. Pitt [the Elder]; and that spirit of *hauteur* which prevailed (as too surely it did) even after he left the Council'.[32]

The Times was expressing a standard view when it claimed in 1790 that many wars had 'originated in the injustice, the animosity, or the capricious passions of individuals'.[33] In the first half of the century, the passions had been regarded as momenta for action in such a way that they could be standardized as classifiable and predictable attributes of general behaviour, and it was believed that passions were something that could be subjected to standard norms and rules. By contrast, towards the end of the century, as in *The Times*, passions began to be conceived in the manner in which the philosopher Immanuel Kant (1724–1804) defined them, namely as something that relates only to the individual, counts as unpredictable and cannot be calculated at all.

The role of monarchs and ministers was not restricted to aggressive wars. They also fulfilled their role and gained prestige waging defensive wars. Charles XI of Sweden commanded the army in person in the defence of Scania against Danish invasion, defeating the invaders at Lund (1676) and Landskrona (1677). The importance of monarchs was further indicated by the number of planned, or otherwise apparently imminent, conflicts that did not break out because of the deaths of the monarchs that had planned them. In 1714 the death of the Ahom leader, Rudra Singh, led to the end of his plans for an invasion of Bengal by a confederacy of local rulers.[34]

A modern stress on the particular views of individual monarchs, rather than on 'systemic' interpretations generally of a geopolitical type, can be criticized as entailing a return to the traditions of eighteenth-century historiography, when great events were commonly ascribed to the often trivial views of individuals, or at least to their views and passions. Thus, the first important work on international law in Russian, *A Discourse Concerning the Just Causes of the War between Sweden and Russia*

(St Petersburg, 1717), by the Vice-Chancellor of the College of Foreign Affairs, Peter Shafirov, placed the blame on Charles XII's personality and persistence.[35] This was inaccurate, but it indicated the approach that seemed most appropriate. Since then, it has been usual for scholars of international relations to search for a deeper level of significance, and to adopt a set of questions, and often a timescale, that have tended to replace personal motivation by impersonal trends.

It is important not to contrast the two too sharply, but there is an essential difference between geopolitical explanations that often convey a sense of inevitability, and explanations that would encourage a more diffuse and less certain approach. To stress the role of the court, of concepts of kingship and of the atmosphere in which decisions were taken, is not simply to rely on the *deus ex machina* of the personal predilections of particular monarchs. It is, rather, to suggest that the prevalent ideas of the period played a crucial role in the context within which decisions were taken. These ideas have to be understood to appreciate the views of individuals and groups who sought war, and to realize that war was not, necessarily, the product of diplomatic failure but, rather, something sought because it produced what were seen as benefits.

The last was also true of conflicts between European powers in the transoceanic world, especially India, West Africa and North America. Hostilities there could amount to war, without any such conflict being declared. The greater role of local agents led to acts that were not necessarily approved of in home capitals, and were frequently not known about there for months. Such agents were often involved in a competitive struggle for trade and for influence amongst local rulers and tribes. The role of automous trading companies with semi-sovereign rights, such as the British and Dutch East India Companies and the British Hudson's Bay Company, increased the degree of local initiative.

The ability to reconcile transoceanic struggles between Europeans with peace in Europe became less easy as the patterns of bureaucratic authority and control became stronger within European empires, formal and informal, and as regular forces were committed to imperial policing. British and French regular forces came to play a greater role in India and North America from the mid-eighteenth century. The first major British regular army unit arrived in India in 1754.

The transoceanic deployment of forces played a central role in the breakdown of Anglo-French relations in North America in 1754–5. Mirepoix, the French Ambassador, had claimed in 1751 that only commercial and colonial issues could now lead the two states to war.[36] In its issue of 14 January 1761, *Lloyd's Evening Post* stated that the war 'was begun by the unjust encroachments and depredations made by the French and their Indians'. The territorial ambitions of Anglo-America also bore part of the blame, but the newspaper, like other British commentators, was correct to argue that French colonial policy was the issue, not the unauthorized actions of local agents. The ambitious British military response, directed from London, was also instrumental in the outbreak of war.[37]

From 1756 until 1792 there was a fundamental change of emphasis in French policy. France acted as a 'satisfied power' in Europe; its gain of Lorraine in 1766 was a working-out of the Third Treaty of Vienna of 1738, and its other acquisition, Corsica in 1768, was already an area of strong French interest. Instead of pursuing gains in the Low Countries or the Rhineland, as under Louis XIV, France sought to protect and develop its maritime, commercial and colonial position.

To use a hackneyed image, this brought her into collision with Britain. To a certain extent, the image is misleading. These were not two powers competing for the same section of road: in many respects, France and Britain could pursue separate goals. Yet there was an inherent 'structural' struggle for imperial primacy and this affected, indeed exacerbated, some of the 'spatial' disputes, particularly because the belligerent domestic political context in Britain made compromise, over North American territory in 1754–6, as, although to a lesser extent over North American political pretensions in 1774–8, very difficult.

On the French part, the escalation of confrontations with Britain into war in 1755–6 and 1778 can in part be traced to geopolitical shifts, specifically her alliance with Austria from 1756, which brought peace to France's European frontiers. However, it is also important to place weight on changes in influential opinion, particularly a greater emphasis on the role and potential of commerce and colonies, and on a sense that the British had to be humiliated in order to sustain French grandeur. In one sense, war with Britain appeared 'rational', whereas conflict with Austria could be presented as 'feudal' and, thus, anachronistic.

Nevertheless, the rationality was questioned. Voltaire condemned the British and French for fighting over the barren wastes of Canada during the Seven Years' War. Johnson asked in 1771,

> what continuance of happiness can be expected, when the whole system of European empire can be in danger of a new concussion, by a contention for a few spots of earth, which in the deserts of the ocean had almost escaped human notice?[38]

Johnson, like Swift in 1711, also attacked the 'monied interest' for benefiting from warfare:

> how are we recompensed for the death of multitudes and the expense of millions, but by contemplating the sudden glories of paymasters and agents, contractors and commissaries, whose equipages shine like meteors and whose palaces rise like exhalations. These are the men who, without virtue, labour, or hazard, are growing rich as their country is impoverished; they rejoice when obstinacy or ambition add another year to slaughter and devastation; and laugh from their desks at bravery and science, while they are adding figure to figure, and cipher to cipher, hoping for a new contract from a new armament, and computing the profits of a siege or tempest.

Aside from the moral revulsion towards those who profited from the sufferings of others, Johnson also thus offered a classic Tory critique of financial activity, of those who made money at their desks and from 'figures'. This looked back on a rich tradition, but it was in many respects outdated in a society where such activity and wealth were of growing importance. As Edmund Burke claimed in 1790, although he made the point theoretically and in a totally different context, that of the international response to the French Revolution, 'the age of chivalry is gone. That of sophisters, economists, and calculators, has succeeded'.[39]

In fact the pressure for commercial and colonial gain, for what *The Westminster Journal*, on 1 April 1749, termed 'the principle of take and hold in America', was wider in its origin than a governmental shift in favour of a foreign policy of naval power and imperial mercantilism, especially in Britain. The Seven Years' War was about not only the wastes of Canada but also its furs, the fish of Newfoundland, and, eventually, the sugar of the West Indies, and the trade of West Africa and India. It was the war of a society that understood the politics of economic competition.

For Britain, this was a major shift in priority. From the Reformation until 1713 foreign policy, by both design and necessity, had been essentially defensive in character, motivated primarily by concern about the intentions of the two most powerful states in western Europe, France and Spain, and, specifically, by their intentions towards the overlapping questions of the survival of the Reformation, the British question (the relationship between England/Wales, Scotland and Ireland), and the succession to the throne, both in the sixteenth century and from 1688. Thus, for example, a temporary lull in Franco-Habsburg hostilities after the Truce of Nice (1538), which enabled the papacy to press for action against England, led Henry VIII to construct a chain of coastal fortresses, increase the fleet and turn to the German Lutheran princes for allies. French troops were sent to Ireland in 1689, to help James II resist William III, and to Scotland, to help Charles Edward Stuart during the 1745–6 Jacobite rising. Anglo-French rivalry in this period in particular reflected domestic developments within the British Isles, and the position of the powers with reference to other states, especially Spain. Thus Elizabeth I sent troops to assist the French Huguenot (Protestant) leader,

Henry of Navarre, Henry IV, in 1589–97, in large part because he was opposed to Spain; this was the crucial factor after Henry's reconversion to Catholicism in 1593.

In the somewhat teleological account of British foreign policy that is regarded as axiomatic, conflict with France, a struggle for oceanic, colonial and commercial supremacy, has been seen as the national destiny. The situation was, in fact, more complex. The search for primacy might define the context within which interests were discussed, but, for long, there was little agreement about the discussion. Any close reading of Anglo-French relations, especially during the period from 1697 until 1754, suggests that the staple foreign policy item of the Whig creed – political, religious, cultural and economic hostility to France – was not matched by any consistent government policy. Such a discrepancy is applicable to many other historical situations.

Whig propagandists, both then and subsequently, used hostility to France as a means to fashion a politically convenient discourse of national interest, as had been done with some success from the early 1670s against, first, Charles II and, then, James II. The seizure and development of the anti-French case by particular groups of politicians was of growing significance in the last 40 years of the seventeenth century, as hostility to Spain and the United Provinces became less valid as a basis of foreign policy and less significant as a domestic political issue. This discourse of national interest was central to much contemporary discussion of international relations in systemic terms, and this has been taken up by later writers concerned to explain these relations and the conflicts of the period.

It was, in fact, the Whig hero, William III, who negotiated the two Partition Treaties with Louis XIV (1698, 1700), by which the Bourbon dynasty was promised substantial territorial gains in the distribution of the dominions of the Spanish monarchy on the death of the last male Spanish Habsburg, Charles II (1665–1700). From 1716 until 1731 Britain and France were allies and Britain was governed by Whigs. In 1733–5 and 1741 the Whig government refused to act in favour of Austria when it was attacked by France. As with Italy and Austro-Hungary at the close of the nineteenth century, two rivals maintained their rivalry and yet allied. It was in part this very willingness of the Whigs to accept a European role for France, combined with the French acceptance that Jacobite claims should not be pushed in peacetime, that led to peace and, at times, good relations between the two powers from 1713 until the early 1740s.

This essentially European agreement was wrecked by the revival, during the War of the Austrian Succession, of French aggression (1741) and of countervailing military intervention on the Continent by a bellicose British ministry (1742), a shift that prefigured that of 1792–3, although the ideological and domestic contexts were then very different. However, the western question was settled for over 40 years by the 1748 peace settlement – thereafter there were to be no territorial shifts in the Low Countries, Rhineland or Northern Italy until the 1790s. It was possible, within a context of rivalry and competing alliance systems or attempted diplomatic alignments, for Britain and France to work out a *modus vivendi* in western Europe, a process eased by the extent to which France no longer had to fear her continental neighbours as she had ever since the demise of English ambitions at the end of the Hundred Years' War.

It proved impossible, however, to make comparable progress over extra-European differences, and this helped to keep Anglo-French relations volatile from the 1750s until the check the French received in the Dutch crisis of 1787, and then, again, during the nineteenth-century heyday of imperial territorialization. In Britain, hope and anxiety, ambition and identity, were increasingly focused on imperial, colonial and maritime issues. In 1754 hostilities began over control of the Ohio River basin in North America, and in 1778 over French support for the American revolutionaries. Although Britain went to war with both Revolutionary France and Napoleon over European issues, the oceanic and colonial struggle with France played a central role during the subsequent wars. Such struggles could be incorporated in existing theories of international relations. Mechanistic perceptions allowed the addition of various coeval international systems and their juxtaposition as if they were machines in the same room. The world could be comprehended as an extension of Europe.

The so-called 'mid-seventeenth-century crisis' witnessed civil conflict across much of the world, including in Ming China, Mughal India, Ottoman Turkey and much of Christian Europe. Thereafter, although civil wars ocurred in some areas, such as the Kingdom of the Kongo (1665–1718)[40] and Manchu China (1674–81), there was a widespread re-creation of domestic order and a consolidation of territorial sovereignty. Yet, this process was resisted in some areas, such as eastern Europe. There, the period witnessed the unsuccessful and often intense[41] struggle of a number of groups, especially Hungarians, Transylvanians, Ukrainians and Cossacks, for independence. The fluidity of territorial boundaries there gave greater opportunities for these groups, as did the existence of buffer zones between the major empires. In such a situation, the identification of a sovereign authority capable of declaring war is largely an irrelevant question and may involve a measure of teleology.

The situation on the Chinese borderlands and in much of Europe changed from the 1680s to the 1750s. Formerly independent or autonomous regions were brought under control. China took over Formosa (Taiwan), Mongolia, Tibet and Xinjiang. The attempt to create an independent Ukraine under Mazepa and an independent Hungary under Rakoczi failed in 1709–11. Austria, Russia and China had no real interest in semi-independent buffer zones. This was also true of Mughal India under Aurangzeb (1658–1707). Pressure was exerted around the perimeters of Mughal power, for example in the Himalayan chain and in Afghanistan. However, Aurangzeb's successors could not maintain his position. The crushing of Catalan autonomy in 1714 helped the new Bourbon monarchy in Spain to show that it also was unwilling to tolerate semi-independent regions, while the defeat of the Jacobite risings of 1715–16 and 1745–6 brought greater British central control over the Scottish Highlands and Islands.

Thereafter, it could be argued that the distinction between foreign war and domestic rebellion was clearer in most of Europe, although in some areas, particularly Poland, the position was still ambiguous. The attempt by Prussia, Bavaria, France, Saxony and Spain to partition the Austrian Habsburg empire in 1740–42 entailed the transfer of territories between sovereign states rather than the creation of new ones by encouraging rebellion.

Rebellions and civil wars could involve high levels of conflict. Twenty thousand French troops were sent to put down the Breton rising of 1675, a force greater than the armies of many independent states. Far larger forces were sent to oppose the Rebellion of the Three Feudatories in China in 1674–81, and by Aurangzeb against the Marathas in India. In the Rakoczi rising 85,000 Hungarians were killed in battle, and in 1711 the number of Austrian troops deployed in Hungary may have reached as many as 52,000, nearly half the entire army.[42] Twenty thousand troops were needed in 1729 to suppress a rebellion in Egypt against Ottoman control. The Pugachev rising by frontier peoples and serfs in Russia of 1773–4 led to pitched battles.

This was even more the case with India in the eighteenth century. The collapse of Mughal power left a number of regional powers, often controlled by leaders who nominally held office under the Mughals. This was especially true of the Nizam of Hyderabad and the Nawab of Oudh. Any account of warfare in India has to comprehend invasions from outsiders, most significantly Nadir Shah's attack in 1739 and that of the Afghans from 1752 until 1761, war between the Mughals and their Indian assailants, especially the Maratha wars of the 1730s, or the Jat war of 1774, war between Indian polities excluding the Mughals, such as that between the Nizam of Hyderabad and the Marathas, and civil war within the Mughal 'state', especially the civil war of 1753–4 between rival viziers, Safdar Jang of Oudh and Imad-ul-Mulk. Similarly, the disastrous wars between Maratha houses at the end of the eighteenth century had much to do with the declining relative ability of the Maratha central government to arbitrate disputes.[43]

Such conflicts again raise the definition of war. To limit it to the sovereign state seems inadequate. It is possible to suggest that war involves a challenge to the authority and power of the state, a challenge that may be domestic or foreign, in so far as the two can be distinguished, in an age of multiple kingdoms, and of less clear-cut notions of sovereignty than those of the late nineteenth century.

However, such domestic challenges could take the form of food riots or large-scale smuggling, and, although it is possible to describe these in terms of social, indeed class, war, it is not clear that the inclusion of such struggles in the category of warfare is helpful. There is an analogy of social tension and specific acts, such as riots, comparable to that of hostility and war. Nevertheless, in internal violence, the 'state' was frequently not the opponent; indeed, it wielded far less power than its nineteenth-century European descendants. Instead, many riots were designed to elicit the favourable intervention of central government at the expense of the locally powerful, or to distinguish between elements in the central government, classically by attacking the agents and policies of unpopular ministers in order to lead the monarch to replace them. This played a role, for example, in the Madrid rising of 1766.

The cases of the Cossacks and the Marathas raise the issue of warrior-peoples and the extent to which their real or attempted absorption in imperial state structures affects the relationship between inter- and intra-state conflicts. This issue was to revive in a different form after 1945 as the dismantling of imperial colonial powers left sovereign units, such as India and Nigeria, that encompassed many peoples and cultures. War was endemic, useful, profitable and necessary to warrior-peoples. The self-definition of both Cossack and Maratha grew through military service. In seventeenth- and eighteenth-century India, military service was the most viable form of entrepreneurship for the peasants, shepherds, ironworkers and others who coalesced into the Maratha caste. Other ways of advancement, such as trade or loaning money to the government, were not available to these groups. Campaigns were held every year.

CONCLUSIONS

Episodes of domestic violence frequently, but by no means always, lacked a clear-cut origin. Attacks on individual tax officials or army recruiters could become more persistent and large-scale. Again, the situation in international conflicts might be similar. Small-scale hostilities could become more serious, or could be contained. This was particularly the case in the colonies, for example between Spain and Portugal in South America. In addition, states could attack others without any declaration of war. The British attacked a Spanish fleet off Sicily in 1718 and a French squadron in the Atlantic in 1755, and did not declare war subsequently for several months in either case. Furthermore, it was possible to engage in wars as auxiliary powers. The British and the French fought in Germany on this basis in the summer of 1743; war was not declared by France until the following year. William Pitt the Elder told the House of Commons in December 1755,

> An open war is already begun: the French have attacked His Majesty's troops in America, and in return His Majesty's ships have attacked the French king's ships in that part of the world. Is not this an open war? The ceremony of a declaration of war may be necessary for giving notice of the rupture to neutral powers, but it can no way be necessary for giving notice to either of the contending parties to prepare for defending themselves, or for annoying the enemy.[44]

Declarations were often delayed for diplomatic reasons, or never made because the use of military force was seen as a reasonable intervention in the domestic affairs of another power or as a short-term expedient. As most alliances contained provisions for defensive mutual assistance only, it was frequently felt necessary on many occasions to avoid the first declaration of war. There might also be domestic reasons for such a course of action. This did not necessarily preclude actions that might be judged aggressive, as in the case of Britain in 1755, and it did not prevent states from being deserted by some of their allies, as Austria was in 1733. Certain states claimed a right to intervene in the affairs of weaker neighbours, as eighteenth-century Russia did in those of Poland, and their military actions were deliberately not accompanied by any declaration of war.

An emphasis on the views of rulers, on the expectation that monarchs should and would wage war, and on the role of *gloire*, helps to explain why differences led to disputes and why unresolved disputes led to wars, but does not explain why particular wars broke out on specific occasions. This was a matter of the interaction of dispute and opportunity, an interaction in which perceptions of domestic and international circumstances by both parties played a crucial role in the attitudes and politics of brinkmanship and confrontation from which wars emerged. A sense of threat, a preparedness for war and an acceptance of conflict in international relations were all important. Asked in 1727, at a time of Anglo-Spanish tension, by a Secretary of State to report on 'what may be done against the Spaniards in the West Indies', Lieutenant-Colonel Alexander Spotswood explained the need for the seizure of Havana:

> it will be the support and bulwark of all our islands in the West Indies, which at present be too much at the mercy of the French and Spaniards, whenever it enter into their heads to make use of their West India strength to dislodge us from thence, and especially Jamaica is in imminent danger.[45]

Such an attack was not staged until 1762; despite differences, the two powers avoided war until 1739 and were allies, albeit poor allies, in 1729-33. Spotswood's suggestion, however, captured the sense of concern that characterized international relations in this period, and the resort to self-reliance in what seemed an anarchic world. He had continued by warning of the danger not only from Spain but also from Britain's then ally, France.

Concern, confusion and self-reliance can also be seen in the outbreak of war between Russia and the Turks in 1735. Neither power planned for a major conflict, and both had responded in 1733-4 to what were regarded as provocative actions by the other without fighting. Far from following a 'forward' policy of aggression towards Islamic neighbours, the Russians, by the Treaty of Gence of March 1735, had returned Baku and Derbent to Persia and recognized Persian suzerainty over the Daghestan region of the eastern Caucasus. The Turks, however, responded by ordering their protégés, the Crimean Tatars, to assert the Turkish claim to Daghestan, a move that would take them through Kabardia, an area claimed by Russia, and that would repeat a step which had led to clashes in 1733. The Russians were unwilling to accept the Turkish claim to Daghestan.

Far from there being any confident Russian plan for a long-term war to drive the Turks back, the Russians were anxious over the views of others, uncertain over their own response and, in part, affected by the defensive mentality that had earlier led to a refusal to provide assistance for Vakhtang VI of Georgia in his struggle with the Turks in 1724–5, and to the withdrawal from Persia. Nevertheless, in 1735 the Russians attempted to seize Azov, in order to block the Tatars from expanding into Kabardia. They failed, but the following year they declared war and seized Azov. The War of the Polish Succession had finished, and the Russians were now free to attack the Turks in force. Their uncertainties were played out within a context of a willingness to fight.

A lack of clarity and ready consistency can be seen not only in the situation and plans of contemporaries but also in the classifications that can be used by modern analysts. This is the case not only of wars in Europe but also of those further afield, although many of the latter have not been studied. In one that has, the Tibetan-Ladakhi-Mughal war of 1681–3, the immediate cause of the war was a religious quarrel between two Buddhist states over the position of the Dalai Lama, the spiritual leader of Tibet, who then declared war on Ladakh. The Tibetans successfully invaded in 1681, leading the Mughals to come to the support of their vassal, Ladakh. Yet this apparently familiar pattern was far from simple:

> . . . this particular case was a matter of self-defence. Besides being bound in honour to help their vassal, the Mughals could not allow the Ladakhi kingdom to be superseded by a far more powerful neighbour, absolutely new to that portion of the Himalayas and fundamentally hostile to them for religious motives. And moreover (perhaps, although not avowedly, the strongest reason for all), the control by this new power of the wool-trade route spelt the doom for the shawl industry of Kashmir, on which much of that country's welfare depended . . . there is always looming up as an incentive, in the form of a right to be defended or of a tribute or monopoly to be imposed, the wool trade.[46]

Alongside the theme of continuity in this period, it is also appropriate to stress elements of change, particularly in Europe. This can be seen by contrasting Louis XIV and Frederick II. Both sought to gain glory in and through war and were not too scrupulous in the pursuit of their interests. However, Louis XIV based his claims to German and Spanish territories, and eventually the Spanish crown, on feudal or dynastic titles. Some of these titles were spurious, but Louis went a long way to make them seem as plausible as possible.

In contrast, Frederick did not really trouble to establish any legal claims to Silesia which were even remotely plausible. This was not only the case because he was a different man, with a different character to Louis, but also because circumstances had changed. In the eighteenth century it had become natural to seek to trade off claims and titles against each other: Sicily could be exchanged for Sardinia and Naples for Parma. It proved impossible to exchange Bavaria for the Spanish, later Austrian, Netherlands (Belgium), but it was conceivable to seek to do so. Thus, Frederick could believe he could trade off his support for Maria Theresa for one of her provinces.

Such bartering had always existed, as the fate of Charlemagne's inheritance in the ninth century amply displayed, but, in the eighteenth century, it had become much less limited by considerations of prestige and historic titles than in the seventeenth, a shift that made it easier to reach peace settlements after a conflict, but that also made it simpler to begin a war when it seemed convenient. However, as in the seventeenth century, it is necessary to understand this convenience, and the more general issue of intentionality, within the context of a bellicose political culture and belligerent political practices, and, also, to appreciate that, thanks to this bellicosity, it is misleading to think in terms of modern criteria of the rationality of causes of conflict. The timing of individual wars might be unfortunate for particular combatants, but conflict itself was not irrational: it reflected the political dynamics of the age.

THREE

1775–1914: Wars of Revolution and Nationalism

There are two master keys to every Cabinet: interest and passion.

DANIEL HAILES, British Secretary of Embassy at Paris, 1784.

INTRODUCTION

Many of the more important wars of the period emerged from, or were related to, violent changes in domestic political systems; indeed, the domestic situation became even more clearly part of the international system than had been the case over the previous century. This was true of the wars of independence in the New World that began in North America in 1775 and then spread to Saint Domingue and Latin America, of the French Revolutionary Wars that began in 1792 and led to the Napoleonic Wars, and of the wars of German (1864, 1866, 1870–71) and Italian (1848–9, 1858–61, 1866, 1870–71) Unification. These were by no means the only wars in this period. The wars of European expansion associated with imperialism are dealt with in the next chapter, but there were also wars between European powers, such as the Austro-Prussian War of the Bavarian Succession in 1778–9 and the Crimean War of 1854–6, and conflicts between non-European powers, such as the Chinese invasion of Nepal in 1792, the Egyptian invasions of Saudi Arabia, and the wars between Egypt and the Ottoman Empire and between the latter and Persia.

Yet a concentration on the wars of revolution is appropriate because these were amongst the most large-scale conflicts of the period and also those that had the greatest impact on global history. Revolutionary wars, struggles in which the overthrow of structures of authority played a major role, were not exclusive to the modern age, but they were more common in it than hitherto. Furthermore, there are important methodological issues in the discussion of the causes of wars of revolution. The two most pressing are, first, the role of 'ideology' in the cause of the wars, and, secondly, the extent to which it is appropriate to distinguish between wars that began as rebellions or revolutions, most obviously the wars of independence in the New World, and those that began as a result of the international impact of states where revolution had gained hold, most obviously the French Revolutionary Wars.

It might then appear surprising to include the wars of German and Italian Unification, but they can be seen not simply as classic territorial expansionism, in this case on the part of Prussia and the kingdom of Sardinia, but also as conflicts both involving the ideology of nationalism and reflecting the radical intentions of territorial states. Nationalism was also crucial in the conflicts caused by Greek rebellion against Turkish rule and Belgian rebellion against that of the Dutch. 'Ideology' is generally seen as playing a critical role in the international relations of the period, but there has been considerable controversy over its role in causing conflict, as opposed to tension.

AMERICAN INDEPENDENCE

In the case of the American War of Independence (1775–83) there are a number of ideological 'factors' on offer, including an essentially secular explanation of the revolution, focusing on constitutional and political alienation from the practices and precepts of British rule and government, and a religious interpretation that emphasizes confessional division and tension. The limited role of government in colonial life and the general lightness of taxation made demands, that to the British appeared reasonable, seem onerous to colonists. Other material matters, for example restrictions on the advance into Indian lands, underlay what later came to be presented in elevated political terminology by a people who were determined to act with as much freedom as possible.

Yet, while these factors explain rising hostility to the imperial relationship, they alone do not account for the outbreak of war in 1775. For that, it is first necessary to turn to the British government. Faced with disaffection in North America in the early 1770s, Lord North's ministry could have adopted a conciliatory policy. In 1766 the controversial Stamp Act had been repealed and in 1782 a policy of concessions was to be adopted in the face of Irish agitation. Indeed, in 1778 the North ministry followed just such a policy towards the Americans with the dispatch of the Carlisle Commission, although by then it was too late to end the war by offering concessions.

However, in 1774–5 a different course was to be pursued. Acts of disobedience in Massachusetts, especially the Boston 'Tea Party' of 16 December 1773, were seen as requiring chastisement; and harsh legislation, the so-called 'Coercive' or 'Intolerable' Acts of early 1774, was matched by an increasing willingness to consider force. The concentration of authority in the province in the hands of a soldier, General Thomas Gage, the Commander-in-Chief, who was appointed Governor of Massachusetts, accentuated this trend, as did a failure to appreciate the extent and depth of disaffection in what was an increasingly volatile atmosphere. The absence of a civilian police force ensured that the army had to be used to maintain and restore order. Troops were the police, the arm of the state in both international and domestic politics. This helped to encourage a recourse to force. In April 1775 this culminated in violence, when troops were sent to seize an illegal arms dump at Concord.

Other considerations came, and come, into play. North's ministry had won a general election in Britain in 1774. This both led to the election of MPs who wished to see a firm line adopted and gave the government crucial room for manoeuvre in terms of domestic politics. Under the Septennial Act, no other election was due until 1781.

The international situation also appeared promising. Britain was neither at war, nor close to one. France and Spain had been soundly defeated in the Seven Years' War (1756–63) and had backed down, in the face of British naval mobilization, in a recent confrontation over the presence of a British base on the Falkland Islands (1770–71). A possibility of closer Anglo-

French relations had been offered in 1772–3, as France had sought to encourage opposition to the First Partition of Poland by Austria, Prussia and Russia, but the British government had avoided involvement. Thus, 1775 seemed a propitious moment to act in North America and, indeed, there was to be no foreign intervention on behalf of the rebels until 1778, a window of opportunity that should have allowed the British to suppress any rebellion.

Yet, as with so many wars, it was not a war that the British government thought it was beginning in 1775. Aside from the conviction that support for violent opposition was limited, so that the news of fighting at Concord and Lexington was received with great surprise in London, the use of troops and the reimposition of royal authority were not seen as an act of war.

However, although it is possible to attribute the outbreak of the war to the particular position of the British government, this is of limited value. It underplays the question of why arms were being accumulated and why there was a willingness to defy the British at Lexington and Concord. These questions can only be answered by returning again to ideological considerations and, in the last resort, those are most pertinent in the case of this conflict. The sense of the British army as a threat and of force as the way to meet this challenge was crucial, although had the British army not advanced to seize the arms, it is unclear that fighting would have broken out.

The American War of Independence broadened out to include other powers, a characteristic of revolutionary wars. Initially, the French government, keen on revenge for losses during the Seven Years' War, had been ready to provide financial and military assistance to the rebels, but unwilling to commit itself publicly to the cause of revolution and thus war. Vergennes, the foreign minister, hoped that the British would lose and, therefore, that a colonial balance of power would be restored, enabling Britain and France to co-operate in limiting the influence of Prussia, Austria and Russia, and France to re-direct expenditure from the navy. Other French ministers were more interested in the simple idea of weakening Britain. Expenditure on the navy more than quadrupled between 1774 and 1778, as the government prepared for the possibility of war.

Anglo-French tension over French aid to the rebels, specifically allowing their privateers to use French ports, led Vergennes to press Louis XVI in the summer of 1777 for French entry into the war. With war apparently near, the British government responded by seeking to delay French intervention until they had won in America. They switched in July 1777 from their earlier moderation to threats designed to intimidate. These succeeded in distancing France from the privateers in August and September, but French caution was designed to preserve peace until the situation was deemed ripe for war, and did not preclude increased preparations.

The British failure to defeat the Americans that year, culminating in Burgoyne's surrender at Saratoga and Washington's riposte at Germantown, encouraged the French to intervene and led to treaties of Alliance and Commerce with the rebels on 6 February 1778. The notification of the Treaty of Commerce to the British government on 13 March caused the recall of the British envoy, as George III could not accept the recognition of American independence. However, as neither power wished to appear an aggressor to her allies, hostilities did not begin until June when the struggle to control Channel waters commenced.

The war widened in 1779, when France persuaded her ally Spain to join. The French promised to fight on until Spain obtained Gibraltar, thus reversing the loss of 1704. The conflict further widened to include a war between Britain and the United Provinces, two eighteenth-century European 'democratic states', in the sense of countries with powerful representative assemblies. Disputes with the Dutch over their trade with Britain's enemies and over the reception of American privateers embittered relations. The once close alliance had been a casualty of the 'Diplomatic Revolution', the Austro-French diplomatic rapprochement of 1756, which made the defence of the Low Countries against France no longer credible diplomatically or militarily, as well as of Dutch financial exhaustion, war-weariness and domestic divisions, and of lack of Dutch support for Britain's colonial and maritime position. However, British ministers had continued to assume that relations could and should be close; and they believed that, under the defensive treaty of 1678, they were entitled to Dutch help against the Bourbons.

Maritime rights took mutual dissatisfaction to the point of conflict. Catherine II of Russia had issued a Declaration of Neutral Rights in March 1780, designed to protect neutral shipping from British maritime pretensions, which were widely disliked in Europe. Aware of negotiations for Dutch accession, Britain declared war in December 1780, hoping to end the supply of naval stores to France, before the Dutch could accede to the Armed Neutrality and thus acquire a Russian guarantee. The British government also wanted the war to lead to the revival of the pro-British Orangist party, as earlier Dutch defeats in 1672 and 1747 at the hands of the French had led to a revival of Orangist power; but these hopes were to be disappointed.

FRENCH REVOLUTIONARY WAR, 1792

Ideological factors were crucial to the series of conflicts collectively known as the French Revolutionary War. This war dramatically recast European international relations, destroying the Austro-French alliance and leading to the resumption of a French forward policy in the Low Countries, Germany and Italy that had been abandoned in mid-century. Ideological conviction and a search for security were rapidly transformed into a quest for hegemony.

The winter of 1791–2 witnessed a marked deterioration in Austro-French relations, one that was to culminate in April 1792 with both powers taking steps to lead to hostilities, although it was actually France that declared war first: on 20 April. The move towards war reflected specific differences – incompatible views on the rights of German princes, both in Alsace and in harbouring French *émigrés* near France's borders, but these were made more serious by a mutual lack of sympathy and understanding and a shared conviction that the other power was weak and would yield to intimidation. Within France, Brissot and other Girondin leaders saw war as a means to unite the country behind them,[1] a common drive, analysis and policy in revolutionary situations.

Relations between Revolutionary France and Austria were more acute than those between France and other powers, not so much because of their common frontier in the Low Countries as because of the fact that the ruler of Austria, Leopold II, was both Emperor and a brother-in-law of Louis XVI. In his former role, he had to protect the frontiers of the Empire, and the interests of the princes threatened by Revolutionary France, whether because they claimed rights in Alsace, or, more seriously, sheltered *émigrés*. On 29 November 1791 the National Assembly called upon Louis XVI to insist that Leopold II and the Elector of Trier, a neighbour of France, disperse the *émigré* forces on their territories.

The pressure from the Revolutionaries was more acute because it followed a half-century during which French governments had largely ceased to press on their German neighbours, and had certainly abandoned the opportunistic expansion of Louis XIV in favour of conciliation and negotiation, best expressed in a series of border treaties designed to settle disputes and establish a permanent peace. In contrast, there was no element of compromise either in the French demands of late 1791 or in their subsequent policy.[2] Furthermore, these demands were seen as more radical and threatening because of the rhetoric and reality of revolution within France. Louis XVI's authority and power were greatly limited in 1791, especially after his unsuccessful attempt to flee the country and place himself at the head of the counter-revolutionaries.

Leopold decided that a firm Austrian stance, supported by the threat of military force, seemed the best way to protect the principalities in the region from external and internal threats. He rejected the National Assembly's pressure over Alsace, and on 21 December 1791 Kaunitz, the Austrian Chancellor, informed the French envoy that if France acted against Trier, Austria would send military assistance from neighbouring Luxemburg. Such moves were automatically interpreted in France as steps designed to affect domestic as well as international circumstances. Armand Gensonné, presenting the report of the Diplomatic Committee to the National Assembly, argued that Kaunitz's statement reflected Leopold's determination to dominate the French government.[3]

Misleading expectations about the likely response of the other led both powers to war in April 1792,[4] and these suppositions reflected an atmosphere of suspicious and tension. Speakers in the National Assembly returned frequently to the theme of a link between domestic and foreign enemies: each made action against the other more necessary. The actions of the *émigrés*, the real and rumoured Austrian connections of the royal Court, and the obvious sentiments of most foreign monarchs, lent substance to such accusations, as did a strong sense that French interests had been betrayed since 1756 by her Austrian alliance, an alliance for which the fault lay with the Bourbon monarchy. Thus, the Girondin Pierre Vergniaud declared in January 1792, in a vociferous speech in which the threat to the Revolution was stressed and the call 'aux armes' reiterated, 'que la rupture de ce traité est une révolution aussi nécessaire dans l'ordre politique, soit pour l'Europe, soit pour la France, que la destruction de la Bastille l'a été pour notre régénération intérieure'.[5] The declaration of war on Leopold's successor Francis II, on 20 April 1792, was presented as the just defence of a free people against the aggression of a king. It was supported by politicians who hoped that a successful war would rally support for constitutional royalism within France, and by others, pro- and anti-royalist, who hoped that success or failure would serve their ends, for example by leading to the defeat of the Revolutionaries or by discrediting the monarchy.

The context and content of French policy formulation and execution were revolutionary. The new nature of the discussion, formulation and execution of French policy ensured that the suggestion that allies should be sought was not pursued consistently, that it was compromised by attempts to inspire political change elsewhere, and that the new universalist rationale of the French policy, its mission and ideology, made *ad hoc* attempts at compromise, and at the retention of aspects of the *ancien régime* diplomatic system, unconvincing.

In 1793 the French Revolutionary War expanded to include Britain and the Dutch. The causes of the Anglo-French war touched off a major controversy, and the issue has subsequently attracted much scholarly attention.[6] The contemporary controversy was so acute because the issue was politically crucial; it dominated British politics. It was claimed that William Pitt the Younger and his ministry sought war in order to split the opposition Whigs,[7] a groundless charge, as the Whigs were weak anyway and had been divided by their response to the Revolution. Such charges, which corresponded with unfounded French conspiracy theories about Pitt's role, neglected Pitt's sincere attempts to preserve peace.[8]

Scholarly discussion has focused on the questions of whether the war was inevitable, and if so, why, and of where responsibility for the conflict rested. A number of different arguments have been advanced, some claiming that 'diplomatic' causes were responsible for the conflict, but others focusing on domestic causes. Both diplomatic and domestic causes for war have been found on both sides, and full play has also been made of conspiracy theories, a process helped by contemporary accusations.

The mutual antipathy of the two peoples and powers was an important factor in increasing and sustaining tension. Contemporary discussion of the causes of the conflict raised this point. John Gifford argued that an 'antigallican spirit' was always seen as an honourable characteristic of a British mind. John Bowles, similarly, saw it as innate, and as crucial to British prosperity and security.[9]

Nevertheless, antipathy alone did not cause war, and Tim Blanning's recent incisive consideration of the outbreak of this conflict supports the conventional view that it was concern for the Low Countries, specifically the United Provinces, threatened by France after its conquest of the Austrian Netherlands in November 1792, that led to war. The notion of its being an ideological war is dismissed, and Blanning also suggests that governmental fear of French subversion led to hostility to France, but not to war. Furthermore, he argues that the fate of the Low Countries was also decisive for the French. In 1795 George Canning, an up-and-coming politician, focused on this issue, when seeking to win support for the war in Britain: 'Tell me if any statesman that ever lived, on being shown that France was mistress of the [Austrian] Netherlands and of Holland – no matter whether with Louis XIV – or with [the Revolutionary] Tallien . . . would not exclaim at once, "Then England *must* be at war with her".'[10]

However, this approach can be queried. It is clear that the Low Countries provided the occasion for war, and it is always important to examine closely the actual steps by which conflict broke out. It is, equally, clear that the British government had revealed a marked disinclination to become involved in the cause of counter-revolution when the French Revolutionary War began in the spring and summer of 1792, and this lends support to claims that it was not motivated by ideological considerations. Indeed, the chronology of confrontation points directly to that conclusion.

Yet Blanning too readily separates British governmental fear and resentment of French support for subversion, from their pursuit of a 'forward policy' against French expansionism.[11] Furthermore, his accurate stress on the effects of mutual miscalculations, that led each side to overestimate its own strength and the problems of its rival, is somewhat vitiated by his unwillingness to consider adequately the extent to which ideological issues were also responsible for the failure to negotiate a compromise. Fear, as much as, if not more than, miscalculation, was crucial. This fear derived on the British part from a distrust that arose from the perception of the French government as being unwilling to accept limits to its ambitions and revolutionary pretensions. Even the opposition leader, Charles James Fox, noted, 'The French disclaim any intention of interference in Dutch affairs, but whether their disclaimer, even if sincere, is much to be relied upon, I doubt'.[12]

Furthermore, the British were aware of the strength of their rival. The emphasis on misunderstanding, on the mutual miscalculation of the power relationship, is not only too schematic but also unfounded. Whatever its possible limitations, French power was readily apparent after France's victory over the

Austrians at Jemappes in November 1792. As Bowles pointed out in 1794, 'the evidence of peace is security';[13] none was offered by the policies and pretensions of Revolutionary France. War was entered into through necessity, not as a consequence of the illusions of what Blanning termed the 'Coppelia effect', after the misleading magic spectacles used by the operatic character Dr Coppelius.[14]

The points in dispute between Britain and France at the close of 1792, principally the navigation of the river Scheldt, the closure of which had been established by international treaty, and the territorial integrity of the United Provinces, were negotiable, as preliminary discussions in the winter of 1792–3 revealed. War can thus be explained by mutual miscalculation, the Coppelia effect, war by accident, error, misjudgement and illusion.

This was certainly the view adopted by certain of the critics of the Pitt ministry, especially when they focused on the failure to maintain formal diplomatic relations. The British refused to keep Earl Gower at Paris or to replace him, and they were unwilling to recognize the Republic when it was declared, and to continue receiving Chauvelin as an accredited envoy. In response to the execution of Louis XVI on 21 January 1792, news of which reached London two days later, the Privy Council, meeting with George III present on 24 January, ordered Chauvelin to leave by 1 February.[15]

When the expulsion was reported to the National Convention on 30 January, Lebrun, the French foreign minister, described the move as a declaration of war, and it has been seen in that light by some modern commentators.[16] Yet, to see such a step as the move towards war is a comment on the atmosphere of the period rather than on the necessary course of negotiations. Serious breaches in diplomatic relations had occurred over the previous century without the outbreak of war, for example between Britain and Russia (1719–30) and Britain and Sweden (1748–63). Nevertheless, in the context of Anglo-French relations in early 1793, with the fate of the United Provinces an immediate issue, and with French politicians vying to prove their revolutionary credentials in a bitter battle for power, such a breach could indeed be seen as akin to a declaration of war.

However, this is not a view supported by the British ministerial correspondence of the period. It was not so much that, as with Anglo-French relations in 1755, passion and prejudice were greater factors in the drive to war than the formal issues in dispute, but rather that for the British ministry distrust became the central issue and that this distrust entailed keeping the French at a distance.

That distrust can be treated either as 'rational' or as 'ideological', a somewhat false counterpointing. It was both. There was a 'rational' assessment that the overall thrust of French policy was aggressive, in cause and/or consequence, whatever the willingness of French agents to offer or suggest compromises on particular points, and also an 'ideological' perception of this challenge. This had two dimensions: first, a rigidity in the British response to French innovations and, secondly, a perception of French policy as ideological in its determination to new-model international relations. The tone of French policy was different both to that of Britain and to that of *ancien régime* France. This was brought home vividly to British diplomats by the unconventional conduct of their French counterparts, and by the manner and content of French public diplomacy, the 'megaphone' nature of the discussion of foreign policy in the National Assembly and the Convention. Much of the language there was of struggle. War was declared often by speakers long before the reality of actual conflict was launched.

The avowed agenda of French policy was a more serious problem for the British government. Treaties were to be recast to conform to the eternal verities of human nature, as interpreted in Paris, and the peoples of Europe were to be given their voice, enfranchized in a new diplomatic order, organized by France and supported by the bayonets of her victorious troops. This threatened Britain as much, if not more, than its immediate manifestation in the opening of the Scheldt. The threat was less concrete and less apparently immediate, but it was one that greatly concerned the British government, especially the Foreign Secretary, Lord Grenville. He made it clear that it was the general thrust of French policy, as exemplified by their claim alone to judge the continued applicability of treaties, that was central. The willingness of the French to sponsor or encourage discontent and sedition was not separable from this, not a distraction from the vital question of the Low Countries, but an indication, both of the essential objectives of French policy and of the means by which they sought to effect them. Domestic sedition in Britain was thus important, not only for its impact on British capability but also, apparently, as a vital sign of French intentions. In May 1791 Montmorin, the French foreign minister, noting the belief that the French wished to force 'tout l'univers' to adopt their new regime, had instead argued that it was up to each nation to judge what was best for itself.[17] Eighteen months later it was credible to argue that the French had bridged the two propositions by defining other nations in terms of revolutionary and pro-French populaces.

The subversive policies, sentiments and contacts of many French agents was a crucial source of distrust, encouraging the view that none could be trusted. If individual French agents, or indeed ministers, differed in private from aspects of the policy outlined above, that was of limited consequence, because they were unwilling and unable to stop it in the electric public forum that was now so crucial to its development. Far from French intentions being secondary to the fact of power, it was these intentions that were the issue. It was not a question of suspicion, for hostile intentions were proclaimed in France without hesitation and equivocation. It was not only that in late 1792 the United Provinces were threatened and British policy perforce shifted, a 'non-ideological' cause of conflict, but also that in late 1792 Revolutionary France demonstrated its resilience, vitality, unpredictability and radicalism, thus lending force and focus to 'ideological' fears. The rapid changes in France from July to September of 1792, especially the overthrow of the monarchy and the September Massacres, combined to make the new Republic seem dangerous, sinister, violent and radical to an extent that could not be comprehended in British terms.

Military success at the expense of Austria and Prussia in 1792, and the radicalization of the Revolution, made the French example appear more threatening. The need to block future French progress appeared more important than the specific points in dispute, precisely because the Republic could not be trusted. Lord Auckland, the influential envoy in The Hague, argued that the navigation of the Scheldt was not, itself, of much importance, as the channel was not good for navigation, but that was not the point, for, as Auckland noted, the rights of the Dutch to insist on the continued closure of the Scheldt were clear in international law, and the French had unilaterally abrogated them. French victory made the revolutionary threat apparent and concrete, at the same time as the Revolution itself seemed more alien, in no fashion a replica of the British and American revolutions of 1642 and 1775. British politicians were obliged to determine and express their views in response to a series of statements from Paris that appeared hostile and without likely end. Each individual declaration was less significant than the series, and they were proclaimed without any sense that conciliation and negotiation were a necessary part of any process of change.

Just as the avoidance of war involves the preservation of peace, and it is useful to try to explain both, so also with the outbreak of war and the end of peace. In the context of the 1790s, the preservation of peace would have entailed acceptance of a threatening French hegemony in Western Europe, and that was implausible. It would have been possible only if the analysis advanced in France, of a feeble Britain threatened by domestic radicalism, had been accurate, but it was not. French talk about their desire for an alliance was of scant assistance, as it was clear that opinion in Paris was divided as to whose alliance in Britain should be sought. The Republic's attitude to treaties scarcely encouraged any reliance on French assurances, and, as the instability of her politics affected her diplomatic personnel and policy, conspicuously so in the case of her representation in London, it was difficult to see whose assurances were to be sought.

Any Anglo-French understanding would have been of an uncertain duration, might have encouraged radicalism in Britain, and would have made it difficult to develop links with other powers or to influence their views. And yet, as French constancy, both domestic and international, could not be relied upon, such links would be necessary for Britain, not least to guarantee any Anglo-French agreement. Such an agreement would have been viable in the long term only had it been part of a larger international settlement.

Distrust is a constant in international relations, but there are types and degrees of distrust. In 1792–3 it was no longer a question of seeing the French threat in traditional and quantifiable terms, such as naval preparations. Instead, the unpredictability and potency of French aspirations, and the links, both real and imagined, between British radicals and France made the situation appear far more threatening.

The nature of British policy ensured that her confrontation with France would be made to appear 'non-ideological'. It was necessary to put policy in the best light possible for both domestic and international reasons, and this could be done by being seen to come to the defence of an ally in accordance with treaty obligations. Yet that was far from the entire story, as previous failures to support allies indicated.

'Ideology' was not simply at stake on the British side. The declarations by the French, and the debates they sprang from, reflected the application of philosophical idealism to international relations, with all the cant and the self-righteous response to the views of others that was to be anticipated. The new utopian society that was being advocated and created in France was not essentially designed to be formed with reference to the concept of the territorial state. In so far as the new politics and ideology illuminated the policy of the French government, they did not encourage the limitation of policy aspirations nor compromise with the interests of territorial states. The Foreign Minister Lebrun's instructions revealed an unwillingness to accept the validity of other perceptions, and his wish to maintain peace with Britain was not accompanied by any consistent willingness to compromise with her to any serious extent. There was no sustained attempt to explain to the Convention the views of other powers.

French domestic developments helped the move towards confrontation by creating an institution – the National Assembly and, later, the Convention – and a didactic and violent political culture that encouraged both the public expression of specific views on foreign policy and attempts to influence policy with these. The public debate on foreign policy in Revolutionary France in 1791–3 had a similar effect to that within non-revolutionary Britain in 1739 and 1755: it encouraged those ministers and politicians who wished to fight, and made others hesitant about expressing their opposition. More cautious French ministers lost the ability to push through their own ideas, and foreign governments were aware of this.

The idea that domestic change within France could be accepted so long as she renounced proselytism was not one that enough French politicians were willing to accept and fight for to make it credible. Compromise over international issues was no more on the table in Paris with those who were setting the pace of French politics than was compromise over Louis XVI's head. To compromise was to betray the Revolution, a shallow, harsh and destructive thesis. Subsequent French policy scarcely revealed a willingness to accept limits, although that was also true of other powers, as shown most clearly with the three Partitions of Poland (1772, 1793, 1795). In northern Italy, initial French victories led to pressure for further conquest in order to satisfy political and military ambitions and exigencies.[18] The Directory government (1795-9) believed war necessary in order to support the army, to please its generals and, for these and other reasons, to control discontent in France, not least by providing occupation for the volatile generals. Military convenience, lust for loot, the practice of expropriation, political conviction, the political advantages of a successful campaign, and strategic opportunism all encouraged aggressive action, as with the occupation of the Papal States and Piedmont, and the invasion of Switzerland in 1798. Distrust, rather than the specific points at issue, similarly proved the crucial element in leading France and Austria to renew hostilities in 1798.

THE NINETEENTH CENTURY

The seizure of power in France by Napoleon in 1799 might seem to reflect a return to *ancien régime* patterns of diplomatic activity and, thus, causes of war. The inexorable scope of his ambition and his vainglorious capacity to alienate others can be seen to repeat those of Louis XIV. Just as his regime marked the end of radicalism within France, so it can be seen as reflecting and sustaining an abandonment of revolutionary objectives and methods in international relations. This would, therefore, suggest that a fundamental divide came, not with the final fall of Napoleon and the Vienna peace settlement of 1815, but, rather, with his rise to be First Consul (1799) and then Emperor (1804). Such an approach can be taken further by suggesting that there was, therefore, a fundamental continuity throughout the nineteenth century: Napoleon III (President of France 1848–51, Emperor 1852–70) could, justifiably, look to the example of Napoleon I.

Such a continuity, however, did not mean that the return of France to a monarchical system under Napoleon I entailed a return to an *ancien régime* system of international relations. Instead, a characteristic feature of warfare, both in the Napoleonic period and subsequently, was a degree of popular mobilization that was greater than that of the pre-revolutionary eighteenth century and one that owed much to measures to obtain a favourable public opinion. This focused on nationalism understood both as a positive force for identity and cohesion, and as a negative xenophobic response to others, both other nation states and incorporating international forces, most obviously Napoleonic France. This response led to violent episodes that could be presented as incidents justifying hostilities or the threat of war. Thus, in 1797 the French embassy in Rome was occupied by papal police during a riot, and a French general killed, while in the following year the flag of the French embassy in Vienna was insulted by a crowd, leading to a demand for satisfaction.

The need for domestic support in wartime encouraged not only propaganda but also an explanation of conflict that would appear acceptable. Combined with the contemporary emphasis on the nation, this led to explanations that hinged on the defence of national interests and honour; but such a defence could well be advanced and presented in aggressive terms.

Napoleon's foreign and military policies were not only a continuation of those of the 1790s in the reliance on popular mobilization. There was also a similar unwillingness to accept compromise, a desire to remould Europe, and a reliance on the politics of expropriation that had led not only to gains by Revolutionary France but also to the three Partitions of Poland (1772, 1793, 1795). Napoleon showed himself unwilling and unable to maintain peace. The Treaty of Lunéville with Austria (1801) and that of Amiens with Britain (1802) were followed, not by any serious attempt to control disputes, but by military consolidation and political aggrandizement that were rightly perceived as threatening. Napoleon broke the clause of the Treaty of Amiens in which he had agreed to respect the neutrality of the Batavian Republic, formerly the United Provinces.

He was happiest with force; his character, views, ambitions and ambience did not lend themselves to accommodation, other than as a short-term device. Thus, having signed the Treaty of Amiens, which included a provision for the French evacuation of Egypt, Napoleon sent Colonel Horace Sébastiani to report on the possibility of a reconquest. His positive report was published in the official *Moniteur*. This was not the conduct of a ruler willing to accept territorial or procedural limits on his hegemony, and it exacerbated British distrust, leading to a refusal to evacuate Malta despite having agreed to do so. Napoleon sought satisfaction, not as part of a process of negotiation and conciliation, but as something to be seized.

As a result, he wrecked the hopes of those who had hoped for partnership, or at least co-operation, with France, such as Alexander I of Russia. Alexander's peace plan of 1803 was rejected because it would have required France to evacuate Hanover, Italy, Switzerland and the United Provinces. In the early 1800s the Austrian government sought to accommodate itself to French power and adopted a conciliatory approach towards extensions of Napoleon's power in Germany and, in particular, Italy, only to find, in August 1805, that France demand Austria demobilize and formally declare its neutrality – in other words, surrender its capacity for independent action. Neutral Naples and Hanover were both occupied in 1803. Portugal was invaded in 1807, despite its attempts to appease Napoleon, because he insisted on closing it to British trade and saw its conquest as a way to increase the French military presence in Iberia. The assault on British trade was a unilateral policy formulated and executed without consultation with client states, allies and neutrals, and this hurt them badly. An economy policy centred on French interests meant that Napoleon's effort to anchor his new dynasty in Europe found no popular roots.

Once conquered, there was no attempt to conciliate the Portuguese. The following year, Napoleon used the disputes between Charles IV and Crown Prince Ferdinand in order to replace the Bourbon monarchy in Spain by a Bonapartist one, that of his brother Joseph. A nationalist rising led to French occupation and a long-standing war. In December 1808 the Austrian government again decided on war, because it felt its safety threatened by French policy and feared a recurrence of the coup method already staged against Spain. Once armed, the finance minister warned that the armaments could not be long sustained,[19] thus increasing the pressure for action, rather as with the Swedes in 1700. There was a sense that there was no choice, that French policy anyway threatened to impose the consequences of defeat, and that war was the sole alternative.

Austria got both war and defeat in 1809, but the Treaty of Schönbrunn left the Duchy of Warsaw, a French client state in Poland, with gains from Austria, and this threatened Russia. For over 250 years Polish weakness had been a condition of Russian strength. Napoleon's refusal to accept a draft convention, negotiated by his ambassador to Russia, guaranteeing that the kingdom of Poland would not be revived, greatly increased Russian distrust and ensured that French actions were viewed through this prism. These included, in 1810, the French annexation of the Duchy of Oldenburg, which had dynastic links with the Romanovs and had been guaranteed in the Franco-Russian Treaty of Tilsit in 1807.

At the end of 1810 Russia left the French economic camp when it abandoned the Continental System; Stalin did not take any comparable step prior to Hitler's attack. Napoleon responded to Russian independence, first with bluster, but also, increasingly, with military preparations. He did not respond positively to Russian diplomatic approaches the following spring. Having assembled a powerful coalition against Russia, Napoleon attacked in 1812, the logic of his system demanding the curbing of his victim. Caulaincourt, a leading courtier, told Napoleon, 'Undoubtedly your majesty would not make war on Russia solely for the sake of Poland, but rather that you should have no rival in Europe, and see there none but vassals'.[20]

Napoleon's will to dominate was both personal and a continuation of that of the Revolution. It ensured that peace treaties were imposed, and that, once made, the French sought further benefits, while their defeated opponents felt only resentment and a determination to reverse the settlement. This, in turn, led to further conflicts. Whereas the European peace treaties of 1763 – Hubertusberg and Paris – had been followed by over a decade of peace between the former combatants, and that of Vienna ushered in a longer period, the years from 1795 to 1814 were a great age of peace treaties, but repeatedly saw them broken. This was due not only to the sense that the French position was unacceptable and that Napoleon could know no limits but also to the conviction on the part of opponents that the French could be held and even beaten: war was unavoidable and victory possible. This inspired not only the attacks of 1792 and 1793 but also subsequent coalitions. Britain, the paymaster, if not pivot, of these coalitions was not offered peace after 1804.

As with other major conflicts, such as the two World Wars of the twentieth century, hostilities spread, and other disputes were exacerbated and subsumed into the greater struggle. Thus the Russian attempt to bring Sweden into the Continental System led to war in 1808, while the momentum of Russian success over France in the winter of 1812–13 led to a wave of popular enthusiasm that pushed the Prussian government into declaring war on France in March 1813. Napoleon's refusal to negotiate peace, or to understand that peace entailed compromise, led Austria to join the anti-French camp later that year.

The Napoleonic regime celebrated power, not least the power of victory, as in Gros' battle paintings, such as *Napoleon at the Battle of Eylau*. A quasi-mystical emphasis on the cult of the warrior can also be seen in the celebration of Ossian, for example in the decorations at Malmaison. The settings of the regime were not those that might encourage moderation. Indeed, the looting of Europe's artistic treasures to glorify its new centre encapsulated the apparent benefits of aggression.

Napoleon's unwillingness to accept limits for any length of time[21] stemmed from his personality, but also from a related assessment of a Europe in which the hegemony of one power – himself – was unconstrained by any outside force. This was the international politics of Imperial China, or of the twentieth-century USA towards Latin America. It created far more problems in Europe, with its traditions of multipolarity, and this ensured that the Napoleonic system and psyche required force, a force that anticipated that of Hitler. Napoleon did not understand compromise, and rejected the excellent advice he received.

Napoleon's views contributed strongly not only to repeated breakdowns of compromise peaces but also, more generally, to a sense that he could not be trusted, a sense that, in turn, affected the attitudes of other rulers to his specific demands. This distrust exacerbated more general problems of misperception. A recent study of the outbreak of war between Britain and France in 1803 argues that the two powers went to war reluctantly as a result of a combination of misperceptions:

> Although the decisive misperception was the British conviction that Bonaparte was planning to send a second expedition to Egypt, the difficulty in maintaining amicable Anglo-French relations owed less to geopolitics and more to misperceptions based upon divergent cultural traditions governing the law and the powers of the state.

This affected French views of the British failure to act as Napoleon wished against critical *émigré* writers. In turn, the British were unwilling to mould their laws to suit the French government. Each side became certain of the other's hostility.[22] The nature of Napoleonic government, at once authoritarian and radical, greatly increased the chances of such cultural misperceptions.

AFTER THE VIENNA SETTLEMENT

Bellicism was not banished when peace was restored to Europe in 1815 by both the Congress of Vienna and Napoleon's defeat at Waterloo. Aside from traditional warlike constituencies in royal courts and landed aristocracies, the emphasis on national honour was not one that lent itself to compromise, while the growing habit of discussing nation as well as, or instead of, dynasty did not lead to a more pacific approach. 'Nations' might have interests that were every bit as urgent as those of dynasties. Indeed, national honour in the form of resentment at the high-handed treatment of American shipping, sailors and territorial waters as part of the British commercial conflict with France led to the War of 1812 between the two powers.[23]

A further cause of confrontation stemmed from the ideological legacy of the Revolutionary and Napoleonic period. The search for new principles and practices of international relations to replace dynasticism and religion entailed great difficulties, not least because these principles and practices were expected to deal with a volatile situation that was greatly different to that of the *ancien régime*. The theory of a collective security system had existed prior to the French Revolution and, indeed, considerable efforts had been made in the 1710s and 1720s to ensure that such a system would preserve the Peace of Utrecht (1713). However, the theory and practice of collective security received a great boost from the Revolutionary/ Napoleonic period, both because such a system appeared necessary in order to protect states from the advance of Revolutionary France and because the threat of radical domestic movements led to pressure for action against the foreign source and support of such movements. Edmund Burke had pressed for intervention against the French Revolutionaries as a legitimate defence of order within the parameters of the Commonwealth of Europe.[24]

Paul Schroeder has suggested that the Vienna system satisfied the essential requirements for peace, namely mutual awareness and restraint, both between states and, more generally, within the system. He argues that such restraint had not existed during the late eighteenth century, and that, indeed, the balance of power theme of the period served principally to destroy the interests of lesser powers by fostering the notion of equivalence of gains for the stronger, as in the partitions of Poland. To Schroeder the Vienna system reflected a collective mentality that grasped the importance of common responsibility to certain standards of conduct in international relations.[25]

However, Friedrich von Gentz, the Secretary to the Congress, recorded the protestations of Prince Metternich, Austrian foreign minister, and other participants about the nobility of their aims while they grabbed what they could. They were only restrained by intelligent self-interest, a desire for stability in order to ensure their own survival and security. For Metternich, consensual politics were an obvious way to compensate for Austria's limited resources in relation to her commitments. Several of Alexander's advisers saw the congress system as an instrument in the hands of Russia's rivals to manipulate the Tsar to their advantage. Fear of France, Bonapartism and revolution were the prime causes of such unity as existed. Moreover, financial exhaustion after the extensive and expensive warfare during the period from 1792 until 1815 may have been as important in keeping the peace as the understanding of the need for restraint that Schroeder discusses.

A collective mentality of sorts persisted after the Congress of Vienna of 1814–15. As a result, states combined to resist apparent aggressors, as in the Crimean War of 1854–6, and sought to limit revolutionary movements and their foreign sponsors, as with the Holy Alliance of 1815 and the Congress System. The Crimean War illustrated the potential gap in apparent magnitude of seriousness between the ostensible cause of an international dispute and the motives that impelled some of the participants. French interests in the Near East led to support for demands by Catholic priests for access to the Holy Places. Turkish concessions led to matching demands from Russia, the protector of the Orthodox clergy, but Russian pressure was resented by the Turks, who had a long tradition of rivalry, and suspicion of Russia was shared by Britain, with its concerns about the route to India, and France. Both welcomed the opportunity to defeat Russia, but war only started after a failed attempt to intimidate Russia into leaving Wallachia and Moldavia, which it had occupied.[26]

NATIONALISM

The extensive redrawing of boundaries in Europe in the Revolutionary/Napoleonic period encouraged an attitude towards territory in which traditional claims played a far smaller role than in the eighteenth and, still more, seventeenth centuries. This led to a search for new legitimacies, in which nationalism played a major part, and also a willingness to support territorial aggrandizement that was conceived and presented as of benefit to states rather than dynasties. In place of historic claims, the rationality of expansionism focused on a logic of national identity and state interest. The two were sometimes seen as similar, as for example in the case of France, but in multinational empires, such as Austria, the emphasis was on the latter, and dynastic considerations continued to play a greater role in the definition of state interest.

Liberal nationalists, especially the founder of the Young Italy and Young Europe movements, Giuseppe Mazzini (1805–72), argued that the suppression of nationalities and nationalism led to conflict, that people were naturally pacific, and that if the peoples of Europe had governments of their own choice there would be a pacific federation of nations. Thus, according to Mazzini, war resulted from the oppression of peoples by dynasties denying the precepts and practice of liberal nationalism. He also argued that wars of liberation – populist, just wars – would be necessary to produce peace.

However, nationalism conflicted with the attempt to maintain the peace system created by the Congress of Vienna. There were direct clashes, as with the suppression of nationalist movements in Naples (1821) and Spain (1823) by Austria and France respectively, but the issue was complicated as some major powers came to support nationalist movements. Thus, Prussia came to the support of rebellious German subjects of the King of Denmark in Schleswig-Holstein in 1848, and Russia intervened in the Balkans against the Turks, although as the Turks were not seen as an integral part of the European system this can be seen as a separate case in which traditional cross-cultural rivalries played a major role. Russian support for Greek independence led the Sultan to declare a holy war in 1828. Russia also intervened in 1877 in order to protect Serbia and Montenegro, which had attacked Turkey the previous year, as a crisis, began by risings in Bosnia and Bulgaria in 1875, spread. Publicity about the massacre of rebels and their supporters in Bulgaria led to pressure for international intervention and an unsuccessful attempt to reach a diplomatic situation in 1876–7 by imposing a programme of reforms. In 1912 the Bulgarian government was, in part, encouraged to attack the Turks by popular pressure on behalf of compatriots in Macedonia.

More generally, Bulgarian warfulness reflected the nationalist imperative. The goal of Bulgarian policy was the restoration of the boundaries of the Great Bulgaria as this was designated by the preliminary Treaty of San Stefano in 1878, before this was revised by the Congress of Berlin of that year. 'Bringing the scattered people together', if necessary by force, was in accordance with the nationalist policies of Italy, Prussia, Serbia, Greece and other states. Bulgaria's wars, down to her participation in World War Two, can be seen as attempts to achieve 'national unity'. Most Bulgarians – the ruling elite and the ordinary people as well – believed, with decreasing intensity due to successive defeats, that this was a 'just cause', which did not require even an attempt at justification. In contrast, all Bulgaria's neighbours suspected her of hegemonic ambitions, as the scope of Bulgaria's ambitions would have led to a Bulgarian preponderance in southeastern Europe.

The fate of nationalist movements became entwined with that of tensions between the great powers. The gain of independence by a protégé nation thus came to play a role akin to that of placing a member of a ruling family on another throne in the seventeenth and eighteenth centuries. Both were honourable, led to a major gain of prestige, and did not revolve around the direct acquisition of territory. Russian and French support of Greek and Belgian nationalism respectively, including the movement of French troops into Belgium in 1832, led to concern on the part of other powers in the 1820s and 1830s, but they intervened to contain the crises rather than to use them as an opportunity for a major war. Britain and Russia imposed an end to fighting in Schleswig-Holstein in 1848. Thus, suspicion, even confrontation, did not necessarily lead to a situation in which conflict spiralled out of control. Austria and Prussia stayed out of the Crimean War. Whereas competing interests and anxieties in the Balkans had precipitated and, in part, been responsible for the Crimean War, Britain did not fight in the next Eastern Crisis: in 1878, Anglo-Austrian pressure led to Bulgaria gaining far less territory from Turkey than had been anticipated, without Bulgaria's patron Russia beginning a war, and seven years later the Bulgarians took over Eastern Rumelia, leading the Serbs to declare war on them. Bulgarian victory was again contained, in this case by Austrian pressure.

The pursuit of state interest did not, and does not, have to lead to war; indeed, it was, and is, usually pursued peacefully, but in the nineteenth century it was, again, affected by a bellicist culture. Nationalism was glorified as a struggle, and not seen as only for pursuit by peaceful means. Much of the conflict of the period was directly related to struggles for national liberation and national liberalization, and these struggles were articulated in a political language of war. A hostility to compromise was widespread, and the limits to the consensual policies discussed by Schroeder were, increasingly, apparent. The Treaty of Paris of 1856, which ended the Crimean War, sought to promote such behaviour, only for it to be followed, almost immediately, by a string of wars and crises which largely ignored its recommendations and the concert.

Nationalism was not only important in Europe. A sense of new nationality also encouraged popular mobilization in the Latin American Wars of Liberation. Napoleon's seizure of Spain in 1808 collapsed established patterns and practices of authority and power in Latin America, and encouraged local seizures of power, beginning in Venezuela and Argentina in 1810. When, however, Spanish partisans sought to reimpose control, especially after the Bourbon restoration in Spain in 1813, large-scale warfare broke out, Spain regaining much of Latin America by 1816. However, as in France in 1792, it proved impossible to re-create the previous world. Furthermore, once revolution had a base, the collapse of Spanish power in particular colonies became as much a matter of war with forces from this base as of overthrow by local rebellion. Thus, forces from Argentina helped defeat the Spaniards in Chile in 1818, and their counterparts from Chile did the same in Peru from 1821.

Nineteenth-century national identity was, in part, expressed through martial preparedness, most obviously with conscript armies. These, in turn, made it easier to wage war, because the states were always prepared for it, or at least less unprepared than in the past. The scale of preparedness encouraged anxiety about increases in the military strength of other powers and a bellicose response in crises, as, more specifically, did the process of mobilizing reservists, for mobilization was seen as an indicator of determination and, once it had occurred, there was a pressure for action.

These factors can be seen as playing a role in the wars begun by Napoleon III of France, Bismarck's Prussia, and the Kingdom of Sardinia during the Risorgimento (the struggle for Italian unification). It is also possible to present these as regimes, both that had policies they considered worth fighting for, and that were to some degree precarious, or, at least, felt that the successful pursuit of an aggressive foreign policy and war would lead to a valuable accretion of domestic support. The regimes of nineteenth-century Europe were operating in an increasingly volatile situation in which urbanization, mass literacy, industrialization, secularization and nationalism were creating an uncertain and unfamiliar world. The temptation to respond by the use of force, to impose order on the flux, or to gain order through coercion was strong. A growing sense of instability both encouraged the use of might to resist, or channel, it, and provided opportunities for 'unsatisfied' rulers and regimes that wished to overturn the diplomatic order. Napoleon III's decision to support Piedmont in 1859 owed much to his wish to unravel the 1815 peace settlement.[27]

In addition, successful wars could be a valuable way to win domestic prestige and support, although the desire for such support ensured that *realpolitik* was generally less blatant than in the eighteenth century. Napoleon III found it easier, more conducive and more appropriate to seek backing by waging wars, or launching expeditions, in Russia, Italy, China and Mexico rather than by broadening his social support by domestic policies. These expeditions coincided with a period of domestic peace after 1848; civil war in France, in the shape of the Paris Commune, did not resume until after serious failure in foreign war. Having demonstrated and sustained a role by leading the Risorgimento, Victor Emmanuel II, King of Sardinia and then of Italy (1849–78), found it useful to declare war on Austria in 1866, in order to head off pressure for reform from left-wing politicians. Similar domestic problems encouraged Wilhelm I of Prussia to press for war that year, and had the same effect on Franz Joseph of Austria, although the unsettled nature both of the Austro-Prussian condominium of Schleswig-Holstein and of the political situation within Germany were themselves a cause of serious dispute.

Indeed, Austrian policy can, in part, be viewed in terms of the relationship between domestic politics and war. Success in the latter encouraged a more authoritarian politics, as in 1849 and 1865. War in 1866 seemed the only solution to the domestic political and financial problems of the Habsburg state, and the sole way to tackle fissiparous nationalism, most obviously in Venetia.[28] Austria was also widely regarded as stronger. In the case of Prussia, but not Austria, success in war encouraged a reliance on force, a repetition of the situation in France under Napoleon I.

Nationalism was both a genuinely popular sentiment and one that could be manipulated to legitimize conflict. It encouraged a sense of interest and superiority against and over others. Politicians and newspapers could stir up pressure for action, as with American entry into the popular American-Mexican War of 1846–8,[29] or when the Chilean press and opposition attacked the 1878 compromise with Argentina over the Straits of Magellan, leading to riots. The following year, similar pressure over Bolivian financial demands on the Chilean nitrate company operating in the Atacama Desert, in breach of an 1874 agreement over taxes, led the government to send troops into the disputed region. Nationalism also developed in the Afrikaner republics of Transvaal and Orange Free State, leading them to oppose Britain's attempts to dominate both them and southern Africa. In 1899 the two republics declared war on Britain. Bellicose political pressures within the USA helped lead to a war with Spain in 1898 that the government did not want.[30]

Within Europe, public opinion played a role in crises, unsurprisingly so in societies where mass participatory politics were becoming more common. In Britain, cumulative Russophobia helped to push a dithering government towards entry into the Crimean War. Public opinion in France and Germany played a role in creating an atmosphere favourable for war in 1870. This opinion had been manipulated when the German Chancellor

Bismarck edited a telegram, recording a meeting between Wilhelm I of Prussia and the French ambassador Count Benedetti at Bad Ems, in order to make their discussion over a Hohenzollern candidature for the vacant Spanish throne appear acrimonious and threatening. Certain leading figures in Paris, notably the foreign minister, Gramont, were easily provoked, or simply lost all sense of proportion. In contrast, the strongly nationalist Adolphe Thiers thought French honour had been satisfied by the first meeting of Wilhelm I and Benedetti. Bismarck, like Franklin Roosevelt in 1941, was determined to have full national support if there was a war. Both also liked to have several options open to hand, and often left it to others to bring matters to a head. Napoleon III, who was hostile to growing Prussian power, did so by declaring war.

Given the political culture of the period, it was possible to gain a favourable public for government policies by adopting an aggressive stance abroad, as Bismarck did when Prussia invaded Denmark in 1864,[31] and, in many situations, it appeared not only possible but also necessary. Although there was opposition to militarism in some circles, especially on the left politically, it tended to succumb to nationalism during crises. The diaries and letters of German participants in the Franco-Prussian War reveal widespread support and enthusiasm for the conflict. In August 1914 the German Social Democrats decided to support their government in the war.[32]

Changes in military thought and practice encouraged warfare. The development of Prussian strategy under Helmuth von Moltke the Elder, Chief of the General Staff from 1857 until 1888, was based on a determination to envelope the enemy forces and to destroy the enemy's military effectiveness. This totality of war encouraged a sense of war as a testing ground of states. The application of reason to war, as in Moltke's development of a railway mobilization plan, was related to an understanding of war as reason. In nineteenth-century political culture the traditional cultural bellicosity of the European landed elite was linked to a more 'modern' planned warfulness.

The volatile politico-social situation in European countries also affected the attitude towards the use of force in domestic political disputes. Revolution and Counter-Revolution were important legacies of the Revolutionary/Napoleonic period. They came to a height in 1830 and 1848, and, also, interacted with the struggles for national unification in Germany and Italy. The pace of socio-economic change exacerbated tensions and created a disorientating sense of uncertainty and movement in many parts of Europe.

Thanks in part to domestic political contexts and to the nature of ideological confrontations, many issues were no more amenable to negotiation and compromise than those of religious conflict had been in the sixteenth and seventeenth centuries. This was true of the quest for independence for Greece and Poland, and for national unification in Italy, although less so of the struggles for influence and control between Austria and Prussia, and France and Prussia. Religious disputes continued to play a role in some areas, leading in 1847 to civil war in Switzerland, as the outnumbered forces of the Catholic *Sonderbund* launched an unsuccessful pre-emptive attack on the forces of the hostile Protestant/radical-dominated Swiss Diet. In the case of weaker powers, major states could intervene, making efforts to impose settlements. Thus, in 1832 the British secretly aided one side in a Portuguese civil war fought over crown and constitution. Russia intervened in the domestic affairs of its Balkan protégés, for example leading to the departure of Alexander Battenberg, the Prince of Bulgaria, in 1886.

In military terms, the mid-nineteenth-century 'internal' crises were very different to those of the seventeenth century. Whereas the military forces of rulers and their opponents had been similar, and in some cases well-matched, in the mid-seventeenth century, as in the British civil wars, the French *Fronde* and the Bohemian (1618), Catalan (1640) and Portuguese (1640) revolts, in the mid-nineteenth century there were greater discrepancies in the military force at the disposal of both sides. Whereas the Habsburgs had lost control of Prague in 1618–20, in 1848 they regained control of the city. Resistance was also crushed in Vienna (1848) and Hungary (1849),[33] as it was in Paris in the case of the Commune in 1871.

However, much of the discrepancy was explained by the strength offered to governments by their control of conscript armies, although that was not the sole factor. An absence of foreign support could also be crucial and, indeed, the stability of the international system, certainly in contrast with that, say, of the early 1790s, emerged clearly in the period between 1815 and 1860. Greece and Italy were both very dependent on the help (or inaction) of certain powers: the British fleet could have sunk Giuseppe Garibaldi's expedition to southern Italy in 1860, but did not do so. The Poles, however, were doomed through the lack of foreign help when they rose against Russian rule in 1830–31 and 1863–4.

At a very different scale, the gold miners who were overcome by British troops and Victoria police at the Eureka Stockade in Australia in 1854 were suppressed by a military system that did not rely on conscripted forces. Rebellion or uncertainty in such forces could threaten governmental stability. The Polish rising of 1830 began with a mutiny in Warsaw. This weakness was not new, but the potential politicization of a citizen army was greater than that of military forces in pre-Revolutionary Europe. The extent to which military lobbies and criteria played a role in international crises was also greater.

The discrepancy in military force was far less in the American Civil War (1861–5)[34] because, prior to the war, the government did not control a conscript army. A combination of the decentralization of a federal system and limited government gave rebels a far greater chance than in the case of European states. The war itself reflected the weakness of the federal structure, the vitality of states' rights, the relative newness of American government, and a political system that could not cope with the strains of big issues, such as slavery and expansion, which became acute in the 1850s, coupled with the need to establish American values in a newish nation.

In Spain, opposition to the government in the Carlist Wars (1833–40, 1848, 1870–76) was helped by traditions of guerrilla warfare that looked back to the struggle against Napoleon.

There was also conflict between rival republican groups: Federalists against Centralists. The bitterness with which Spaniards fought each other stemmed from the War of Liberation of 1808–13. Clerical propagandists transferred earlier calls for action, against France and her supporters, to the new target of the Liberals. Allowing for the importance of regional feeling, Spanish politicians had a strong sense of the identity of Spain and were willing to kill to secure it: nationalism, in short, helped to cause civil rather than foreign war. In China, the Taiping Rebellion (1850–64) proved difficult to defeat, in part because of the zeal inspired by its syncretic Christian/messianic/Communist creed and the more general crisis of Imperial China.

CONCLUSIONS

The domestic use of force was related to foreign wars. Many nineteenth-century rulers had seized power by force, either power within a state, as Napoleon III had done in 1851 and Mehmet Ali of Egypt in 1811, or power over a nation, as the ruling houses of Sardinia and Prussia had done in the case of Italy and Germany. It was understandable that force had an appeal and a logic to such rulers. Furthermore, the analysis of war in a European culture increasingly prone since the Enlightenment to put a premium on secular rationality served not to present war as unnecessary or an aberration but rather to present it as logical. Thus, in his influential *Vom Kriege* [On War] of 1833, the Prussian general Karl von Clausewitz emphasized the politicality of war – the belief that war should be dominated by political considerations and should be an instrument of policy.[35] This was not conflict as dynastic whim. Scientifically analysed, war had to be prudent and rational.

The readiness to wage warfare has always, in part, relied upon a belief in military superiority. In the nineteenth century this was increasingly rationalized with a more precise quantification of the relative strengths and numbers of armies and navies, a reliance on conscription and, thus, on a well-scrutinized and controlled population, and the greater precision in communications stemming from the use of railways, steamships and telegraphs. Information made it easier to plan for war.

In addition, in the second half of the century, force appeared central in any understanding of international or domestic politics in the Darwinian sense of a struggle for survival; and increasingly so in a European world in which the alternative to force – customary legitimacies and traditional practices and attitudes – were condemned unless they could be defended as utilitarian. The struggle for space was central to *Die Erde und das Leben* [The Earth and Life] (1902), by the German geo-politician Friedrich Ratzel. Conflict was also central to much analysis of social relations within states. Furthermore, it was important to the notion of will-power as an organizing force and purpose in society and politics.

An emphasis on will could be encouraged when states were attacked, but it was more often deployed as an adjunct of offensive strategies. Such an emphasis discouraged any suggestion that conflict should be avoided by a measurement of resources, for will was seen not only as a resource but as a force superior to resources. Intellectual and cultural interest in war, rather than peace, in turn affected political and military leaderships: war was seen, both consciously and subconsciously, as normal. There was a peace movement – indeed, in Britain the Peace Society was founded in 1816 – but the movement was small-scale.[36]

The wars of the mid-nineteenth century, both domestic and international, have a far greater sense of familiarity to modern commentators than those of a century earlier. In part, this is a reasonable response to the development of industrial warfare, the increased monopolization of power and organized violence by states,[37] and the mass politicization of the age of nationalism. The totality of mid-twentieth-century conflict was prefigured in Napoleon's 1806 Berlin decree which declared Britain as under blockade, ordered the arrest of its subjects, and prohibited all trade and post links. In part, however, there was a major difference, in that the bellicist culture of the period ensured a greater willingness to kill and be killed than in Western society in the 1990s.

Several of the themes raised in modern discussions of the causes of war were voiced by contemporaries. When in 1870 the

French emissary Wimpffen met Bismarck and Moltke in order to discuss terms for the French army surrounded in Sedan, he argued that generosity was the sole possible base for a lasting peace, only for Bismarck to reply that it was particularly difficult to rely on the gratitude of a people. Wimpffen stressed the pacific tendencies arising from French capitalism, but Bismarck drew attention to the bellicosity of the press and population of Paris.[38]

FOUR

1783–1914: Wars of Imperialism

THE EUROPEAN WORLD

This was Europe's age. Between 1783 and 1914 European powers rose to dominate most of the world. Their armies spread their power, their navies charted the seas, and their merchants welded the world together through trade organized to the benefit of the European economy and to the profit of its national exchequers. The major exception was the United States, but it was a state ruled by people of European descent, its economy was closely linked to and partly financed by Europe, and its culture was shaped by European influences.

The impact of Europe on the United States was sustained by migration. European migration also totally altered the politics, land-ownership, economy and ethnic composition of Australasia and Canada, and greatly affected other regions, including Algeria, South Africa and Patagonia. Migration was an aspect of control. It was the product of European power and of the growth in the European population, both absolutely and as a proportion of the world's population. Between 1815 and 1901 the USA took over eight million immigrants from the British Isles. That migration did not involve force on the part of Britain, but imperial power played a crucial role in other migrations, such as the French to Algeria. The new colony was seen as a welcome way to lance tensions created by demographic growth, social disruption and economic problems in metropolitan France. Similarly, Italian governments, later in the century, saw colonies in Africa as a way to deal with domestic problems. Reports of the fertility of Libya encouraged imperialist pressure for its seizure by Italy in 1911.

In many parts of Africa, native peoples were driven from

their land, their pastoral practices blocked by new European settlers or their subsistence agriculture ended in order to produce crops for export, such as cotton in Uganda, and the natives reduced to servile labour, a new slavery. The Europeans were not the only people who moved, but all those who moved long-range only did so with the consent of European and North American states. This was true, for example, of Indian workers moved to East and South Africa, Sri Lanka, Burma and Malaya, or of Chinese emigration to the USA and Australia.

These migrations reflected the potency of new technology. Thanks to the steamship, the oceans shrank. Steamships, refrigerated shipholds, barbed wire and long-distance railways led both to the development of agricultural production for the European market in other temperate climates, and to the ability to move products rapidly without spoilage, so that Europe became part of a global agrarian system. North American grain, Argentine beef and Australasian wool and mutton were crucial. Without imports, Europe could not have fed itself, and the development of its industries would have been limited.

Trade was not restricted to food. The economy of coal/iron/steel/engineering that rose to importance in Europe provided products for the rest of the world. Europe exported vast quantities of investment capital that acted as the engine of this global economy. English became the *lingua franca* of business, the language of profit across most of the world. The growth in the global economy and its inherent volatility ensured a powerful element of instability, as shifts in relative economic strength became more rapid and were more widespread in their effects. This instability was not solely a question of relations between the European (and European-American) powers but also involved the impact of these powers, as the products of new politico-economic-military forces, on states and societies where no such change had occurred.

Nineteenth-century shifts mirrored the situation in the Greek world discussed by the fifth-century BC Athenian general and historian, Thucydides, in his *History of the Peloponnesian War*, a historical classic frequently cited by modern political scientists as the first work to consider the origins of war. He presented the growth in Athenian strength as a destabilizing force within the system. Thucydides described Athens as an economy, state and society transformed and empowered by maritime commercialism, and conservative and landlocked Sparta as unable to respond: as still agrarian and reliant on slavery. This difference was seen by Thucydides, and by subsequent scholars who have used his account as the first text on the causes of war, as responsible both for a destabilizing shift in relative power and for a degree of cultural animosity that made it difficult to adjust disputes. Modern commentators have tended to emphasize the former, although the latter was also very important. A common 'Greekness' did not prevent important politico-cultural differences.

A comparison can be made with the nineteenth-century world, with the European transoceanic empires seen as latter-day Athenian empires. European imperialism in that period is not counted amongst the lists of hegemonic wars that have been drawn up, but the wars this imperialism gave rise to can be seen as wars to determine hegemony, most obviously the Anglo-French conflicts with China, and also as wars reflecting hegemony, in this case European power. These wars, collectively, were for control of the world, and control over more of the world's land surface was formally transferred in the 1880s and 1890s than in any earlier comparable period of time. However, the conflicts were separate struggles, not world wars, in large part because of the absence of bilateral ties between the European powers (as far as transoceanic conflict was concerned) or their opponents, and also because the opponents lacked maritime strength. The nature of alliances within Europe was to ensure that the conflict that broke out in the Balkans in 1914 could not be similarly limited.

The spread of European control and influence in the nineteenth century was far from peaceful. There was violent resistance, especially in Africa, Central and South Asia, Indo-China and China. Yet there was also emulation, an attempt to borrow European techniques and practices. This was most apparent in Japan, but also affected other areas, such as Egypt, or China under the Self-Strengthening Movement (1861–95). Thus, territorial control was not the limit of European power. There was also a process of Europeanization that encouraged change in states such as the Ottoman Empire and Siam (Thailand).

The nineteenth was also a century in which humanity increasingly sought to use advances in knowledge in order to mould the environment. Scientific breeding of plants and animals affected species and transformed economies, as in the spread of rubber to Malaya. Greater understanding of tropical epidemic diseases, such as malaria and cholera, offered the possibility of their control and, thus, of a safer European presence in tropical lands. More generally, science appeared to hold the key to the future, to the creation and use of goods, new sources of power, new sounds and substances. It ensured a world in which change was constant and possibilities apparently endless. Telegraph, telephone and radio altered distance and increased the integration of economic and political systems, and the extension of control. In 1901 Gugliemo Marconi sent radio signals over 3000 miles across the Atlantic. The first successful powered flight, by the Wright brothers in 1903, led Lord Northcliffe to remark that 'England is no longer an island'. Every innovation contributed to a sense of change that was the most important solvent of former certainties. Such a sense increased ambitions and anxieties.

The period from 1816 until 1913 is sometimes presented as relatively peaceful, in terms of the number of conflicts per year, the degree to which individual states were involved in war, and the length of time when major powers did not fight each other, all in comparison both with the preceding century and the subsequent half-century. This is misleading, even as a description of Europe, because it ignores both the high level of civil warfare and military intervention in the domestic affairs of other states, especially from 1816 until 1849, and the degree to which European powers were engaged in colonial warfare. Much of the warfare of this period arose from the expansion of European power, but it would be misleading to suggest that the sole expanding powers were European or, indeed, that most of the warfare of the period involved Europeans. Prior to the 1840s the European impact on much of Asia was limited, and this was also true of much of Africa before the 1880s.

The list of expanding powers in the nineteenth century included, in Africa, Egypt, Lunda,[1] Abyssinia, Sudan under the

Mahdi, and the Zulus, as well as a series of personal empires in West Africa, such as that of Touré Samory, the 'Napoleon of the Sudan'. The source of such expansion varied greatly. The *jihad* launched by Usman dan Fodio in West Africa in 1804 was directed against other Africans, especially the – in his eyes – insufficiently rigorous Islam of Hausaland. The result was the creation of the Sokoto caliphate. For a short while, Mehmet Ali of Egypt (1811–49) must have been one of the most successful conquerors of the century. He was motivated by a drive to create a powerful 'modern' state and a new dynasty, and extended Egyptian power into Saudi Arabia, Sudan, Palestine and Syria.

In Asia, China was still able to intervene effectively in Nepal in 1792, and the list of expanding states would include Burma, Siam – for example in the Malay peninsula in the late eighteenth century and in Laos from 1850 until 1892 – and Punjab under the Sikhs, and, later in the period, Japan. This is not an exhaustive list. For example, Dost Mohammed, ruler of the Afghans, advanced south, defeating the Sikhs in 1836.

If this chapter concerns itself most with European expansionism and with wars involving European powers, that is not intended to imply that those were the sole extra-European conflicts or, necessarily, indeed individually the most important ones, but rather that they were collectively crucial in shaping the nature of the nineteenth-century world. Similarly, wars of imperialism were not restricted to this period. European powers launched such conflicts against Ethiopia in 1935 and Egypt in 1956, and similar wars have long been an important category of conflict. Nevertheless, the European imperialist wars of the nineteenth century were particularly important in the history of the world.

LATIN AMERICA AND SOUTHERN AFRICA

Conflicts involving states created by people of European descent form a related category. By 1850, following the Latin American Wars of Liberation, European power on the New World mainland south of Canada was greatly restricted, and surviving European enclaves in British Honduras and British, Dutch and French Guiana did not serve as the basis for large-scale policies of territorial expansion. The breakdown of attempts to create large federal states in Latin America, such as the Peru-Bolivian Confederation of 1836–9, ensured that there was a large number of independent powers, especially in South America. They competed for predominance, and also faced a series of border conflicts that owed much to the need to define new frontiers, and something to the added pressure of economic interests, not least the desire for a coastline, and, thus, for direct access to the international trading economy.

Ideological differences could also play an important role. The conflicts in nineteenth-century Latin America were in part the consequence of post-colonial instability, when not only international frontiers but also the coherence of 'national states' was in dispute. Peruvian support for an attempt to overthrow the conservative regime in Chile in 1836 helped to lead the latter to declare war, although that also owed much to concern about the Peru-Bolivian Confederation and to tariff conflicts. Texan refusal to accept continued Mexican rule led to war in 1836, and that was followed by another as the USA challenged the territorial position of Mexico (1846–8): contrasting political ideologies and antagonistic public cultures exacerbated differences over effective control in a rapidly developing area. Argentina and Brazil competed for control of Uruguay. In the War of the Triple Alliance (1864–70) Argentina, Brazil and the Uruguayan *colorados* fought Paraguay, and in the War of the Pacific (1879–83) Chile, Bolivia and Peru fought to control the valuable nitrate deposits in the Atacama Desert north of Chile and to determine whether Bolivia would retain its Pacific coastline.

Such Latin American conflicts are frequently ignored in work on the causes of war, but they were major struggles: 330,000 died in the War of the Triple Alliance. These struggles also established a pattern of regional hegemonies and agreed frontiers that helped to limit further conflicts. This was assisted by the limited nature of foreign political intervention in Latin America.

The definition of frontiers and regional hegemony also lay behind the Anglo-Boer Wars in southern Africa (1881,

1899–1902). Like the Latin Americans, the Boers were of European descent, and cultural suppositions and political practices were thus different to those affecting European imperialist treatment of non-Europeans. However, whereas in Latin America European imperial influence was essentially economic, in southern Africa there was an imperial power, Britain, that required territorial control. The failure of Napoleon III of France to sustain Emperor Maximilian as a protégé in Mexico in the 1860s indicated the difficulty of any European military commitment to Latin America. Indeed, one of the principal limitations on warfare in this period was the reluctance of European powers to use military force and to expand territorially there. In part, this can be explained prudentially in terms of the value of economic control, the difficulty of the task militarily and the deterrents of British and American hostility to intervention by other powers.

However, cultural factors were also important, not least the sense that imperial power should not be extended over such peoples. The complex of racial, ideological and other factors that contributed to imperialism and to imperial wars did not pertain in the case of Latin America. The Anglo-Boer and American-Mexican wars are important qualifications to any monocausal explanation, for they were imperial wars launched against people of European descent; but the absence of sustained European military pressure on Latin America has to be considered in any discussion of the causes of imperial wars. As ever, the wars that did not happen have to be included in any analysis of the causes of war.

IMPERIALISM

European powers had scarcely been averse to extending their control over distant peoples and lands prior to the nineteenth century, but in Africa and sub-Siberian Asia the major emphasis had been not on territory but on trade, albeit trade the terms of which were affected by the use of violence. This changed in the nineteenth century, as both the ambition and the capability of European states increased;[2] and this shift was emulated by states that Europeanized at least part of their society – certainly their armed forces – such as Egypt and Japan. Long-standing imperial powers greatly increased the intensity of their territorial ambitions. Thus, in Mozambique and Angola the Portuguese no longer sought influence or a presence, but, rather, control and an ability to organize the population to Portuguese ends.

The shift began in the late eighteenth century and was most marked in the case of Britain, the leading imperial power. The India Act of 1784 declared that 'schemes of conquest and extension of dominion in India are measures repugnant to the wish, the honour, and policy of this nation'. Even so, in the ten years prior to Britain's entry into the French Revolutionary War in 1793, the British did make gains at the expense of native rulers or peoples – in Australia and southern India, at Penang in modern Malaysia, and in Sierra Leone. The situation was very different in the case of European powers, for British colonial gain from them would involve a full-scale war. In transoceanic disputes between themselves, European governments sought to avoid resort to force, essentially sought compromises from the outset, and were able to negotiate them because they were dealing with other European powers operating in accordance with familiar diplomatic conventions.

In contrast, even though extra-European territorial goals at the expense of non-European powers were often limited, the mechanisms for establishing a compromise settlement were less ready, and policy was not in the hands of diplomats seeking a compromise. If, as in Australia or the Andaman Islands in the 1780s, no native state was acknowledged, then Britain could act in a bold fashion, taking advantage of established conventions relating to land seen as occupied by 'savages', and thus 'waste' or 'desert'. Similarly, the North American Native Americans were not represented in the 1782–3 peace negotiations between Britain, France, Spain and the USA that reapportioned their land.

The willingness to treat any non-European people or state with respect diminished in the nineteenth century (although Japan proved an exception). This also reflected, especially from the 1880s, greater competition between the European imperialist powers and a reluctance to leave unconquered what might become the victims of their rivals. As in the case of European international relations and war, it is necessary to complement an understanding of a bellicist political culture with a consideration of why particular wars broke out, but, as with Christian-Ottoman relations in the sixteenth century, this can be a misleading approach; it can be argued that in some regions a state of conflict, or at least dispute, was continuous, and that, therefore, the notion of 'war' as something distinct was, and is, problematic. This was in part true of Brazilian and American expansion into their 'interiors' and Russian expansion into both the Caucasus and Central Asia. In these cases, and, indeed, more generally, aggressive local officials, especially military commanders and traders, could exacerbate relations. A contrast between national policy-making and more aggressive private initiatives can be noted in the case of the USA, with the additional complication of widespread and extensive migration. The notion of 'Manifest Destiny' provided a justification for continued American expansion.

British expansionism in India from the late 1790s reflected a new attitude in which Indian polities were seen as dependents whose foreign and domestic policies were to be controllable by British officials. This was unacceptable to Indian rulers and led to a series of conflicts, beginning with the Fourth Mysore War in 1799 when Tipu Sultan refused to accept demands that would have made Mysore a British protectorate. This forward thrust arose in large part from the determination of a number of officials, especially the Governor-General, Richard Wellesley, but it was defended as necessary to prevent French intervention.[3] Such a defence was not without reason. The French had directly supported rebellion in North America (1775–83) and Ireland (1798), and it was reasonable to feel that India would be next. British conquests also increased tax revenues, helping to relieve an increasingly hard-pressed East India Company and to finance military activity.

Imperial wars have also been seen both as the products of a desire for economic control over the world and as a result of competitive deadlock within Europe, rather as stasis between the Soviet Union and the USA, in Europe during the Cold War, can be regarded as encouraging aggressive activities elsewhere. There has been a furious historiographical debate for over

35 years over whether European intervention was the result of surplus European antagonism looking for an outlet or the product of extra-European instabilities created by informal expansion and other changes. In the former case, there was the impetus and opportunity to turn to extra-European expansion. The major powers competed, in part, by expanding their influence and power in non-European parts of the globe, a sphere where rivalries could be pursued and prestige gained with a measure of safety and without too substantial a deployment of resources. The competitive element had been important from early on. Thus, France attacked Algiers in 1830, and in 1834 also decided to conquer the Algerian littoral, in part in order to challenge the British dominance in the Mediterranean. Alleged British ambitions were used to justify French expansion in West Africa in the 1880s and 1890s. Colonial expansion by the leading powers encouraged weaker European empires to expand, the Dutch conquering Aceh in Sumatra and Portugal resuming expansion in Angola and Mozambique. This seemed the best way for them to prevent despoilation by the leading powers: to conquer was to be.

Such an account may appear mechanistic and far removed from the practices of power at the frontiers of empire. Much expansion was locally stimulated, rather than encouraged in Europe. As far as local sources of expansion were concerned, the difference by the late nineteenth century is that there were so many more points of European entry outside Europe, and that the resources for sub-imperial expansion were much greater than in the 1820s. Although the scale of power was different, it is also notable that the period from 1885 until 1903 was a generally peaceful one in Latin America, but without any marked pressure for compensatory Pacific expansion. Yet, such a notion of European competition, driven in large part from the centre, is instructive because there is a recognizable difference between the pace and extent of imperial expansion and warfare in 1885–1903 and that in, for example, the 1820s.

Furthermore, as already indicated in the discussion of Chinese-'barbarian' relations, there was mutual benefit, as well as rivalry, in relations between major empires and their 'barbarian' neighbours. In the 1880s and 1890s such nuances were, in large part, thrust aside by the Europeans, although it was equally true that European imperialism owed much to divisions amongst the non-Europeans and indeed to their military support. However, although this could be crucial, for example in West Africa and South Asia, the decision-making process was very much kept in European hands.

In general, war between European powers was avoided, especially after 1815. Prior to that, for example, Spain and Russia had avoided conflict in the Pacific. Subsequently, the European powers co-operated in the carve-up of Africa and other parts of the world, especially in the Pacific. Sustained disputes were less common than treaties which agreed boundaries between colonies. Despite several war-panics, in which both sides prepared for conflict, there was no war between Russia and Britain after the Crimean War of 1854–6. Thus, in 1885 the two powers prepared to fight, after the Russians seized Merv and advanced south, trying to extend their hegemony over the tribes of the region, in defiance of what the British regarded as an agreement between the two states. The British India army prepared for action, and fighting took place between the Russians and an Afghan force that had advanced north of the Murghab with British encouragement and advisers. Nevertheless, a territorial compromise was eventually negotiated and the British India army did not fight the Russians.

However, there were conflicts between European powers and states formed by people of European descent – the Anglo-Boer wars of 1881 and 1899–1902, the Spanish-American War of 1898, and French intervention in Mexico in 1861–7 – and between these powers and Europeanizing states: the Russo-Japanese War of 1904–5. These conflicts stemmed, in part, from the prestige of imperial states that felt themselves unable to make compromises or accept losses. Thus, in 1898 the Spanish government and army could not face the prospect of abandoning Cuba, although they were aware that the USA was a formidable foe.[4]

British leaders found it difficult to accept Boer views and were willing to risk war in order to achieve a transfer of some power in southern Africa. The Anglo-Boer War of 1899–1902 is often seen as a classic example of 'capitalist-driven' empire-building. However, many capitalists with interests in the region concerned themselves with politics and war only when aggressive business methods did not meet all their needs. Alfred Milner, the aggressive Governor of Cape Colony (1897–1901), was essentially driven by political considerations and his own ambition. Ministers in London thought the Boers were bluffing and would not put up much of a fight if war followed; while the failure of the British to send significant reinforcements persuaded the Boers to think it was the British who were bluffing. The Boer republics declared war after Britain had isolated them internationally and had done everything possible to provoke them. The British ministers were greatly influenced by the fear that if, given the gold and diamond discoveries, the Boers became the most powerful force in southern Africa, it might not be long before they were working with Britain's imperial rivals, especially the Germans in South-West Africa, and threatening her strategic interests at the Cape. The Prime Minister, the Marquis of Salisbury, no mean imperialist, remarked that Britain had to be supreme. Thus, although the Boer War might never have happened had it not been for the gold and diamonds upsetting the economic balance of power, it is necessary to be cautious before ascribing too much to the capitalists: those in business were less important than the capitalists in government, and the latter were concerned about power rather than business.[5]

Competing Russian and Japanese interests in the Far East interacted with domestic pressures, including the view in some Russian governmental circles that victory would enhance the internal strength of the government, and a foolish unwillingness to accept Japanese strength, interests and determination. Engaged in a complicated struggle for power and influence in St Petersburg, the Russian leaders were too divided amongst themselves and too intent on their own power struggles to have a coherent Far Eastern policy. The Finance Minister was very opposed to war, but many of the military had served in the Far East, they were linked to commercial adventurers with interests in the region – Russian counterparts of Cecil Rhodes – and were close to the Tsar. The government did not seem to have been looking for a war, but it failed to see that serious dialogue with Japan was necessary if it was to be avoided. The Tsar and his advisers did not think the 'yellow devils' would dare to fight.

Russian behaviour and arrogance did much to create ulti-mate unity in Tokyo in 1904. The 'moderates' agreed that Japan had to fight while she enjoyed a temporary advantage over the potentially stronger Russians; and this was repeated in 1941 in the preparations for Pearl Harbor. The Russians paid the price for treating the Japanese as a lesser people.[6]

Aside from governmental attitudes, popular and political pressures were also important. Nineteenth-century imperial-ism drew on a variety of attitudes, including Social Darwinism and theories of racial superiority, none of which encouraged a sympathetic treatment of non-European views. The risings before 1914 in South-West Africa and Tanganyika against German control led to debate over imperialism within Germany. Matthias Erzberger was jeered in the Reichstag when he announced that Africans also had souls. Imperialist senti-ment led the critical Social Democratic Party to lose votes in the 1907 election – the so-called 'Hottentot election'.[7] Confidence in imperial mission and military strength encouraged a resort to force. In addition, governments that were prepared to use force against their own citizenry were ready to apply it elsewhere. Thus, General Bugeaud, who suppressed a rising in France in 1834, was given command in Algeria two years later. French colonial generals, widely known as the *Algériens*, were used to suppress domestic unrest on a number of occasions.

Although humanitarian considerations did play an important role in European attitudes and policies, as in Christian prose-lytism and moves against the slave trade, these considerations arose from the potent interaction of a conviction of superiority and a sense of mission. Thus in Algeria, invaded by France in 1830 largely in order to win prestige for the Bourbon monarchy, and annexed in 1870, the French appropriated nearly four million acres by 1900, including much of the good land, and introduced Christianity, civil law and education, and a secular state.

The purposes and parameters of diplomacy were thus dif-ferent to those affecting international relations within Europe. War was not a product of the breakdown of diplomacy, as much as an activity that made as much, if not better, sense of the nature of international relations. In Algeria, the French progressively pushed their control south towards, and into, the Sahara. The Russians justified their expansion into Central Asia on the grounds of the 'imperious necessity' to establish a stable border. This seemed readily comprehensible to Lord Curzon, who discerned a physical inevitability in the Russian advance:

> in the absence of any physical obstacle and in the presence of any enemy whose rule of life was depredation, and who understood no diplomatic logic but defeat, Russia was as much compelled to go forward as the earth is to go round the sun.[8]

Expropriation and continual pressure also characterized the treatment of the Native population in the USA, that of the Aborigines in Tasmania, and that of the Native population in some of the Latin American countries, for example in Brazil, and the 'pacification', 'Conquest of the Desert', campaigns of the 1870s in Argentina, especially that of 1877. Treaties were imposed, ignored or arbitrarily abrogated. In 1866 the American government manipulated the situation to negotiate a treaty opening the Bozeman Trail through Sioux territories. The Sioux responded by attacking the army. Australia and New Zealand adopted expansionary policies in the Pacific that reflected the racism of their culture and of leaders such as Richard Seddon, the New Zealand Premier (1893–1906). The situation in Canada was less violent. Contempt, hostility and racialism can also be seen as playing a role in Japanese pressure on China from the 1890s. The Sino-Japanese War of 1894–5 largely stemmed from Japan's determination to supplant an apparently anachronistic China in its client state, Korea. Europeanization thus led to imperialism.

The sense of mutuality that was, and is, crucial to the successful operation of the international system was absent. This was clearly seen in 1798 when Napoleon's invasion of Egypt, still part of the Ottoman Empire, almost casually led to war with the Turks. The French had invaded Egypt in order to be better able to challenge the British position in India. They had assumed that the Turks could be intimidated or bribed into accepting French action, which, indeed, followed a whole series of provocative acts. These assumptions were coupled with a contempt for Turkey as a military force. Napoleon's sense of grandiloquence and his belief that the Orient was there to serve his views emerged from his recollection:

> In Egypt, I found myself freed from the obstacles of an irksome civilization. I was full of dreams . . . I saw myself founding a religion, marching into Asia, riding an elephant, a turban on my head and in my hand the new Koran that I would have composed to suit my needs. In my undertakings I would have combined the experiences of the two worlds, exploiting for my own profit the theatre of all history, attacking the power of England in India and, by means of that conquest, renewing contact with the old Europe. The time spent in Egypt was the most beautiful in my life, because it was the most ideal.[9]

Reality was to be otherwise. The Turks resisted and, in alliance with Britain and Russia, did so successfully. The French cultural supposition of superiority and arrogance of power had led to a lack of sensitivity that caused the war. Although it was Selim III who declared war on France, there was no viable alternative response to the invasion of Egypt.

Similarly, in 1787 and 1806, the Turks declared war on Russia in response to aggressive Russian policies in the Caucasus and the Balkans respectively, although on neither occasion was the actual outbreak of conflict welcome to the Russians. Catherine II, the Great, made no secret of her determination to make Russia a major power on the Black Sea. She had occupied the Crimea in 1783. Four years later, the Emperor Joseph II of Austria met her at the new Russian Black Sea naval port of Kherson and found her 'dying' to fight with the Turks.[10]

Trouble developed, however, in the Caucasus, where Turkey, Russia and Persia had competed for control or influence for over 50 years, and where there were religious and ethnic rivalries, an absence of clearly defined boundaries and a lack of control over rival local protégés. Russia had moved into an area that Persia and Turkey had been disputing since the sixteenth century. On 24 July 1783, by the Treaty of Georgievsk, Erekle (Irakli) II, ruler of Kart'li-kakhet'i, the principal Georgian state, who had actively sought Russian intervention, placed himself under Russian protection, and in November 1783 Russian troops entered Tbilisi. Erekle swore allegiance to Catherine, the Russians promised to regain for Georgia what had been lost to the Turks in the sixteenth century, and, in 1784, a military road through the Dariel Pass, linking Russia and eastern Georgia, was completed. These moves alarmed the Turkish frontier pashas, especially Sulayman of Akhaltsikhe, and in 1785 he and Omar Khan of Avaria raided Georgia, leading to Russian complaints. The Russians had upset the balance of power, and they and the Turks were drawn in to support competing protégés as conflict spread in the region. In the North Caucasus, Sheikh Mansur Ushurma, a Chechen Naqshbandi sheikh, launched a holy war against the Russians in 1785.

By 1786 Russo-Turkish relations were deteriorating rapidly. Russian actions were in breach of the Treaty of Kutchuk-Kainardji of 1774, which had established that all Georgians were under the protection of the Sultan, though the Russians argued that the treaty was an error and that they had only intended to recognize Turkish suzerainty over part of Georgia. In addition, the treaty had been ambiguous about the status of the Black Sea coasts of the Caucasus region, which included both Circassian and Georgian lands.

In May 1786 Bulgakov, the Russian envoy at Constantinople, presented an aggressive memorial demanding compliance with Russian views in Georgia. The following January he renewed the Russian demand for a consul at Varna, a step that the Turks feared would lead to an extension of pro-Russian agitation in the Balkans, and demanded that the Turks prevent the Kuban Tatars and the people of the Caucasus from committing hostilities against Russia and her allies, demands that the Turks were determined to reject. A week later, Turkish troops were sent to reinforce the crucial Black Sea fortress of Ochakov, and on 1 February 1787 the Reis Effendi, the Turkish minister responsible for the negotiations, was dismissed and a less pacific replacement appointed. In addition to the issues already mentioned, there were a host of others, including Russian anger about the expulsion of a sympathetic Hospodar of Moldavia by the Turks and disputes over the return of deserters.

Ministerial changes in Constantinople were important. On 24 January 1786 Koca Yusuf Paša, a Georgian convert and the Governor of the Morea, became Grand Vizier. He was a supporter of immediate war with Russia, which he saw as a major threat to the Turkish empire. His influence was increased by the departure of the cautious Grand Admiral, Gazi Hasan Paša, to Egypt in order to restore Turkish authority over the Mamelukes. The Sultan, Abdulhamit I (1774–89), does not appear to have taken a forceful role. On 15 August 1787 Koca Yusuf Paša demanded formally from Bulgakov the return of the Crimea and, on the following day, he was sent to the fortress of the Seven Towers, the traditional method of declaring war. The Turkish government decided to fight on until the Russians had been driven from the Caucasus and the Crimea.[11]

The intimidatory and threatening nature of the Russian advance was clearly important in raising Russo-Turkish tension, but so, also, was the nature of Turkish political culture. Aside from the emphasis on martial values, there was scant sense of the value of compromise. Furthermore, although Turkey in the 1780s was long past the glory days of Ottoman expansion, there was, nevertheless, still a sense that Russia and Turkey competed as essentially aggressive and aggrandizing states and regimes. Conflict was even more likely when states, polities or peoples that were in a more active condition of expansion competed, as with China and the Dsunghars in the 1690s, the Afghans and the Marathas in the 1760s, or the British in India and, on the other hand, Mysore, the Marathas and the Sikhs, and, in the nineteenth century, the British, the Boers and the Zulus in southern Africa. The First Anglo-Burmese War of 1824–6 began with a declaration of war by the East India Company because the aggressive, expansionist kingdom of Burma, keen to consolidate its frontiers and end disorder in neighbouring principalities, clashed with the Company's fears and its defensive determination to protect British protectorates in north-east India. Burma and the East India Company had a common frontier, as a result of the Burmese conquest of Arakan in 1784. The unsettled nature of the frontier and the disruptive role of Arakenese refugees gave rise to serious disputes and created distrust. When, in the 1850s, the French attacked the Tukolor empire of al-Haji Umar in West Africa, it was expanding to the east at the expense of the states of Kaarta, Segu and Macina.

Thus, alongside the notion of war as a struggle for hegemony between rising and declining states, as when Italy invaded Turkish-ruled Libya in 1911, can be placed the suggestion that a crucial aspect of warfulness at the level of international systems was the nature of the relationship between expanding polities. There was a growing belief in the late nineteenth century that the world was destined to be partitioned or dominated by just a few empires or powers, and it was necessary to ensure a place in that premier league. Thus, to struggle and expand was to be, and to claim a stake in the future.

Expanding polities were, by their very nature, likely to be bellicose; indeed that was almost a condition of their expanding power, but this bellicosity did not have to lead to war with other expanding polities. Instead, the relationship between war at the expense of non-expanding polities and war with expanding polities was important in the nature of warfare. From 1816 until 1913 much, but not all, European warfare outside Europe was in the former category, while within Europe more of the conflicts were waged between powers that were, if not expanding, at least not in decline.

Transoceanic European intimidation can be seen in the Anglo-Chinese Wars. The first, the so-called Opium War of 1839–41, arose from the Chinese attempt to enforce their prohibition on the import of opium. The seizure of opium held by British merchants and their expulsion from Canton led to pressure within Britain for a response. The demand for compensation was backed up by force. Freedom of trade had been enforced at the expense of China's ability to regulate its economy and society. The first war was followed by a second from 1857, as Britain pressed for an extension of commercial rights and the Chinese refused to accept a revision of the Treaty of Nanjing of 1842. The incident that led to hostilities was the arrest in Canton on charges of piracy of the crew of the *Arrow*, a Hong Kong ship flying the British flag. The British sought monopoly of trade. Chinese ignorance of the capabilities and intentions of the Europeans hindered good relations, but it proved possible to assimilate the treaty ports and treaty system to an indigenous concept of how to conduct relations with 'barbarians'.[12]

The context was very different, but a similarly one-sided process can be seen in other episodes of European imperialism, for example the Maori Wars in the North Island of New Zealand from 1860 until 1872, the Cape Frontier Wars (formerly known as the Kaffir Wars) in southern Africa, growing European intervention in Syria and Lebanon, and the Russian pressure on Persia.[13] Much of this pressure was cumulative: the advance of European powers rarely stopped. Thus, the Russians advanced in the Caucasus and Central Asia, one gain serving as a prelude to another, and the British followed a similar course in Burma, southern Africa, and, as they created, the North-West Frontier of India. This led directly to warfare and also ensured that fighting appeared the most sensible response to powers threatened by European advance, as when Sher Ali of the Afghans' suspicions of the British led to the Second Afghan War of 1878–80.

Furthermore, European advance led to religious-cultural disquiet and disorientation that produced movements of religious reaction, as amongst the North American Natives, the Moslems of Libya, Sudan, the Caucasus and Sumatra, the Pathans of the North-West Frontier in the 1890s, and amongst some Africans, for example in the Fifth Cape Frontier War, in Matabeleland in 1896, and in Tanganyika in 1905–7. A *jihad* against the French invaders of Algeria was declared by Abd el-Kader in 1832. The issue of perspective in distinguishing between war and rebellion, as discussed in earlier chapters, again plays a role; in this case, the context of indigenous opposition to colonial power. Shifts in assessment stemming from decolonization have enlarged the number of wars, not least by treating as thus what were regarded by colonial powers as rebellions or lawlessness.

Even if, at a particular moment, the European power did not want a full-scale conflict, the general tenor of its policy was such that it could be seen as aggressive and a threat. Therefore, when the situation appeared propitious for a violent response, a war could be launched, as by the Turks in 1787. That such a moment was often one of hesitation, even conciliation, on the part of the imperial power apparently confuses the issue of responsibility, but the inherent cause in such cases was the general aggressive attitude and policies of such powers; a parallel to the question of how far Napoleon and Hitler were responsible for the wars in which they were involved.

The greater control of states over their peoples and the extension of the world of officialdom into border zones ensured that government agents and, in most cases, the agents of central government played a greater role in frontier regions and border warfare than, for example, in the sixteenth century. This shift was true of regions such as the Balkans. The greater uniformity of individual armies also played a role. Frontier regions were less characterized by autonomous armed forces than in the past, and, as such forces were integrated into regular armies, so their commanders' capacity for independent initiatives was lessened. Thus, despite the role of 'men on the spot', local agents of imperial power, in encouraging action,[14] this was less the case than in the sixteenth century. Advances in communications, especially the telegraph, further increased the control of central governments by reducing the ability of frontier commanders to determine the content and flow of information.[15]

A cult of order, epitomized by straight lines drawn on maps to create frontiers between colonies that paid no heed to ethnic, economic or geographical links, reflected the desire for 'rationality' and control that characterized much governmental policy. Greater control ensured that it is more appropriate to think of wars, rather than continual warfare, certainly as far as the central governments were concerned. This can be seen in Mozambique in the mid-1890s. Although Antonio Enes, the Portuguese Royal Commissioner (1895–6), was determined to crush the kingdom of the Gaza Nguni, he did so with the support of the metropolitan government. The nominal cause of the war was a rising in 1894 by Tonga chieftains against Portuguese taxes and interference in a succession dispute, and the refusal of their overlord, Gungunhana, the Gaza Nguni ruler, to hand them over. The war then began with a Portuguese invasion, including troops recently arrived from Portugal.

However, in some areas, the men on the spot were very much in control. Thus, in West Africa, the *officiers soudanais* of the

French marine corps dramatically increased French territory in the 1880s and 1890s, despite a lack of governmental support. Russian commanders in Central Asia were similarly responsible for aggressive action. In both the French and the Russian cases the incoherence of the policy-making machine was important. In the case of Britain, Sir Bartle Frere, Governor of Cape Province and Commander-in-Chief for South Africa, adopted an aggressive stance towards the Zulus in 1878, launching an offensive the following January against the wishes of the Colonial Secretary. Brigadier-General Frederick Lugard, High Commissioner for the Protectorate of Northern Nigeria, was pressed by the government to keep the peace with the Sokoto Caliphate, but he was determined on war and he got it in 1902. The pretext was the murder of a British officer and the failure to hand over the murderer, but other justifications included the continuation of slave raiding.

The Europeans sought to impose their definitions and rules as well as their interests, and to deny that non-European powers and peoples had any that were comparable or of equal validity. Piracy and the slave trade were both greatly limited. In 1856 the British seized Awadh [Oudh] in India under the pretext that it was misruled. In 1871 the Dutch sold their forts on the Gold Coast to Britain without any heed to the views of the king of Ashanti, Kofi Kakari, who saw these forts as trading bases under Ashanti sovereignty. Resentful of past Ashanti victories and of Ashanti commercial policies, the British failed to heed Ashanti views, leading to war in 1873 – a war that was welcome to Edward Cardwell, the Secretary of State for War, Lord Kimberley, the Colonial Secretary, and General Sir Garnet Wolseley. More generally, the effective denial of sovereignty to many non-European polities ensured that conflict with them was treated as little different from the suppression of rebellion. In India,

> except for the different scale of the operations needed to control them (police rather than army), the East India Company's servants made no great distinction between rebellion and frontier wars, and the gang violence they called 'dacoity' in nominally pacified areas.[16]

The lack of concern with the rights of colonial peoples led to a harsh response to rebellion. The advance of European power, and its increased territorialization, brought Western concepts of sovereignty, suzerainty, frontiers and conflict into dispute with those of other societies. Thus, British pressure for free trade clashed with Ashanti defence of controlled monopolies. This was also true of the British and, first, Mysore[17] and, later, Burma, and there was also the serious problem with the latter of differing notions of sovereignty and borders.[18] In 1806 Lord Grenville, the British Foreign Secretary, referred without irony, when issuing instructions for the seizure or destruction of the Turkish fleet, unless the Turks yielded to British views, to 'the insensibility of the Turkish Government to those sentiments which restrain states in a more advanced stage of civilization from acts of outrage against the Law of Nations'.[19] Warfare and its causes were, therefore, increasingly defined in European terms.

FIVE

1914-45: Total War

This is not a question of fighting for Danzig or
fighting for Poland. We are fighting to save the
whole world from the pestilence of Nazi tyranny
and in defence of all that is most sacred to man.
This is no war for domination or imperial
aggrandisement or material gain; no war to shut any
country out of its sunlight and means of progress. It
is a war, viewed in its inherent quality, to establish on
impregnable rocks, the rights of the individual, and it
is a war to establish and revive the stature of man.

WINSTON CHURCHILL, House of Commons,
3 September 1939.

The cause that I and a handful of friends represent is
this morning, apparently, going down to ruin, but I
think we ought to take heart of courage from the fact
that after 2,000 years of war and strife, at last, even
those who enter upon this colossal
struggle have to admit that in the end force has not
settled, and cannot and will not settle anything.
I hope that out of this terrible calamity there will
arise a real spirit, a spirit that will compel people to
give up reliance on force, and that perhaps this time
humanity will learn the lesson and refuse in the
future to put its trust in poison gas, in the
massacre of little children and universal slaughter.

GEORGE LANSBURY, pacifist former leader of
the Labour Party, House of Commons,
3 September 1939.

Total war was industrial war, the war of annihilation with the capacity to annihilate. The movement away from subsistence societies ensured that there were more discretionary amounts of everything, including manpower and weaponry. Total war began with World War One (1914–18), although earlier conflicts, most obviously the American Civil War (1861–5) and the Russo-Japanese War (1904–5), prefigured it. The rationale of total war led to the atomic confrontations of the period from 1949, and, although the atom bomb was never used during these years, the mass devastation that it threatened greatly affected international relations and planning for war.

The greater destructive capacity of warfare, represented not only by the enhanced ability to kill large numbers on the battle-field but also by the potential of airpower and submarines to affect civilian life and effect civilian death, did not prevent conflict and, in one respect, indeed encouraged it. Knowledge of the destructive capacity of opponents' forces and of the speed with which they could act, and belief in the military advantages of the offensive, led to pre-emptive strikes as with the Israeli attack on its Arab neighbours in 1967. Furthermore, pre-emptive action and the notion of a preventive war as a means of redressing a perceived strategic imbalance can be seen as playing a large role in the German decision to attack in 1914.[1]

The development of improved administrative methods was also important. The ability to manage war efficiently facilitated war-making. The technical capacity for sustained mass mobilization within a modern economy was crucial to total war, and that was related not only to wealth and administrative capability but also to mass ideology. Range, as well as destructiveness of weaponry, was an aspect of total war. Range was not new – European warships had sailed the oceans since the fifteenth century – but it was more intense and insistent, due to developments in naval and aerial capability.

Furthermore, the political range of European power was also more intense and insistent than hitherto. Thus, most of the world in 1914 was under the control of European powers or of peoples of European descent. A war between such powers involved conflict around the world, as was indeed the case in 1914–18. This control also ensured that the concept of wars across cultures became, temporarily, less valuable. There was little of such conflict when European power reached its apogee.

Yet that situation was to change as European power declined with, first, challenges in the 1920s and then the wars of de-colonization from 1945. Furthermore, the ideological and politico-social unity of Europe fractured, with, first, Commu-nism and then Fascism deliberately focusing hostility on different European societies. Thus, warfare across cultures came to mean as much the Soviet assault on Poland in 1920 or the Nazi invasion of France in 1940, as the British campaigns against the Faqir of Ipi in Waziristan on the North-West Frontier of India in 1936–9. This altered the analytical context of warfare, for the former category of conflicts were those between powers with essentially similar military systems and practices; although it was true that differences in weaponry and its use could still be very important. Both Germany and France had tanks and aircraft in 1940, but they were different and employed in differing fashions. Indeed, these differences illustrate the problems of employing a statistical approach. The military systems of Germany and France in 1940 can appear similar, and certainly were so in contrast with those of the Faqir of Ipi, but it was the differences between them that were to prove crucial.

The cross-cultural aspect of intra-European conflict also ensured that, as earlier with the French Revolution, there was an uneasy mixture of, on the one hand, the conventional language, content and processes of diplomacy and international relations, and, on the other, others that were more radical in both content and form. Furthermore, as earlier with the French Revolu-tionary Wars, there was the question of the role of ideological considerations in the cause of war. This has been of great weight in scholarship on the causes of the World War Two and the Cold War. First, however, it is best to turn back to earlier struggles.

World War One began very like two recent conflicts, the First and Second Balkan Wars, and indeed, in part, was a continuation of the assertiveness and ambitions revealed in those conflicts. Like them, it arose from the ethnic and territorial rivalries of a Balkan world where violence was the principal method of pursuing disputes. World War One was different because other and 'greater' powers intervened forcefully and from the outset. Yet the very fact that intervention by these powers had been very different in type and intention in the two previous Balkan wars, and, indeed, in earlier crises, such as those of 1876-7 and 1908, suggests that terms such as inevitability need to be handled with care, and therefore also directs attention to the events of the years immediately preceding the war, especially the diplomacy of 1912-14.

If Europe was a 'powder keg' waiting to go up, it is worth asking why it had not done so earlier; a point similar to that about the inevitability of the Thirty Years' War. It is interesting to ask why Germany had not fought (or made greater demands at the risk of war) when she had enjoyed a clear military advantage in Europe, especially after Russia's defeat by Japan in 1905 and the Russian revolution of that year. Indeed, significant sections of the German leadership had favoured a Continental war in 1887-8 but were kept in check by Bismarck and Kaiser Wilhelm I. Similar war talk in Vienna gradually died down, in part because of the recurrent Austrian difficulty of finding the resources to fight a major war. Earlier, Metternich had wanted war against the Orléanists of France in 1831, but had been reminded of Austria's financial weakness. More recently, tension over the position of Serbia had led Austria and Russia to deploy troops in threatening positions from the autumn of 1912 until March 1913, but the forces were then withdrawn.[2]

The comparison with the Thirty Years' War is instructive, because, as in that war, the central question is not why there was a rising in Bohemia in 1618 or a clash between Austria and Serbia in 1914, but rather why other powers became involved; why, in short, the crisis bridged divides. This issue has produced shelves of scholarship, much of which is of great value for general discussion of the causes of war. The most prominent individual work has been Fritz Fischer's *Griff nach der Welt macht: Die Kriegszielpolitik des kaiserlichen Deutschlands, 1914–1918* (Düsseldorf, 1961), a book translated into English as *Germany's Aims in the First World War* (1967).[3] Fischer and his followers asserted 'den Primat der Innenpolitik [the primacy of domestic policy]', the need to search for foreign policy in social structures and dynamics, most centrally the challenge that rising Socialism posed to the Conservative elite. This was not a value-free dissection because the social structures that were seen as pernicious were those of conservatism and capitalism. More specifically, the theory was designed to condemn Wilhelmine Germany and thus to undermine it as a model for post-1945 Germany.

The ideological project illuminating the work of much of this school helped to account for its tendentious character, but there were also flaws in the analysis, not least the reification of social forces, the underplaying of the autonomous nature of the diplomatic and military processes, and, more seriously, the failure to consider international contexts.[4] An explanation centred on aggression in one state does not explain the responses of other powers nor, necessarily, the conjunctural nature of the conflict. This is particularly important in a situation where a number of powers are involved. Although there is a sense in which there was a core decision on which all subsequent events hinged, to explain why Germany went to war in 1914 does not account for why Britain chose to come to the assistance of Belgium or why Italy deserted Germany or the USA intervened in 1917. Indeed, the *Innenpolitik* account is of limited value not only for the outbreak of war in 1914 but also if the war is understood, as it should be, not as a single conflict but rather as a series, as a war with multiple entries. Each can, of course, be discussed in terms of *Innenpolitik*, but once initial hostilities had broken out, the role of diplomatic and military considerations became even more pressing. The same was true of World War Two.

However, such an account does not imply that an analysis that focuses on *Innenpolitik* is without value, but, rather, that it is necessary to consider the domestic politics and pressures of a number of states and to show how and why they interacted in a certain fashion in particular international circumstances. The latter is a necessary caveat, because an accumulation of *Innenpolitiks* is of only limited value and could be actively misleading if it suggested that international relations was their sum. This is implied by the Marxist-Leninist approach, for war therein is seen as an adjunct of social structure and one largely motivated by economic considerations: the pursuit of the factors of production by other means. This approach argues that the inherent economic nature and problems of capitalist societies lead to aggressive policies.[5] Again, the autonomy of diplomacy and the military are underrated, for they become, simply, an aspect of the superstructure of the socio-economic system. Furthermore, the Communist labelling of states as feudal, bourgeois, or proletarian is unhelpful, because, as in the age of European religious conflict, there were rivalries within these categories, while, unlike in that earlier age, many societies and states did not see themselves in terms of this classification. In 1914 most bankers and merchants supported peace. Some industrialists benefited from the greater demand for armaments, but there was no capitalist pressure for war.

German leaders from the formation of the Second Reich in 1871 thought quite often that their interests could be advanced without war as long as the balance of power favoured them; they were encouraged by the prospect of Anglo-Russian and Anglo-French wars. Long-standing and ongoing imperial rivalries amongst Britain, France and Russia had contributed to peace in Europe, working in particular to the advantage of Germany from the 1880s. The Germans did not always appreciate this, notably in 1887–90, but they were not panicked by the Franco-Russian military agreement of 1894 into the sort of alarmist and adversarial thinking and actions that characterized the run-up to the outbreak of World War One.

Instead the Germans, and Austria, courted Russia to some effect. There was a German as well as a British version of the 'free hand' in the 1890s; this is hardly a phrase which suggests powers being locked into an alliance system or denied much freedom of manoeuvre. The expectation persisted in Berlin until about 1904–5 that, thanks to extra-European disputes, Britain would ultimately find herself at war with France and/or, more especially, Russia, a view that encouraged a belief in the viability of German naval plans.

Such confidence in Berlin that time was on its side only declined as Russia began to grow rapidly in strength shortly before 1914. The prospect of a loss of Germany's overall advantageous position threatened a real balance of power, or even an imbalance to her detriment, that might frustrate her ambitions in Europe as well as in the wider world.

A consistent growth of German belligerence dated from the start of fears that the balance would be or was being altered to the advantage of her opponents. In the early 1910s, powerful figures in the German political and military elite felt threatened by the build-up of Russian power and by encirclement by the Russo-French alliance. In 1912, during the First Balkan War, the Russians carried out a trial mobilization. Growing Russian military strength, not least the development of her strategic railroad net, led to pressure for a pre-emptive war. This railway system benefited from French investment specifically designed to improve the ability of Russia to mobilize and to act once mobilized. This would make it less likely that Germany would be able to fulfil the Schlieffen plan and defeat France in the West before confronting Russia. On the eve of World War One the Russians were outspending the Germans, and political disputes over fiscal policy made it unlikely that the Germans would be able to respond. Count Helmuth von Moltke, Chief of the General Staff from 1906 until 1914, pressed for war because he feared that Germany might not be able to win a war with Russia later.[6] The sense of threat was exacerbated by Turkey's defeat in the First Balkan War and by German knowledge that the British had agreed to open negotiations with Russia, although Britain's likely actions in the event of war were difficult to evaluate. A belief in the inevitability of war encouraged a desire to begin it at the most opportune moment. Furthermore, Germans could look back with pride and confidence to successful recent wars. There was no equivalent to the earlier experience of defeat and occupation that played a part in memories of the Wars of Liberation against Napoleon.

Yet these pressures did not explain Austrian, Russian, French and British policy. The Austrians were also concerned about a worsening situation – in their case, Russian-supported Serbian assertiveness, and its challenge to Austria's international position in the Balkans and the stability of Austria's Balkan possessions. There was a growing frustration amongst the Austrian leadership at not being able to shape their own destiny in external affairs, and Serbia had a great deal to do with that feeling. Serbia had been economically dependent on Austria, but that began to change, starting in 1906, when Serbia signed a trade treaty with Bulgaria. A boycott of her livestock failed to reduce Serbia to Austria's terms. The Austrians wished to preserve Bosnia and Herzegovina, which they had annexed in 1908, from Slav ambitions: the Serbs were pressing for a Serb-led Yugoslavia. Austria had been completely unable to realize any of its aims, some of them very unrealistic, during the Balkan wars. This was blamed, in part, on insufficiently strong German support.

Moreover, the same anxiety about being powerless was no less strong in respect to internal politics. The Austrian leadership was, increasingly, unable to get their way in respect to relations with Hungary, and the increasing tendency by various groups, from the Slovenes to the Czechs, to use parliamentary obstruction did little to make the aristocracy, who still had a fair amount of real power, comfortable with developments. In addition, the military was the only institution that was still able to promote a sense of purpose for the Habsburg Empire with any credibility, and there was a feeling that if the military were able to take control it could put things right. The cautious Friedrich Beck was no longer Chief of Staff. Before the assassinations at Sarajevo, more and more of the Austrian leadership began to feel that war against Serbia was the sole answer to the empire's domestic problems – if only Berlin would agree. Russian support for Romanian interest in the Romanians living in Transylvania, part of the Austro-Hungarian state, also aroused anxiety.[7]

The Russians, in contrast, were both encouraged by Serbian success and ready to see Serbia as a crucial protégé. They had encouraged the formation of the anti-Turkish, anti-Austrian Balkan League in 1912 and were closely associated with the Serbian premier, Nikola Pašić. The Russians also opposed growing German influence in Turkey. Thus, Austrian threats to

Serbia, in the aftermath of the assassinations of the Austrian heir, Archduke Franz Ferdinand, and his wife Sophia, in Sarajevo on 28 June 1914, were a challenge to Russian interests and the Russian perception of international relations in eastern Europe.[8] The assassinations were carried out by terrorists under the control not of the Serbian government but of the Black Hand, a secret Serbian body pledged to the overthrow of Habsburg control in South Slav territories. 'Apis', Dragutin Dimitrijević, the head of Serbian military intelligence, was a crucial figure, able to ignore his government's efforts to contain the activities of the Black Hand.

French support for the entente with Russia remained strong and the French sought to strengthen it, both by improving Anglo-Russian relations and by increasing the size of the French army.[9] Indeed, the French President visited St Petersburg in July 1914 and made France's backing for Serbia clear.

Domestic pressures within Britain had focused on France for most of the previous century. France was the traditional enemy and rival, and colonial rivalries provided fresh fuel to keep fear and animosity alive. In 1898 both powers had come close, in the Fashoda Crisis, to war over the fate of the Sudan. Many British commentators would have agreed with Joseph Chamberlain, Secretary of State for the Colonies, in his view that Britain and Germany were natural allies, their peoples of a similar racial 'character'.

And yet the two powers went to war in 1914. Chance played a central role: a major European war broke out at a moment very different to those of heightened Anglo-French and Anglo-Russian colonial tension in the later decades of the nineteenth century. Defeat in the Russo-Japanese War of 1904–5 had weakened Russia as a balancing element within Europe, thereby exposing France to German diplomatic pressure, and creating British alarm about German intentions, as in the First Moroccan Crisis of 1905–6. This crisis, provoked by Germany, was followed by Anglo-French staff talks aimed at dealing with a German threat.

Their consequences were to play a major role in leading Britain towards World War One. In 1907 British military manoeuvres were conducted for the first time on the basis that Germany, not France, was the enemy. That year, fears of Germany contributed to an Anglo-Russian entente. Yet, as was customary, political opinion was divided. Alongside hostility to Germany in political and official circles, there were politicians who sought to maintain good relations. Furthermore, the ententes were not alliances.

As in 1792–3, Britain did not go to war as soon as her allies, although in 1914 the speed of events and the nature of Britain's diplomatic alignments were such that her entry into the conflict was far less delayed than on the previous occasion. In 1914, as in 1792, it proved difficult for the British government to make its position clear, thus encouraging France in 1792 and Germany in 1914 to hope that she would not act.[10] The government was, indeed, very divided in 1914.

'Ideology' might seem to be a major difference between the situation in 1792–3 and that in 1914. However, it would be mistaken to see the latter crisis simply in terms of the interests of competing states. As in 1792–3, distrust and the willingness to fight owed much to cultural and ideological factors. The Social Darwinism of the 1870s and beyond, with its emphasis on natural competition, encouraged a belief in a world that was necessarily red in tooth and claw. Militarism appeared natural. Late Romanticism glorified war and struggle as a means to discover identity and purity through pain. The educated elites believed in the moral value of war, and the role of nationalism ensured that war between nations was seen as natural. There was little interest in internationalism, except amongst the unempowered left.[11] As in 1792–3, these cultural/ideological suppositions do not explain the conflict, but they do help account for the way in which differences were allowed to escalate.

Thus, to the Serbian-backed terrorists who were responsible for the Sarajevo assassinations, it seemed appropriate to follow a violent course. When the news reached Vienna, shock and the customary response to an unexpected and dramatic event – a call for action and a sense that a display of action was needed – interacted with an already powerful view that war with Serbia was necessary.

The Austrians then turned for, and received, a promise of German support. This reflected a wish to satisfy the views of

Germany's closest ally, but also, again, a sense that a forceful response was necessary, appropriate and desirable. As a result, Germany found itself involved in a crisis in which it was not controlling the parameters or the timetable. German backing helped Austrian proponents of force to overcome the opposition of the Magyar [Hungarian] premier Tisza. Thus, the international situation influenced the policy debate within Austria, maintaining the cohesion of the Austro-Hungarian state.[12]

The Austrians believed that a limited war was possible, that German backing, promised on 5–6 July, would deter Russia from war, and that the international and domestic situations were propitious for conflict with Serbia. On 23 July an ultimatum was presented to Serbia which the Austrians believed the Serbian government could not accept. Indeed, the Serbs were determined not to accept any infringement of their sovereignty, and this unwillingness to yield helped to cause war. Their reply of 25 July to the Austrian ultimatum conceded many of the demands, but refused to accept a police investigation. The Austrians rejected the Serbian reply as inadequate and declared war on 28 July, beginning hostilities the same night. Furthermore, the Austrians were not interested in the proposal, floated on 29 July by a German government increasingly concerned that it would not be possible to localize the struggle, that they stage a limited war and merely occupy Belgrade.

The Russians responded to the ultimatum with military preparations on 26 July. They were confident of French support and believed it necessary to act firmly. The Russian leaders had agreed during the Balkan Wars that it was too early to risk war, but felt in July 1914 that – although Russia was not fully prepared to fight – she was too strong to allow herself to be humiliated again. Their preparations amounted to a partial mobilization, and they were noted in Serbia, Austria and Germany, helping to encourage a sense of developing crisis and pressure for action. Efforts to contain the crisis, and localize the conflict, were pre-empted by its escalation. On 30 July, rather than abandon Serbia, Russia ordered a general mobilization against both Austria and Germany, although only after Tsar Nicholas II had been persuaded to reverse a decision to rescind the order.

This put pressure on Germany. Its war plans called for action against France before Russia could act. The refusal of both Russia and France to stop their preparations thus led the German government – unwilling to back down and as if trapped by its strategic concepts – to attack. General mobilization was implemented on 1 August. Despite the international recognition of Belgium's perpetual neutrality in 1839, it was invaded on 3 August, in order to permit an advance on Paris from the north-east.

Military considerations and the army leaderships themselves played a major role in pushing governments to act, because mobilizations were seen as the crucial indicators of intentions. The military were especially important in Austria, Germany and Russia. In Austria, Conrad von Hötzendorf, the Chief of Staff, wanted war with Serbia. He believed it necessary, and it has been suggested that he was motivated by a wish to be a military hero in order to obtain the woman he wanted. He got the woman, but not the victory he sought.

Military pressure rested on the argument of necessity. War was not seen as an easy challenge but as a danger in which it was necessary to act first. While very few before 1914 expected a general European war to be a long war, one of the great myths of World War One literature is the old truism that the army leaders did not expect heavy casualties. From 1905 onward, based upon the lessons of the Russo-Japanese War, they fully expected that they would be heavy. This expectation dramatically changed thinking on manpower requirements and provided the impetus for programmes in all countries to expand the size of their armies. These programmes interacted with an increase in armaments to produce by 1914 a major growth in military preparedness. States increased their military capabilities to match those of their neighbours in an arms race that did not lead to effective deterrence.[13] The establishment of general staffs led to systematic peacetime military planning – continual preparations for war. It is not, therefore, surprising that it has been argued that the war-plans, with their dynamic interaction of mobilization and deployment, made war 'by timetable' difficult to stop once a crisis occurred, and that a major war was not intended.[14] The German war-plan required that hostilities rapidly follow mobilization.

However, this interpretation has been challenged by an emphasis on the role of politicians in affecting the development of the crisis, especially in its early stages – in short, an argument that politicians were not trapped, and that their role and preferences were important.[15] Indeed, there was such a role. It can in part be seen by hypothesizing counter-factuals. The civilian ministers could have stood up to Conrad and pressed Franz Joseph on the risks of war. The French leaders could have urged caution when they visited St Petersburg. A very awareness of precarious domestic and international situations did not have to lead to war. Internal pressures within Austria-Hungary would indeed have been better resisted had there been no war. Again, alliances did not dictate participation in the war. Although France and Germany kept the alliance of Russia and Austria respectively, the Triple Alliance did not survive the onset of war. Italy did not come to the aid of Germany and Austria, and, instead, joined their opponents the following year. King Carol of Romania, a secret ally of the Triple Alliance, also abandoned them.

An awareness of risk and risks had helped to prevent former crises from leading to war. In 1914 the situation was different because Austria chose to fight, Germany to support her, and Russia to respond. The Austrians made a deliberate choice for war, and had the Russians not responded they would have lost their influence in the Balkans and the prospect of a two-front war against Austria. Austrian action reflected frustrations – especially frustration at a situation in which Balkan powers were becoming more assertive. Their support for nationalism within the Habsburg Empire already seemed an attack. Unlike Irish or Indian nationalism within the British empire, that within the Habsburg dominions had powerful foreign support. Yet the very reluctance of Tisza to support action in July 1914 indicated that there was nothing inevitable about the war or about the views of the decision-makers. Like their counterparts in other states, Austrian leaders were worried about their situation and fearful of their future, but, in the context of bellicose elites, this led to pressure for action rather than a reliance on caution. German leaders sought to use the crisis in the Balkans to change the international balance of power in Germany's favour. They were willing to risk a war arising out of the Sarajevo incident because no other crisis was as likely to produce a constellation of circumstances guaranteeing them the commitment of their main ally, Austria, and the support of the German public.

Once the war had started, neutral powers were placed under great pressure from both sides, being offered inducements and cajoled with the possible consequences of the other side winning. Thus, Italy in 1915 was offered gains at the expense of Austria,[16] the Bulgarians backed Germany from 1915 in return for the offer of all of Macedonia and most of Thrace, and – in part, thanks to Germany's crass wartime diplomacy – the USA was persuaded of the dangerous consequences of German strength and ambitions and entered the war against her in 1917.[17] In a similar fashion, major conflicts of the past, such as the wars against Louis XIV or the Austro-Turkish war that began in 1682, had spread to encompass states not initially involved. The role of empires in World War One also ensured that the struggle encompassed and encouraged separatist movements, as with German support for Irish separatism, British backing for the Arab revolt against the Ottoman Turks that began in 1916, and Allied support for nationalist movements within the Habsburg empire, especially in Bohemia, the centre of the future Czechoslovakia.

The USA was not a belligerent culture, society or state by European standards, it lacked a large standing army and a powerful military-political nexus, and it had a strong tradition of neutrality and isolationism. This did not mean a pacific culture nor an aversion to war and the use of force, as Spain had noted in 1898. The commemoration of the Civil War lent heroism and purpose to the notion of conflict. Frontier wars against the Native Americans played a major role in the definition of national identity, contributing to a society that was violent and bellicose even if its politics were not particularly belligerent.

Furthermore, in 1905 President Theodore Roosevelt proclaimed the 'Roosevelt Corollary', a supplement to the Monroe Doctrine, by which the 'wrongdoing' or 'impotence' of any state in the western hemisphere could require American intervention. As a consequence, Nicaragua was occupied in 1912,

Haiti in 1915 and the Dominican Republic in 1916, and troops were sent into Mexico in 1916. This was a politics to match that of imperial China during its heyday: the USA was to look on states bringing it tribute through economic colonialism, and to intervene if there was disorder. Such states would not be dignified by declarations of war. Thus, in 1914 the Mexican port of Veracruz was shelled after what was seen as an insult to the American navy. The invasion of the Dominican Republic in 1965 by the 'Inter-American Peace Force' – an army of US marines ordered to determine local politics – was in this tradition.

In 1914 there was active hostility to the idea of participation in the European war. It was seen as alien to American interests and antipathetic to her ideology. However, over the next three years German actions, especially the unrestricted submarine warfare that sank American ships and the apparent German willingness to support Mexican revanche against the USA, led to the shift in attitude that caused entry into the war in 1917.

THE 1920S

As after 1945, the decade after the end of World War One in 1918 was one of war, not peace, and that despite the creation of institutions – the League of Nations and the United Nations, in 1919 and 1945 respectively – that were designed to maintain peace. Furthermore, the Peace of Versailles of 1919 included a clause that fixed the responsibility of the war on Germany, and this 'war-guilt' issue, and the associated reparations (financial retribution), were designed to discourage further aggression. Similar clauses were included in the treaties with Austria and Hungary.

However, from the outset force was involved in the settlement of the new order. Thus, in 1919 the Czech army took Slovakia from the Hungarians and a German strike in the Sudetenland against the new state was harshly suppressed, while the Romanians suppressed the Communist regime in Hungary, and the Poles took Vilnius from Lithuania. The peace settlement for the Turkish Empire led to a bitter war, as Greek attempts to gain part of Anatolia were defeated.

In the 1920s there was large-scale war in China, Turkey and Russia, as well as conflicts in Afghanistan, Iraq, Saudi Arabia and Morocco that were less extensive. There was a mix of 'traditional' causes of conflict, as with the struggles between warlords in China following the collapse of central authority from 1916, between tribes in the Arabian peninsula, and between tribes and state authority in Iraq and Persia; and conflicts in which new political and ideological projects played a major role, as in Russia, Turkey and China.

In the last, the determination of the Kuomintang to produce a united state led to a series of wars as, under Sun Yat-sen, they sought to exploit warlord divisions. This helped cause the first (1922) and second (1924) Chihli-Fengtien wars, named after competing warlord cliques. In 1926 Sun's successor, Chiang Kai-shek, launched the Northern Expedition against the warlords in central and northern China, achieving by October 1928 an uneasy unity for much of China. It is difficult to present this major warfare other than in terms of the anarchic self-interest of the warlords, their kaleidoscopic alliances and a Kuomintang which, despite a measure of idealism, came, under Chiang, to act as a form of successful warlordism with national pretensions. China in the 1920s is a useful corrective against any assumption that the bases of politics and warfare were necessarily different to those of the fifteenth century.

In Russia, the project of 'modernity' ensured an unwillingness to compromise on the part of the Communists. This was the case not only with opponents within Russia but also in encouraging a determination to dominate surrounding countries, formerly parts of the Russian empire, such as Central Asia, the Caucasus, the Ukraine, the Baltic republics and Poland. The first three achieved a precarious independence, only for it to be destroyed in the latter stages of the Russian Civil War, as the Communists regained control over most of the Russian empire.

As most of the struggles of the 1920s entailed conflict for control of individual states, this was not a period in which warfare can be measured by declarations of hostilities. Both the Russian Civil War and warlordism in China entailed not only civil war, in the sense of struggle for control over an established state, but also conflict as an element of state formation and dissolution. Foreign intervention was important, especially in Russia and Turkey, but, again, declarations of war cannot measure the conflict: issues of legitimacy and recognition helped to ensure warfare without the legality of war. Success in such warfare encouraged new aggressive 'adventures'.

Civil conflict was a matter not only of major wars, such as those in China and Russia, but also of uprisings, attempted coups and violent strike action in many countries. This was especially true of those defeated in World War One. Thus, in Germany there were left- and right-wing uprisings in 1919 and 1923.

THE 1930S

Ideological conflict and warfare without declarations of war remained the position in the 1930s, most obviously with the situation in China, which was affected both by serious and sustained conflict between Nationalists and Communists and by Japanese expansionism, and with the Spanish Civil War of 1936–9. Nevertheless, there were also more 'conventional' wars, both the Chaco War between Bolivia and Paraguay (1932–5), and the Italian invasion of Ethiopia in 1935–6, the last of the European wars of colonial annexation. However, the attack on Ethiopia was launched in a different context to that which had characterized much European expansion in the seventeenth century. Although its impact was limited, international opinion, especially in the shape of the League of Nations, an international adjudicating body, and the public opinion of states such as Britain and France, had to be considered, and Mussolini's Italy was therefore careful to present an excuse for its actions in the shape of 'incidents' that apparently required action: Ethiopia was accused of aggression on its frontier with Italian Somaliland. Mussolini explained his invasion of Albania in 1939 by referring to the need to 'restore law and order' there.

The Italians had in fact been responsible for disturbances in the country, but the notion of a mission to maintain peace and stability reflected the imperializing nature of power in this period. It was a crude and unilateral perversion of the attempt to use international bodies for such ends. However, as with the Spanish Civil War, the decision of Britain and France not to intervene was important to the character and course of the conflict in Ethiopia. This adds another dimension to the issue of wars which did not break out.

In 1931 the Japanese invaded Manchuria, claiming that the Chinese had been sabotaging the Japanese-financed South Manchurian Railway. They attacked Shanghai in 1932, stating that it was necessary in order to protect Japanese residents from possible attack, and in 1937 widened their aggression to a full-scale invasion of China, after a clash between Japanese and Chinese troops at the Marco Polo Bridge in Beijing. The Japanese had had a presence in Manchuria for several decades, but the extension of their activities elsewhere indicated that they were not prepared to accept limits. This was imperialism like that of Russia in Central Asia in the late nineteenth century, an imperialism no longer welcome to world opinion in the age of the League of Nations. The Japanese had been disturbed by the expansion of Kuomintang power and pretensions, and were also inclined to despise their opponents.

However, the consequences of the Marco Polo Bridge incident can also be seen as an example of unintended war. The unplanned incident occurred at a time when many leaders in Tokyo, including some influential generals, were convinced that Japan should concentrate on the preparation of her army for war with the USSR; this was a very different matter from fighting China. Ideally, China should be persuaded to accept her fate as a junior partner of Japan, and the ensuing diplomacy was designed to show Chiang he had no alternative. It was Chiang's uncooperativeness which prompted Tokyo to try to give him a short sharp lesson. The Japanese were misleadingly confident that China would fall rapidly.

In addition, it is important not to suggest a greater coherence and continuity in Japan's policy than was the case. The factionally riven character of the governments and armed forces of Japan in the 1930s did much to confuse the course of events. There were to be major battles between Soviet and Japanese forces at Changkufen (1938) and Nomonhan Bridge (1939), but they did not broaden out into a war, declared or undeclared.

A pattern of bluster, deceit and intimidatory gambling was to be followed by Hitler's Germany, for example in the attack on Poland in 1939 and, more generally, in the intimidation and despoilation of Czechoslovakia in 1938–9. Hitler defended the invasion of Bohemia and Moravia in 1939 by claiming that its German population were suffering 'violent excesses' and were appealing for help, a spurious pretence also employed when Poland was attacked. The cynical creation and manipulation of 'incidents' and opinion by a leader and government that asserted its desire for peace ensured that the public explanation of policy bore little reference to its governmental formulation and execution. Mussolini wrote in 1939 of the need to 'talk of peace and prepare for war'.

Such manipulation was not a novelty of the age of dictators. In 1788 Gustavus III of Sweden wished to present his attack on Russia as a defensive step. Accordingly, Swedish soldiers disguised as Russians staged a border incident at Puumala on 28 June, enabling Gustavus to declare war on 6 July. In 1792 Russian troops invaded Poland under the pretext of supporting the Confederation of Targowica, a Polish noble league that Catherine had inspired. The resulting Russo-Prussian Second Partition of Poland the following year prefigured the Hitler-Stalin pact of 1939, although without the latter's genocidal consequences.

The attitudes of leaders such as Mussolini were of particular importance because the dictatorial systems they created lacked effective institutional and political restraints on the leaders, and, indeed, increasingly lost an ability to offer any reasonable range of policy options. A recent study of Mussolini's decision to intervene in the Spanish Civil War in 1936 has noted the bypassing of diplomatic experience and the 'tendency for foreign policy to be concocted out of his whims'.[18] Thanks to this intervention, an essentially domestic conflict within Spain overlapped into the international sphere.

As with many leaders, Mussolini appears to have evaluated information about various aspects of the situation, most significantly the intentions of other powers and the progress of the war, before deciding to act in accordance with his instincts.

Such conduct is common: the purpose of 'rational' analysis is often to select arguments to support instincts, and systems of explanation and deterrence predicated on such analysis are, therefore, limited in accuracy and effectiveness.

The protectionist economic policies and emphasis on self-sufficiency that were particularly strongly adopted in interwar dictatorships severed much of the commercial links between countries that gave them mutual interests. This process exacerbated, and was exacerbated by, the economic slump of the 1930s. This slump encouraged social and political tensions and helped to lead to the rise of anti-democratic political movements which by their very nature relied on crisis and violence, to waves of strikes, and to coup attempts, as in Finland in 1930 and Austria in 1934. It also accentuated the Japanese desire for self-sufficiency, which encouraged a determination to control the raw materials, first of Manchuria and, eventually, of South-East Asia.

WORLD WAR TWO

In the case of Germany, the 'government' shrank essentially to Hitler, and his motives have been a subject of extensive debate. They can be traced to his long-term views on the role of Germany and the Germans, and, also, to the interaction of these views with the short-term opportunities and anxieties presented by international developments in the late 1930s. Opportunities and anxieties themselves do not exist in the abstract; they are sensed and created, and Hitler's ideology played a major role in this process. His notions of racial superiority and living space ensured that he took different views towards his eastern and western neighbours. Far from being a nihilist without plans, simply seeking opportunities for conquest – a twentieth-century caricature copy of a dated view of the 'barbarians' – Hitler had a long-term aim and saw war as its realization, a war for the extirpation of what he regarded as a Jewish-dominated Soviet Union. To that end, he sought to control eastern Europe, to end the threat of a war on two fronts by defeating France, and to reach an agreement with Britain. The destruction of the USSR was to be accompanied by the annihilation of the Jews, the two creating a Europe that could be dominated by the Germans, who were to be a master-race over the Slavs. This agenda began long before the outbreak of World War Two with the violent suppression of political and economic freedoms, organizations and entities within Germany, including strikes, left-wing parties and Jews. Hitler might not have wanted a major conflict in 1939, but he anticipated such a war within six years and planned his economy accordingly.

Yet, having argued that World War One should not be explained simply by reference to the internal dynamics of German leadership and society, it is inappropriate to ignore this argument for World War Two. As with the former conflict, it is necessary to take due note of the dynamics of the international system, for example Soviet policy, especially the willingness to co-operate with Germany in attacking Poland. It is also important to note the shifts in Anglo-French policy, not least the abandonment of appeasement in 1939. For much of the 1930s it was by no means clear to many commentators in Western Europe whether Nazi Germany or Soviet Russia was more of a threat, and it was also unclear as to how best to confront the threats. The eventual outcome – alliance with Russia from 1941 and then cold war with her – was far from inevitable.

Furthermore, the role of Hitler has been qualified by suggesting that his regime and its aims should be seen as a continuation, in many respects, of those of the Wilhelmine Reich. Certainly, Hitler did not invent racialism, anti-Semitism, the notion of *Lebensraum* (living space) or aggressive warfare. Yet they were combined to genocidal effect and given dynamic force by his evil genius. The argument that the Nazi regime represented the essence of German history is facile. The suggestion that German strength was the crucial post-1871 geopolitical problem, causing repeated confrontation and eventual war, is also unhelpful, for it fails to address the question of the purposes of power.

Similarly, although Italian unification had introduced a new element into Mediterranean politics, and Mussolini's adventurism can be seen as another stage of that shown by Italy at the expense of the Turks in 1911–12, the nature of Mussolini's regime and ideology was such that the politics of prudence that had generally characterized earlier Italian policy was from 1935 replaced by a rhetorical foreign policy with an emphasis on force and power, often for their own sake. The Fascist glorification of war[19] and the notion of rebirth through conflict came to have greater effect on Italian policy, accentuating the consequences of an already extreme nationalism. Unlike nineteenth-century Liberals, and contemporary Communists and Socialists, the Fascists did not see the abolition of war as possible or desirable. The cult of the leader was not a way to restraint, for, like Louis XIV and Napoleon, Mussolini and Hitler surrounded themselves with the trappings of unconstrained power, literally strutting a stage as they soaked up their own bombast. Fascism created a history for itself in which struggle and martial images played a major role, most obviously with Mussolini's March on Rome of 1922. There was also a major build-up of military power. Germany resumed general conscription in 1935.

The belief that the German army had not lost World War One, but had been stabbed in the back by traitors and weaklings, preceded Hitler's rise to power, but he gave it a position of political centrality. The same was true of Mussolini and the Italian belief that they had not gained their legitimate spoils, that, instead, they had suffered from a mutilated peace.

Ideological considerations were also important in the case of Poland, for the ethos of the Polish government made compromise impossible in 1939: there could be no recurrence of Czech acceptance of the Munich terms. Poland would not accept client-state status. Indeed, the Poles had actually seized Teschen from Czechoslovakia in October 1938, just as their eastern border with the Soviet Union rested on military victory in 1920. Colonel Josef Beck, the Polish Foreign Minister in 1939, had played a major role in the seizure of Teschen.

Initially, the British and French governments had hoped that Hitler would be tamed by the responsibilities and exigencies of power, or that he would restrict his energies to ruling Germany. There was also a feeling in Britain that the Versailles terms had been overly harsh on Germany and that it was, therefore, understandable that Hitler should press for revision. It was anticipated that German revisionism could be accommodated, and that Hitler would be another episode in European power politics, rather as Napoleon III, the reviser of the Congress of Vienna, had been, and, possibly, less threateningly so. Furthermore, in both Britain and France pacifism was strong and fiscal restraint even stronger, although outside Europe both powers used troops to sustain their imperial interests. Similarly, the Americans intervened militarily in Central America and the Caribbean.

Nevertheless, the military situation was very different in Europe. The British government, especially under Neville Chamberlain, thought it both necessary and possible to negotiate with Hitler, and it took time for the government to appreciate that it was not possible and, instead, dangerous. By 1938 Hitler, indeed, appeared a threat, and British intelligence, if anything, exaggerated German military capabilities vis à vis Britain and Czechoslovakia. In 1939 there was a breakdown of confidence in negotiating directly with Germany, but the attempt to create a powerful opposing alliance left Britain offering guarantees to the exposed states of Poland and Romania, unable to prevent the USSR from joining Hitler and, instead, reliant on the French, who were to be revealed in 1940 as a flawed ally, both militarily and politically. Had the negotiations for a triple alliance of Britain, France and the Soviet Union succeeded, then Hitler might have been deterred from acting. They collapsed, however, in August 1939, largely because Britain and France could not satisfy the Soviets on the issue of Polish and Romanian consent to the passage of Soviet forces in the event of war. Earlier, the idea of a four-power declaration by Britain, France, Poland and Russia had fallen foul of Polish opposition.

This failure reflected the nature of the Anglo-French alliance system in eastern Europe, particularly the concern of Britain, France and their actual or potential allies that the Soviet Union itself represented a threat – a view that was strongly held by the Polish government. In terms of what happened in eastern Europe, both in 1939–40 and from 1945 until 1989, this was a reasonable supposition. Soviet support for Germany was crucial, given the failure of Italy to act in Hitler's support and the unexpected determination of Britain and France to fulfil their guarantees to Poland. Chamberlain underestimated the possibility of a Russo-German understanding and was concerned about the possibility of a revival of German–Polish links.

Chamberlain essentially followed the same policy in 1939, both before and after the outbreak of war. Poland was a stage, not a turning-point. Once Hitler had seized Bohemia and Moravia, Chamberlain sought to create an alliance system capable of intimidating Hitler. However, despite the guarantee of Polish independence, Hitler persisted. He believed that Britain and France would not fight, especially as a result of his pact with Stalin, and indeed the British Chiefs of Staff had advised that it would not be possible to offer Poland any direct assistance. After war had broken out, Chamberlain hoped that it would be possible to achieve the same goals by a limited war that was far from limited in terms of the aspirations towards a blockade of Germany. It was hoped that such pressure would lead Hitler to negotiate or would lead to his overthrow. This policy did not collapse until Hitler's *blitzkriegs* in the West in 1940.

If the initial outbreak of the war can be variously presented, the same was true of the series of subsequent conflicts that also form part of the war. As with World War One, the explanations advanced to account for the initial outbreak of these struggles are in part still valid, but it is also necessary to place due weight on the vortex-like nature of a major war, the heightened pace of fear and opportunity that accompanies such a conflict, and the unwillingness of the Germans to try to translate initial victories into a peace that was acceptable to more than those who had shared in the conquest and to the elements of the vanquished that could be persuaded to accept dictated terms. In 1939 Hitler turned the defeat of Poland into an opportunity for better relations with the Soviet Union, but, despite Hitler's Reichstag speech of 6 October calling for peace with Britain and France, no real attempt was made to compromise with them, let alone Poland. Britain and France were determined to fight on to prevent German hegemony, and this led Hitler to plan the attack on France eventually launched in May 1940.

A year later, Hitler's over-confidence and his contempt for different systems, combined with his concern about Stalin's intentions in eastern Europe, led him to attack the (from 1939 neighbouring) Soviet Union, despite the fact that Britain was undefeated. Until the summer of 1944 there was no Western front to compare with that of 1914–18. Hitler was confident that the Soviet system would collapse rapidly and was happy to accept misleading intelligence assessments of the size and mobilization potential of the Soviet army. Hitler's refusal to accept what others might consider objective diplomatic and strategic considerations ensured that local wars he had won militarily were, from 1941, transformed into a world war he could not win. Yet such adventurism and conceit rested on more than his warped personality; it was also the product of a political-ideological system in which conflict and hatred appeared natural, and genocide all too possible.[20]

The American President Franklin Delano Roosevelt had responded to the escalation of Japanese attacks on China in 1937 with a speech urging 'a quarantine of the patients in order to protect the health of the community against the spread of the disease'. Such a policy eventually proved impossible for most of the world in the early 1940s. The vortex-like character of a major war can be seen at work in the extension of the German war, with, for example, the entry of Italy in 1940 and the German attack on Yugoslavia and Greece in 1941, and also with the outbreak of the Pacific war. In the former case, German successes in 1939–41 led other states, willingly or otherwise, to become allies and protégés, and to provide military resources to help the Germans, most obviously against the USSR when Germany attacked it on 22 June 1941. Romania, Hungary, Slovakia and Finland made major contributions against the USSR, while other allies, such as Italy, also sent troops. The composite force launched against the Soviet Union was similar in that respect to that led by Napoleon. The neutrality of states such as Belgium (1940) and the Netherlands (1940) was casually violated to serve strategic convenience.

Despite his alliance with Hitler, Mussolini had initially taken no part in the war, but in 1940 he joined in because he feared that he would otherwise lose the opportunity to gain glory and territories: Mussolini sought gains from France and the British empire, and greater power in the Balkans. He felt that Italian greatness required a new Imperial Rome that could dominate the Mediterranean anew, and, to this end, thought British defeat necessary. This policy, however, was not based on a reasonable assessment of the capabilities of the Italian military machine, and this failure was to lead to a series of disasters in 1940 when Britain and Greece were successively attacked.[21]

It was not only Axis powers, however, that led to a widening of the war in its early stages. Soviet aggression, most prominently the attack on Finland in November 1939, can, in part, be seen as an extension of the Axis after the Molotov–Ribbentrop pact. The Soviets had first demanded 30-year leases on bases that would leave Finland strategically bereft and had then staged an incident that offered them a pretext for invasion. British plans to stage an 'uninvited landing' in Norway, as a prelude to sending troops to help the Finns, was a response. They were not implemented, but in 1940 the British mined Norwegian waters in order to prevent the transport of Swedish iron ore to Germany. This, however, was overshadowed by the surprise German invasion of Denmark and Norway that April, an invasion intended to end irritating British moves in Scandinavia and to challenge British control of the North Sea.

Like Hitler, the Soviet Union, Hungary and Bulgaria wished to revise the post-World War One peace settlement, while Italy and Japan were also dissatisfied powers. All had territorial motives for overturning the international situation in 1939, but in the case of Germany, Italy, the Soviet Union and Japan there were also powerful psychological reasons: their political cultures rested on the idea of struggle and on defiance of the existing global order. Furthermore, success encouraged intervention in the war. Mussolini hoped to follow up earlier successes in Abyssinia (1935–6) and Albania (1939).

In contrast, Franco's Spain, which did not intervene in World War Two, had been badly battered by civil war in 1936–9. Spain also benefited from its distance from the German–Soviet battleground in eastern Europe. Bulgaria supported Germany and was given some of conquered Yugoslavia and Greece, but it was not a full ally and did not help in the invasion of the USSR. Nevertheless, Britain declared war in December 1941 and the USA in 1942.

Having joined the war, it was difficult to leave it. Defeated France agreed armistice terms on 22 June 1940. Part was occupied, the remainder becoming a neutral state with its capital at Vichy. This, however, was not accepted either by the Free French or by Britain. British anxiety about the French fleet at Mers-el-Kebir in French North Africa, and its possible effect on the Mediterranean balance of power, led to a demand that it scuttle, join the British or sail to a harbour outside possible German control, and when this was refused it was attacked on 3 July 1940. The death of 1300 French sailors did not lead to a declaration of war, but it set a pattern for hostilities, including the invasion of Syria and Lebanon in 1941 and of Madagascar in 1942. Both were motivated by fear – of German influence in Syria and of possible Japanese submarine bases in Madagascar – reflecting the way in which strategic position was seen as a possible threat and as a reason for action. Thus, the British overthrew a pro-German government in Iraq in May 1941, and that August British and Soviet troops entered Persia in order to gain control of supply routes. Elsewhere, resistance ensured that conflict continued across much of the area already conquered by Germany, leading in some regions, especially much of Yugoslavia, to civil war.

Soviet victories in 1944 led to abrupt shifts as Soviet troops advanced into eastern Europe. Thus in September 1944, under the pressure of the Soviet advance, Bulgaria declared war on Germany, although as the USSR was also then at war with Bulgaria, the latter for a few hours was at war with all the major powers, bar Japan.[22] The Romanians had changed sides the previous month. The new Italian government that replaced that of Mussolini had already declared war on Germany in October 1943.

The collapse of France and the Netherlands in 1940, and the weakening position of Britain, already vulnerable in the Pacific, created an apparent power vacuum in East and South-East Asia, encouraging Japanese ambitions southwards into Indo-China and the East Indies, while leading the Americans to feel that only they were in a position to resist Japan. Japanese aggression and expansion helped to trigger American commercial sanctions, specifically an embargo on oil exports that, in turn, encouraged the Japanese to act, in order to protect their position. They were confident of rapid military advantage and hopeful that the difficulties of driving them back would out-weigh greater American strength. As with Hitler and Britain and France, a conviction of the weakness of the opposing system led to a failure to judge resolve.

The issue of 'cause' in the Pacific war is problematic. The Japanese were unwilling to accept limitations to their activity, unless fought to a stop, as by the Russians in 1939, a defeat that led in April 1941 to a non-aggression pact between the two powers. At that stage the Soviet Union was still allied to Germany, to the anger of Japan, and Japan had not been informed of the planned German attack.

The Americans considered themselves entitled to take a view on events on the other side of the Pacific, a position enhanced by their control over the Philippines, conquered from Spain after a war of aggression in 1898. Such a remark is not intended to imply any equality of action, responsibility or guilt between America and Japan, but simply to note that both had wide-ranging views on their own position, interests and rights, and views that it was difficult to accommodate through diplomatic means. Each was based on a different 'globalism', a sense of interaction with the outside world in which there was little room for mutuality but varied approaches to the use of force.[23] Each power not only had a sense of rectitude but also a feeling of racial superiority. America acted as an imperial power, but did not see itself as one.

Neither power wanted to fight the other, but the Japanese government and military, although divided, were determined to expand at the expense of others, particularly from 1940 in South-East Asia, 'the southern resources area', and the American government was resolved to prevent them. The occupation of northern Indo-China in September 1941 led the Americans to limit trade, and the occupation of the South the following July led to a trade embargo. They also demanded that the Japanese withdraw from China. The Japanese decided to begin war if diplomatic approaches failed to lead to a lifting of the embargo. On 7 December 1941 they attacked Pearl Harbor.

Each side failed to apply deterrence successfully. Economic deterrence failed the Americans and, more specifically, their poor use of their extensive intelligence resources was insufficient to prepare them for the initial Japanese attacks: as with the Russians in 1904–5, the Americans interpreted likely Japanese conduct in light of their own presuppositions. In turn, the initial Japanese ability to mount successful attacks and to gain territory, in the face of weak and poorly led opponents, failed to deter the Americans from the long-term effort of driving back and destroying their opponents. The American government and American public opinion was not interested in the idea of a compromise peace with the power that had attacked Pearl Harbor. As with the war in Europe, that in Asia had a vortex-like quality that culminated in its closing stages with the Soviet attack on Japan: the USSR declared war and invaded Manchuria on 8 August 1945, two days after the first atomic bomb had been dropped on Hiroshima.

World War Two opens up a question that caused great interest in the 1990s: namely, whether democracies were less prone to start wars than dictatorships. In the longer-term historical context there was relatively little to support this view: although they did not begin the war, in 1914 France and Britain were not reluctant to fight, and the imperial democracies of the late nineteenth century, particularly Britain and France, but also Italy and the USA, had proved willing to support the use of force in order to extend their global sway – trade and the flag followed the Gatling gun. The situation was more complex in 1939–45. A reluctance to fight lay behind appeasement, and in 1939 France and Britain came into the war as guarantors of a state, Poland, not as members of an aggressive pact. The same was even more apparent in the case of America, attacked by Japan, without any prior declaration of war, and then declared war upon by Germany. Revisionism can and will chip away, but the overwhelming picture is again cultural: the democratic powers lacked the aggressive ethos, ideology, methods and alliance systems of their dictatorial counterparts. There was considerable weight behind their propaganda claims.[24]

SIX

1945–90: Cold War and the Wars of Decolonization

INTRODUCTION

World War Two was followed by a period of extensive warfare in which most conflicts can be allocated to two often related categories: wars of decolonization and wars between Communist and non-Communist powers. These two categories do not explain the conflicts, for much decolonization took place without warfare, as in most of French Africa, while Communist and non-Communist powers could also co-exist without war, and could indeed co-operate or ally. President Nixon's success in creating better relations between the USA and China was crucial to international relations from the early 1970s. Nevertheless, these two categories explain much of the cultural and ideological dynamics behind the warfare of the period.

CONFLICT WITHIN EUROPE

In contrast, European powers did not wage war with each other. This was not simply a matter of them waging a surrogate struggle in the shape of the Cold War. In addition, the powers within the two competing blocs generally did not fight each other, but, rather, took steps to increase military, political and economic co-operation within their own blocs: the successful Soviet invasions of Hungary in 1956 and Czechoslovakia in 1968 were designed to maintain such Soviet-directed co-operation and control in the eastern European bloc. These were not seen as wars by the Soviets, except in so far as Communism presupposed a continual struggle between what were seen as progressive and reactionary forces. As far as the Soviets were concerned, they were responding to developments that threatened to subvert the Communist bloc – in short, particular domestic policies carried out by governments within the bloc constituted a form of rebellion.

This internationalism implied both that Hungary and Czechoslovakia were and should be statelets rather than states, and that the defence of the Soviet system rested on ideological integrity as much as territorial control. Thus, to indicate the former, the reformist Dubček government of Czechoslovakia remained within the Warsaw Pact, and Communist politicians throughout eastern Europe believed that it had to do so.

More generally, in both cases, a psychological inability to accept change, rather than a prudential assessment of likely developments and threats, was crucial to the decision to invade. The very notion of a Party and of Communist orthodoxy introduced the issue and terminology of deviance into discussion of political differences. It also put pressure on the Soviet leadership to be seen to maintain the true path. The brutalization of domestic groups judged unacceptable – Communism's large-scale social and political 'cleansings' – encouraged a reliance on force.

Both invasions indicate the difficulty of classifying war. The invasion of Hungary was a short, but bloody war. The massive military invasion of Czechoslovakia by Soviet, Polish, East German, Hungarian and Bulgarian forces was far less bloody, in large part because it was so overwhelming. The invasion had been planned to coincide with a seizure of power by Czech sympathizers, leading to a public invitation by the Czech Praesidium for allied forces to help put down a 'counter-revolution'. Instead, although the vastly outnumbered Czech army was not in a position to resist, the invasion's Czech allies were less successful in staging their coup, and the Praesidium condemned the invasion as a violation of international law. However, the Czechs received no foreign assistance.

American intervention in western Europe was not comparable: funds were provided to sympathetic parties, but the different nature of the two blocs was illustrated by the absence of any policy of destabilizing the independent-minded President de Gaulle of France in the 1960s. European powers that were in neither bloc, such as Austria, Sweden and Switzerland, not only remained neutral but also peaceful. Frontiers did not change and European states avoided support for revolutionary movements within other states in the same alliance system, such as those in Corsica, the Basque country and Ulster. The sponsoring of subversion in the opposing bloc became less frequent as the frontiers of the Cold War became more clear, and by the 1960s was largely limited to support for propaganda and peaceful movements.

The absence of full-scale conflict between the two competing blocs owed much to the deterrent power of atomic weaponry and also to the role of alliances and the, consequent, creation of strong and clear diplomatic and military front lines. It was not a result of the internationalism that had led in 1945 to the formation of the United Nations with the accompanying hopes of an end to the traditional politics of aggression and the customary deterrence through competing alliance systems.

DECOLONIZATION

In his utopian novel *L'An 2440* (Paris, 1770), Louis Sébastien Mercier had foretold the struggle for decolonization. He imagined a monument in Paris with a depiction of a black man, his arms extended and a proud look in his eye. Around him lay pieces of twenty broken sceptres, and the pedestal read 'Au vengeur du nouveau monde'. The wars of decolonization began soon after the appearance of this novel – in the Thirteen Colonies in British North America, then Haiti and finally Latin America – but, elsewhere, until the twentieth century, it was rather a case of resistance to advancing colonization, not its overthrow. In the twentieth century there were important risings in the interwar period, especially in Morocco, Syria, the Dutch East Indies and Palestine, and a more sustained series of wars of decolonization began soon after the end of World War Two, in fact as attempts were made to reimpose European colonial power, more particularly by the Dutch in the East Indies (later Indonesia) in 1945 and the French in Indo-China in 1946. Elsewhere, conflict was delayed, but important wars against colonial powers began in Algeria in 1954 and in Portuguese Africa (Angola, Mozambique, Guinea) from 1961.[1] The British also faced conflict across much of their colonial world, including Aden, Cyprus, Kenya and Malaya.

This category of conflict was swiftly joined by that of wars fought not against the colonial power but, rather, over the spoils following the departure of that power. This was the case with the Indo-Pakistan conflicts over Kashmir in 1947–9 and 1965, the Arab-Israeli war of 1948–9, the Burmese Civil War of 1948–55, civil war in Indonesia from 1950 until 1962, war between the Viet Cong and the government of South Vietnam from 1959, the Congolese civil war of 1960–67, and civil conflict in Cyprus from 1963.

Such wars interacted with the struggle between Communism and anti-Communism. The latter played a major role in a number of conflicts, including the Greek Civil War of 1944–9, the Chinese Civil War of 1946–9, the resistance to the establishment of Communist rule in Poland in 1945–8, the Malayan Emergency of 1948–60, the Korean War of 1950–53 and the Cuban Revolution of 1953–9. In the case of the first five, patterns of authority had been affected by recent war and imperial occupation. Thus, in Greece the opposition of the Communist party to pre-war right-wing regimes, especially the dictatorship of General Metaxas in 1936–41, had been transformed by Nazi German conquest. This led to a delegitimation of authority, to an active resistance in which the Communists played a major role, and to a situation in which violence came to be the means of political discourse and debate. German evacuation in 1944 led to an accentuation of conflict between left- and right-wing guerrilla groups, and then, in order to thwart a left-wing takeover, to military intervention by the British on behalf of the right. Attempts to reach a compromise were wrecked by partisanship, leading to a second stage of the war in 1946–9. Again, foreign intervention was crucial, particularly the provision of American aid to the right and the eventual cutting of aid to the Communists, especially after the Tito–Stalin breach of 1949.[2] The Chinese Civil War was a continuation of a struggle that had begun in the 1920s, while within Yugoslavia the conflict between Communists and non-Communists had led to bitter fighting between resistance groups from November 1941.

The struggle was also central to a large number of *coups d'état* in the post-war world, for example the Communist seizure of power in Czechoslovakia in 1948, the anti-Communist military coup in Indonesia in 1965, and the reactionary military coup in Greece in 1967. There was, and is, not always a clear-cut separation between coups and civil wars, and this complicates the analysis of civil war. For example, the Spanish Civil War began in 1936 as an only partially successful coup.

COLD WAR

The struggle between Communism and anti-Communism was also important to the general tension between a large number of powers, a tension summarized by the term Cold War.[3] The Cold War was not a formal or frontal conflict, but a period of sustained hostility involving many proxy wars. The major powers intervened in other struggles, providing arms, advisers and, at times, troops. Such intervention sustained the Cold War, and made it 'hot' in many areas. Although it was not necessary to the confrontation between highly prepared and expensive forces, both in Europe and in terms of nuclear weaponry, conflict in the Third World, generally between surrogates, sustained attitudes of animosity, exacerbated fears and contributed to a high level of military preparedness. Dr Strangelove, the fictional exponent of nuclear hype, did not need Castro, but anxieties aroused by the activities of Soviet-supported forces contributed directly to American phobias. Such activities apparently made specific a more general sense of threat. Just as nineteenth-century theorists had seen war, not peace, as normal, or, at least, had concentrated on conflict, so their Cold War successors concentrated on confrontation rather than conciliation, affecting both the public, and political and military leaders: strategic theory was given a formal role, including institutional continuity and a place in decision-making processes.

A feeling of weakness on both sides, of the fragility of military strength, international links, political orders and ideological convictions, encouraged a sense of threat and fuelled an arms race that was to be central to the Cold War. Indeed, in many respects the arms race *was* the Cold War. Aside from the competition between the USA and the USSR to produce and deploy more and better weapons, there were also subsidiary arms races between the competing services of individual states.

Militarily, the Soviet Union initially lacked the atom bomb, but its army was well-placed to overrun Western Europe. Ideologically and culturally, in 1945 each side felt threatened by the other. The American offer of Marshall Aid to help recovery after World War Two was rejected as a form of economic imperialism, and this created a new boundary line between the areas that received such aid and those that did not. The Soviet abandonment of co-operation over Germany and the imposition of one-party Communist governments in Eastern Europe led to pressure for a response.

Thanks to the apparent global threat of Communism and Soviet power, the USA abandoned its tradition of isolationism and played a crucial role in the formation of the North Atlantic Treaty Organization in 1949. That year, the Senate ratified the North Atlantic Treaty by 82 votes to 13. To the Americans, the Cold War had been launched by the USSR, and NATO and other steps were necessary responses. The establishment of NATO was followed by the creation of a military structure, including a central command, and, eventually, by German rearmament. Substantial American forces were stationed in Europe, thus increasing US commitment to the region.[4] An analysis of World War Two that attributed the war and Hitler's initial successes to appeasement led to a determination to contain the Soviet Union. Atomic bomb attacks on Soviet cities had been planned from October 1945. By the early 1950s the requirement and strategy for atomic defence and war in Europe were in place: the American forces there had to be protected.

The Korean War (1950–53) ensured that the Cold War could not be confined to Europe. The Communists had won in the Chinese Civil War, but they were not to be allowed further gains in East Asia. Big-power intervention exacerbated differences in a number of areas, particularly the Middle East and sub-Saharan Africa. Warfare in both of these regions received far more global attention than conflict there in earlier periods.

The location of war in the world was very different to that in the period between 1914 and 1945. The Middle East and sub-Saharan Africa were not geographically close to the major powers – the USA, the Soviet Union and China – and, partly as a result, these powers did not intervene in conflict there as frequently and, generally, as directly as they did in regions of uncertainty and dispute near their frontiers, although they provided the armaments with which the wars were conducted. Tank and aerial warfare in the Middle East would have been impossible without foreign arms supplies. Thus, the USSR sent troops into Afghanistan in 1979 and, thereafter, fought a bitter war there,[5] but it did not engage in comparable activity in Africa or the Middle East, although its Cuban surrogates did in Africa. China intervened in the Korean War, and clashed with India, North Vietnam and the USSR, but, again, it did not fight further afield: the Communists maintained the cartography of Imperial China to its greatest extent, although Taiwan in particular eluded them.

The Americans, however, followed a different pattern. Not only did they intervene in Latin America – sending troops to the Dominican Republic (1965), Grenada (1983), Panama (1989) and Haiti (1994) – but they also contributed the largest contingents to the United Nations armies in Korea (1950–53) and the Persian Gulf (1990–91), and sent a large army to Vietnam (1965–73), a force that also intervened in Cambodia in 1970. Troops were also sent to Lebanon in 1958 and 1982–3, and Libya was bombed in 1986, an act of war although not the prelude to one. This range reflected American military capability and economic strategic interests, and also a sense of global concern and mission. Arguments of consequences and credibility were used to support pressure for action, as with the bombing of North Vietnam in 1965–8. The commitment of forces encouraged pressure for their protection. Apparent attacks on American warships in the Gulf of Tonkin off Vietnam in 1964 led Congress to pass a resolution permitting the president 'to take all necessary measures to repel any armed attack against the forces of the United States and to prevent further aggression' – in short, to wage war without proclaiming it. This reflected a number of factors, including Lyndon Johnson's wish to avoid an explicit choice between war and disengagement, and the American reliance on the strategic concept of graduated pressure.[6] Failure in Vietnam led to a more circumspect stance in the late 1970s, but in the 1980s this was replaced by the 'Reagan doctrine': secret operations against Communist or left-wing states, particularly in Latin America.

The interaction of decolonization, ideological confrontation and the intervention of the major powers lay behind much of the conflict of the period. This was true of Latin America, although there political (as opposed to economic) decolonization was not an issue, and the civil conflicts did not always relate to a clear struggle involving Communism. However, right-wing groupings, especially within the military, saw politics as a struggle against Communism and, as in Argentina, Chile, El Salvador and Guatemala, were willing to use force to achieve their ends. Their Communist counterparts sought to do the same, backing armed revolutionary struggle in countries such as Bolivia.

In Korea and Vietnam, civil war between two ideologically contrasting authoritarian regimes was greatly affected by foreign intervention, sufficiently so for both wars to be generally seen in terms of this intervention. Massive American involvement in Vietnam was supplemented by troops from Australia, New Zealand, South Korea, Thailand and the Philippines, although the war effort was less international than the Americans had wished. Again, classification is a problem, especially in South Vietnam. The Communist Viet Cong began guerrilla activity in 1957 and soon had over 20,000 troops there. Viet Cong strategy switched to that of 'liberating' sections of rural South Vietnam. The degree to which this conflict should primarily be seen as civil war/rebellion, or as an invasion from North Vietnam, was controversial. If the latter, it is also possible to argue that the two Vietnams were really one country and that the entire conflict should still be seen as civil war. Maoist war is the best example of a mix of military aggression and politics, and the best application of that was in the Vietnamese revolution. For most of the war, soldiers spent less than fifty per cent of their time fighting. Military struggle and political indoctrination were seen to act in symbiosis. The soldiers who dragged the heavy guns up the hills around Dien Bien Phu and built the Ho Chi Minh trail were the lowest of the low in military terms, but they believed that they could attain status by doing these menial tasks. They were also taught to believe that if they died – as most did – their descendants would be rewarded, for instance in the distribution of land.

The growing ideological dimension of international conflict was readily apparent. As late as 1917–18 the Russians, Austrians and Germans ultimately came to hate their own governments more than they feared their enemies. Nothing similar occurred in 1939–45, with the possible exception of Italy, and there have been few exceptions since. The ideological clash helped to exacerbate distrust and this ensured that even when international tensions eased, as with the *détentes* that followed the death of Stalin and the latter years of Khrushchev, there was still an uncertainty and a sense that the other bloc was seeking to take advantage. *Détente* was a matter not of the end of the Cold War but of its conduct at a lower level of tension. This sense of flux encouraged military action, as with the invasions of Hungary and Czechoslovakia.

REGIONAL RIVALRIES

There were other causes of conflict in the post-war world. It was not only 'big powers' that intervened in the affairs of other states. Instead, in a reversion to the situation prior to the heyday of European imperial expansion in the last quarter of the nineteenth century, locally powerful states launched interventionist actions. Thus, Egypt sent an army into Yemen in 1962 to try to impose Nasser's Arab Socialism and to advance Egyptian interests. Turkey invaded Cyprus in 1974, Libya intervened in Chad with an unsuccessful full-scale invasion in 1983, and Libya and Egypt in the Sudan, while India, Tanzania and, in the mid-1990s, Nigeria acted as regional 'policemen', although their interventions in nearby states were often heavy-handed, if not aggressive. Furthermore, the pursuit of regional hegemony could greatly increase tension. In 1975 South Africa sent a large force into Angola in order to try to limit the success of the left-wing

MPLA, which was then winning the civil war. Further attacks followed in 1978 and 1979, as the South Africans attacked the bases of guerrilla movements seeking to drive them from South-West Africa (Namibia). Angolan forces were attacked in 1981–8, again without any declaration of war.[7] In 1977 Egypt mounted a successful surprise attack on Libya in order to indicate its anger with Libyan pretensions and policies. Border disputes were also important, as in the Indo-Chinese war of 1962, that between India and Pakistan in 1965, the clashes between China and the Soviet Union in 1969, and those between Ethiopia and Somalia over the Ogaden, the last a conflict greatly exacerbated by big-power involvement.

In part, the conflicts reflected the uncertainties left by imperial powers: both poorly determined frontiers and the departure of a hegemonic power able to ensure that disagreements over frontiers did not lead to war. Thus, Morocco and Algeria clashed over their frontier in 1962–3. However, the propensity of particular elites to regard such disputes as a crucial aspect of prestige was central to the wars. In Pakistan the prestige of the army and of military governments was closely bound up with confrontation with India, while in Greece the security and self-image of the armed forces was identified with resistance to the Left. The bombastic President Sukarno of Indonesia was ideologically committed to conflict with imperialist and 'neocolonialist' forces, and this encouraged him to confrontation with Malaysia in 1963–6, and, then, ensured that he needed to present the confrontation as successful while in turn providing him with an excuse to suppress domestic criticism. Although in 1964 the Indonesians increased their military commitment, sending troops to the Malayan Peninsula, there was no formal war and no retaliatory attack on Indonesian bases.

Another megalomaniac, Idi Amin, military dictator of Uganda from 1971 until 1979, rose to power in a coup, ruled by terror, slaughtering opponents, greatly increased the size of the army, and attacked neighbouring Tanzania, alleging that its government supported military operations by Ugandan exiles. This served as an excuse for attacks in 1971, 1972 and, more seriously, on three occasions in the winter of 1978–9. After the last, the Tanzanians invaded and overthrew Amin.

Conflicts could serve to demonstrate greater strength and regional hegemony. This was an element in Indian pressure on Pakistan and that of China on India. It is also a factor in current disputes over islands and territorial waters in the South China Sea involving the states that border the sea, especially the struggles over the Spratlys. Episodic fighting in the Sea since 1974 involving Vietnam and China, and confrontation, also, involving Taiwan, Malaysia and the Philippines, have not led to war, although they have fuelled naval build-ups.[8]

Rivalries between bordering states could also take other forms. The army of El Salvador invaded Honduras in 1969 after a visiting Honduran soccer team had been attacked in San Salvador and the football victory of El Salvador had been followed by anti-Salvadorean riots in Honduras. The root cause was more complex and owed much to long-standing difficulties, exacerbated by large-scale Salvadorean migration into Honduras. Nevertheless, the specific causes of the conflict in 1969 were important: by inflaming passions, they made compromise appear unacceptable. Risk had been transferred from the international to the domestic context.

Although big-power rivalry played a role, as when the Soviets stirred Egyptian suspicions of Israeli preparations and intentions in 1967, leading first to Egyptian and then to Israeli mobilization, war in the Middle East also owed much to local tensions. The very presence of Israel was unacceptable to many Arab leaders and polemicists. Although the Jordanian rulers were able to reconcile themselves to Israeli existence, their Egyptian and Syrian counterparts found this far less easy. David Ben-Gurion, Prime Minister of Israel from 1948 until 1953, felt able to argue that Israel had no foreign, domestic or economic policy, only a security policy. Feeling under threat, Israeli leaders claimed that successive status quos were dangerous. Thus, in 1956 there was pressure to attack Egypt by, for example, Moshe Dayan, Chief-of-Staff of the Israeli Defence Forces, on the grounds that the armistice agreements of 1949 had left a hazardous situation.[9] Four years later, the prospect of Israeli moves against Syria led the Egyptians to deploy more troops near Israel's frontier. This helped to increase Israeli military concern about the strategic situation. Israel attacked in 1967 because it felt, and indeed was, threatened by the strength and preparations of its neighbours.

Public pressure for a strong defence posture rendered compromise difficult after the Israeli victory in the Six Day War of 1967. The pressure to act against terrorism helped to lead to the Israeli invasion of Lebanon in 1982, although that also owed much to the reliance on force of the Defence Minister, Ariel Sharon.[10] Lebanon itself had been destabilized after the Six Day War, in large part because of the extension of the Arab-Israeli conflict and its interaction with struggles for power in a country much divided by complex ethnic, religious and political rifts. This situation encouraged foreign intervention, as with the Syrian invasion of 1976.

Public pressure was not only present on the Israeli side. Within Arab countries there was also hostility to compromise and a desire for war, as in Egypt in 1948. Dissatisfaction with the status quo could lead to pressure for conflict. President Nasser was affected by popular pressure in 1967, and his desire to retain the leadership of the Arab cause encouraged him to take public steps against Israel, especially the expulsion of the United Nations peacekeeping force from the Sinai frontier and the closure of the Gulf of Aqaba to Israeli ships. Nasser was an army officer by background, had risen to power as a result of the 1952 coup and wished to wipe out the ignominy of defeats by Israel in 1948 and 1956. He had already revealed a propensity to military adventurism in Yemen. However, this was more than simply a matter of opportunism. Nasser also felt under pressure from economic problems arising from his misguided attempt to force-start the economy through state-planning, while the aggressive attitude of the new military government in Syria towards Israel challenged his prestige. Israel's gains in the 1967 war, and the subsequent inability to negotiate a satisfactory peace settlement, helped lead Egypt to stage a war of attrition against Israel in 1969–70, and Egypt and Syria to resume hostilities with Israel in 1973.

The number of independent states rose with decolonization, thus increasing the number of those legally entitled to declare war. Furthermore, the new states faced decolonization struggles of their own, as the principle and practice of national self-determination confronted the inchoate and controverted nature of nationhood across much of the world. Thus, for example, Iraq faced demands for autonomy or independence from both Kurds and Marsh Arabs, and waged a long-term conflict against the former as well as brutally suppressing the latter. Katanganese separatism was suppressed by Zaire. Successive Ethiopian regimes sought to control Eritrea, where a war of secession was waged between 1961 and 1991.[11] Somali support for secession from Ethiopia of the Somali-populated Ogaden region ensured that the conflict involving the Western Somali Liberation Front can be better understood as a war between two states. Indeed, in 1977 Somalia committed regular forces to the struggle. On a much smaller scale, the same approach can be taken to the Shifta War in north-east Kenya in 1963–7: Somali claims to the territory were successfully thwarted.

Across much of the world, force was used to suppress regional separatism. Thus, in 1966 the Ugandan army suppressed a secession attempt by the kingdom of Buganda. In 1997 a separatist revolt on Anjouan, one of the islands in the Comoros, was also suppressed. In Sudan there have been decades of war, as governments based in the Moslem North have sought to suppress the regional autonomy and, at times, identity of the non-Moslem, Black South.[12] Tamil demands caused a war of secession in northern Sri Lanka (formerly Ceylon) from 1983, while India deployed large numbers of troops to resist Kashmiri, Naga and Sikh separatism.

Biafra sought independence from Nigeria in a conflict fuelled by ethnic fear and hatred. The slaughter of large numbers of Ibos – possibly 30,000 – in the massacres that followed the second coup in 1966 led to a collapse of Ibo support for the notion of Nigeria. The new Nigerian government, composed of officers and the product of a coup, were unsympathetic to the Ibo demand for a looser confederation, while the Ibo leadership challenged the legality of the federal government and increasingly took steps towards autonomy, taking over federal institutions in south-eastern Nigeria. In response, the federal government first redrew internal boundaries, and then, after the 'Republic of Biafra' was proclaimed, in July 1967 launched a 'police operation' that became a civil war. This civil war owed much to hatreds engendered and strengthened during the bloody turmoil of 1966. The warfulness of the domestic political situation was readily translated into civil war, not least because of the prominent role of the military in government and because there was, already, a high level of civil violence.[13] The atrocities committed against civilians by both sides in the Biafran conflict were all too common in separatist wars, reflecting the crucial argument of ethnic numbers, the polarization of civil conflict and the commitment of military regimes to holding states together. Such atrocities were also commonplace in civil wars within multi-ethnic states, such as Angola and Mozambique, and the People's Republic of the Congo (Congo-Brazzaville) in 1997.

Another example was the regional conflict within South Africa that became severe and sustained in Natal from 1987, one in which the Zulu Inkatha movement fought the United Democratic Front, which was linked with the then-banned African National Congress. This struggle for dominance involved control over land and employment, and the ability to negotiate with the apartheid government. Police involvement further complicated the struggle, which was at once a war and a disorganized upsurge of ethnic violence and lawlessness, again raising the problem of definition. This was war not as the defiance of the government, but as a conflict between groups within a state where the government could still deploy considerable force. By 1990 Inkatha was deploying thousands of men, weaponry was becoming more sophisticated, and casualties were heavy.[14] More generally, warfare in Africa reflects population increase, competition for scarce resources and the proliferation of light weapons. The largely colonial-drawn frontiers of African states provide arenas for and within which competing groups and factions fight it out. In Chad and Sudan the groupings have Moslem-versus-Christian cultural backgrounds. Elsewhere, they are most often, but not always, ethnic (which carries the culture of the ethnicity) and have links with the past warrior tradition of African societies. In Somalia, for example, inter-clan fighting has a long tradition. The issues between clans – those of grazing rights and waterholes – are very often literally life for the winners and death for the losers. These are now no longer being fought with spears, but with cast-off Soviet and American weaponry.

CONCLUSIONS

New states confronted a world made unstable by ideological tensions, big-power rivalries and the legacy of imperialism. It was also one in which the nature of weaponry made lengthy conflict destructive and expensive. Many conflicts were therefore swiftly over. This was true for example of the Arab-Israeli 'Yom Kippur' war of 1973, the Turkish invasion of Cyprus the following year, the Chinese attack on Vietnam in 1979, and the Falklands war of 1982. Other conflicts, however, were both destructive and lengthy, most obviously the Iran-Iraq war of 1980–88,[15] but more typically civil wars, for example that in Nigeria in 1967–70 or those in Chad, Sudan and Sri Lanka.[16] Such conflicts arose from or broke out in the context of powerful ethnic and religious hostilities that allowed a degree of mobilization of national, or regional, resources and social energy that was no longer possible in 'advanced' liberal societies. In the latter, democratization, disenchantment with violence and glory, individualism, and different concepts of national interests had all contributed to a reaction against war that was deeper-rooted and more sustained than other negative responses over the previous half-millennium.

SEVEN

1990–: War Today

In the American film *Mars Attacks* (1997), the presidential science adviser, played by Pierce Brosnan, explains, on more than one occasion, that the approaching Martians are bound to be peaceful, because no advanced culture would wage war. This is one of the latest instances of an intellectual suggesting that it is possible to advance beyond war. The view had already led to calls for open diplomacy and rational policies from the eighteenth century, and for disarmament, international law and institutions, and the brotherhood of man from the early twentieth. Instead, in *Mars Attacks*, the adviser is presented as a fool, and the Martians are revealed as particularly homicidal, delighting in their destructive capabilities, and implacable, until their explosive demise at the sound of American popular music. Similarly, in the film *Independence Day* (1996), the potent aliens destroy all they can, beginning in Los Angeles with those humans gathered to welcome them, and only stop when they are in turn destroyed. In the American television series *Dark Skies* (1996–7), the advanced powers of the aliens are again deployed for destructive purposes and the seizure of control.

The notion that advanced civilizations of great potency might dispense with war was not one that engaged the imaginative attention of humans at the close of the millennium. To take Hollywood, that vital creator and reflector of popular attitudes, the bellicosity of advanced aliens was different to those of rampaging Tyrannosaurs Rexs only in their cold deliberation and planned determination. However, there were indications that developments were making a number of human societies less keen to embark on wars, more reluctant to inflict casualties and more unwilling to accept losses. This was readily apparent in the increasingly negative response of governments and populations to the commitment of resources abroad, as with the Americans in Somalia. It is unlikely that a similar response would arise if these societies are attacked, and, indeed, the position then might repeat that of the beginning of the century when, despite their internationalism, the overwhelming majority of Socialist leaders supported their countries' participation in World War One. Nevertheless, the modern situation with regard to conflicts that are not wars of national survival is very different to the situation a century earlier, and there was a readily apparent contrast between the American response to the Korean War and that to involvement in Somalia, Haiti or Bosnia.

A reluctance to embark on aggressive, or indeed, any wars did not extend to all powers and did not prevent an assertive global or regional interventionism, as with the American invasion of Panama in 1989 or the dispatch of Indian troops to Sri Lanka in 1987. Nevertheless, however much such episodes might reveal the heavy-handedness and assertiveness of global or regional powers, they were presented not as aggressive, but as designed to maintain legality: war by peacekeeping. In short, armies were to serve as the police force of a benign global or regional order. This was dramatized in the response to the Iraqi conquest of Kuwait in 1990. The Americans were at great pains to ensure that their response was part of a wide-ranging reaction, one far more akin to the UN-supported American-led response to the North Korean invasion of South Korea in 1950 than to American participation in the Vietnam War. This was seen by the governments of the USA and its allies as necessary for domestic as well as international reasons. Thus, America went to war in reaction to the Iraqi invasion, but this war had to be acceptable, in form as much as content, to domestic suppositions. A notion of acceptability underlay the so-called Weinberger Doctrine of the mid-1980s in which the then Secretary for Defence advanced six principles justifying resort to war: just cause, determination to win, right intention, proportionality, popular support, and last resort.

This was clearly not the case in control societies, such as Iraq, Syria, China, Burma or Indonesia, societies where the military determined policy or where politics did not involve much of a dialogue between government and populace. If the politics and culture of the 'absolutist' states of the early-modern period involved force as well as compromise, that was equally true of authoritarian modern societies. Militarism and military forces have played a particularly major role in many of the states that emerged from the European colonial empires after 1945, rather as they earlier did in those that emerged from the overthrow of the Spanish New World empire.[1] In both cases, the use of violence to achieve independence helped to encourage a martial ethos and a respect for the military.

Nevertheless, the limited role of the army in nineteenth-century USA suggests that this was a far from universal trend. In the American case, the defeat of the British in the War of Independence was in large part ascribed to an armed citizenry rather than a professional army. An earlier non-Western example of the role of war in encouraging respect for bellicose elements can be found amongst the Fox tribe of the American Mid-West. Traditionally, war chiefs only played major roles when the tribe was threatened, but the intermittent warfare of the late seventeenth century increased the prominence of such chiefs and diminished that of village chiefs, while the warrior became a more important role model than the hunter or trapper.[2]

An emphasis on the positive role of force also characterized Communist states. Communism in the Soviet Union, China, Cuba, Albania and Yugoslavia stemmed from success in civil war and was sustained by terror, while, in eastern Europe, the expulsion of the Germans towards the close of World War Two was a crucial preliminary. The Chinese Communist government displayed a continued preference for force and an inability to cope with opposition when, on 4 June 1989, it used the army to clear protesting students from Tiananmen Square in Beijing, inaccurately describing the movement as a 'counter-revolutionary rebellion'.

In some modern control societies, governments chose to use military aggression as an aspect of politics; indeed, military aggression *can* become politics. This could be presented in terms of 'rationality', with the argument that such wars were commenced in order to bolster domestic positions. But the wars can, as much, be seen as stemming from cultural suppositions about the role of force and the forces, and the 'rationality' can be presented as constructed in those terms. Thus, the Argentinian invasion of the Falklands/Malvinas in 1982 can be seen as an exercise in which the use of force was a means as much as a goal. The islands would possibly have ended up under Argentinian suzerainty, eventually, by peaceful means, but such a success would have been less desirable than a military victory. In certain societies and political cultures the latter is far more glorious than peaceful diplomacy, and the definition of glory, and many aspects of the practice of politics, had shifted singularly little from that of the nineteenth century.

This was also the case with the ethnic and religious identities and demands that contributed greatly to much of the fighting in the Balkans, the Caucasus and Central Africa in the 1990s. In each case, it was possible to draw attention to frontiers that ignored such divisions, thus apparently explaining or excusing the resort to violence, but, elsewhere in the world, such ethnic and religious divisions did not necessarily lead to conflict. However, in the Balkans and the Caucasus in the 1990s, the collapse of a former political order created the very situation of flux, opportunity and fear that most encouraged and encourages a distrust of negotiation and a resort to violence in bellicist cultures. In the former Yugoslavia, war rapidly developed from a conflict over secession, as the Serb-dominated Yugoslav government sought to prevent Slovenian and Croatian independence, into a far more atomistic struggle for territorial conflict and, eventually, ethnic hegemony and survival, amongst Croats, Serbs and Moslems. A belief in the value of violence rapidly surfaced and force became the crucial means of demographics, economics and politics.

State identities and boundaries tend to be more recent and genuinely debatable in the Balkans than elsewhere in Europe. The states buried under the Ottoman Empire – Serbia, Bulgaria and Greece – which were re-excavated in the modern period had been more deeply buried than Poland or Ireland ever were. This was less true of the Habsburg (northern) Balkans, especially Croatia. In the modern period, with the collapse of imperial structures, the excavated states had to assume a fixed form, and this was difficult. The Serbs of Serbia did not regard Tito's post-war version of Serbia as definitive, but they neither knew what Great Serbia should include, nor, once Yugoslavia had collapsed, did they wish to fight a major and sustained war to create it. There was for centuries a fear of Islam as a powerful winners' creed which could dissolve Serbian identity. This faded after the Turks departed, except as lingering dislike and suspicion where Islam persisted: in Bosnia and the Sandzak. The Islamic revival since the 1960s, and the demographic decay of Serb populations – everywhere, but, especially in Bosnia – helped in the creation of a Serb-national 'angst'. Lacking any version of the sacred borders, the Serbs of Serbia have now largely fallen back on the 1945 borders as the only solid thing they have.

Although there is nothing distinctive in the causes of Balkan wars, there are particular ways of conducting them. All sides have, and understand, an idea of controlled, limited war: war as demonstration and negotiation, as a politics by military means that is so political that any notion of a contrast is a misnomer – a mixture of sudden and brief brutality, truces and convoluted strategies of diplomacy. This conception is rooted in the Balkan tradition of war as in the domain of an Emperor or Sultan, who cannot be resisted if provoked too far, but whose agents can be made to wheel and deal, as, for example, in Albania during much of the eighteenth century. The wars of 1991–5 in the former Yugoslavia contained almost no serious campaigns. They were composed of short advances, demonstrations, pauses and plots. However, there was also a tendency to wage war by other means, as in the rape of Moslem women used as a tool of 'ethnic cleansing'.

In the Caucasus in the 1990s, Armenia and Azerbaijan went to war, while the Georgian army used force to resist separatism by the Moslem province of Abkhazia, but the latter received Russian military assistance. Chechnya rebelled against Russian control.[3] Similarly, in Central Asia, the collapse of Soviet power helped to precipitate a civil war in Tajikistan in 1992. The same resort to violence was true of parts of Africa, both in the era of decolonization and afterwards, for a sense of new uncertainties exacerbated and provided the opportunity for longer-lasting rivalries. The end of the Cold War led to warfare within the former Soviet bloc, although the number of casualties was less than those caused by the policing, or political warfare, of the purges of the 1930s.

In many states, problems were also created by the intervention of armies in politics. This ensured that tensions within the military, both between and within services, were translated into government and affected state policy. Navies played a smaller role than armies in politics. The role of the military also encouraged a violent response to regional disaffection, as in Burma, Indonesia, Nigeria and Sudan, and this, in turn, could increase international tension and lead to foreign intervention in disputes.

The role of the military in government, however, has become less important in major states. Indeed, the twentieth century has witnessed an increasing lack of understanding of military matters by increasingly civilianized governments. 'Soldier kings' may have been amateurs of the craft (many were not), but they had some sense of its parameters. Since 1960 no leader of the USA has had military experience at senior command levels, and the lack of knowledge in other major political and administrative hierarchies is also notable. This may be seen as a factor encouraging intervention – for example of the USA in Vietnam, the USSR in Afghanistan and UN forces in Bosnia. Eisenhower's fear of intervention in Vietnam arose from his knowledge of what jungle guerrilla warfare would be like. But this did not stop him from intervening by other means and thus creating a momentum for intervention which Kennedy and Johnson could not resist. Civilian leaders were less aware of the problems of translating military resources into victory and lasting success.

Yet, over the last decade, the civilian leaders of most major states have also been more reluctant than hitherto to employ force against their citizens. Troops continue to be deployed to tackle regional separatism, as in Ulster, Corsica and Kashmir, but European governments prefer to rely on the police to maintain internal order. The Communist governments of the Soviet Union and eastern Europe used far less force resisting their overthrow from 1991 than they had earlier exerted in seeking to maintain it in East Germany (1953), Hungary (1956), Czechoslovakia (1967) and Poland (1981). The use of troops in labour disputes is less common than earlier in the century. This more hesitant resort to force domestically affects foreign policy.

The absence of military experience at senior, or in many cases any, levels is not restricted to the current leadership of major Western states, but is, more generally, a feature of their political, administrative and social elites. These no longer reflect the ethos (and often composition) of the landowner–warrior nexus that was so important in the West down to the early twentieth century and that in some senses represented a tradition looking back to the 'Barbarian' Invasions. The same tradition could be found in other countries invaded by successful nomads who then created a new landholding and political class without dispensing with customary attitudes and practices, for example the Mongols, Mughals and Ottoman Turks. The tales of epic heroism of the times of Genghis Khan and Richard the Lionheart were repeated in the world of print of the nineteenth and early twentieth centuries, but have largely disappeared since. In Britain, the novels of George Alfred Henty and Captain W. E. Johns – the latter the creator of Biggles – have been replaced in public libraries by exemplary tales of a new political correctness: charitable, humane and, crucially, no longer a masculine preserve.

In addition, the world of the veteran has diminished. Mass conscription ensured that large numbers of men had served, and they helped to make military service appear an integral part of many societies. Veterans were also more likely than others to support the use of force. Although many veterans were not politically extreme, others proved important sources of recruitment to Hitler, Mussolini, Mosley, and the *Action Française*. In the 1920s and 1930s veterans actively deployed pacifism and attacked internationalists. They played a major role in the *squadre* that attacked Socialists in Italy from 1920. Veterans were used the previous year, both by right-wing groups in Germany and by the Hungarian Communists. Hitler had won the Iron Cross.

Within post-war Britain and America, veterans celebrated the military experience. The decline of mass conscription has eroded this collective memory. Whereas the British Legion had many members in the 1960s, by the 1990s they were fewer, older and less influential.

More generally, in the post-1945 world, there has been a growing abstraction of death and suffering, a process linked both to medical technology and to secularism. Particularly, though not exclusively, in the Atlantic world, ordinary people have been more and more comprehensively insulated from personal pain, and are less accustomed to consider it normal and reasonable. In addition, while there has been a growing abstraction of pain and suffering, CNN and other television channels bring conflict directly into the home. This does not necessarily make war-making either easier or more difficult, but it does influence patterns of causation and continuance, especially by constraining democratic governments from pursuing campaigns abroad. The Tet Offensive was probably the first example of television affecting the outcome of a battle. The battle was a victory for the USA, but Americans at home saw their boys in Saigon crying with fear because the Viet Cong was where they were not supposed to be. Support for the war plummeted.

Another relevant, but complex, shift is due to changes in patterns of expendability amongst young adult males. Complex societies depend on them relatively less than muscle-based subsistence societies, and, anyway, thanks to demographic growth, there have been greater numbers of such males. On the other hand, smaller families have made every child precious, and the cult of youth in modern Western consumer culture is not a cult of organized violence. There is no equivalent to the child soldiers of Iran or Somalia. Instead, there is an emphasis on hedonism and individual rights, neither of which are conducive to militarism or bellicosity. The glorification of sacrifice in war that preceded and followed World War One finds few modern echoes.[4] Whereas a military coup in Spain in 1936 received much support (as well as bitter opposition), an attempted military coup in 1981 petered out in a far less violent society.

Instead, anti-war attitudes dominate serious adult literature in the West and have done so for several decades, with war presented as callous disorder in popular works such as Joseph Heller's *Catch-22* (1961).[5] 'War' – i.e. now anti-war – poetry from the period of World War One became popular in the 1960s and 1970s in Britain. It came to play a major role in school syllabuses. Silkin's *Penguin Book of First World War Poetry* was first published in 1979. Such literature affected the attitudes of those who rose to power and influence from the 1960s. It was sustained by fresh calls for peace. In 1997 *Oh Rêve* [Oh Dream], a single by the French rock star Yannick Noah, replaced the call of the *Marseillaise* to raise the 'blood-soaked banner' with a very different version: 'Let us try to open our spirits, across the country, to peace and tolerance. Let us rediscover French virtues'. Within academic circles, peace studies are more acceptable than those of war. The interest in pacifism that had grown earlier in the century, with the foundation of bodies such as the International Anti-Militaristisch Bureau in 1921, became more marked from the 1960s. The destructiveness of modern warfare, particularly the suffering directly caused to civilians, led to growing criticism. The possibility of nuclear conflict altered the ethical debate, especially because of the lasting nature of radioactivity. Pacifism can also be linked to a more cosmopolitan consciousness. The Falklands war of 1982 was followed in Britain by a national commemoration service in which the clergy prayed for the defeated Argentinians. Prime Minister Thatcher's earlier call to 'Rejoice' at success did not strike a universal chord and was heavily criticized in some quarters.

Military changes are also pertinent. The steady decline in the employment of mercenaries and colonial troops by the great powers possibly helped to moderate their behaviour. Modern public opinion is less willing to tolerate the expenditure of professional soldiers, especially conscripts, drawn exclusively from their own nationality. Highly trained servicemen and very expensive military equipment are harder to replace. Pre-industrial societies were capable of sustaining warfare (however that term is defined) for much longer periods than industrialized societies have done. Modern, industrialized societies certainly can conduct warfare on a scale unknown in the pre-industrial war (ultimately by conducting 'total war'), but can do so only for short periods; a few years at a time. Because the destructive capacity of warfare in the early-modern world was limited, states could sustain conflict for many decades; the rapid growth of the destructiveness of warfare in the nineteenth and twentieth centuries has had the effect of shortening wars. And when – in Vietnam in the 1950s and 1960s – the modern, industrialized USA ran up against a pre-industrialized society, it was the latter which held out longest.

The shift away from bellicosity, however, is more than simply a matter of functional possibilities and requirements. There have also been important cultural changes, or at least aspirations. Notions and practices of self-restraint have interacted in the West with changing ideas of social order and masculinity, seen for example in the rising influence of women and female stereotypes, and the public stance and self-image of homosexuals. The military has become a vehicle for sexual emancipation – especially in the USA, where there has been a drive towards politically correct armed forces. The decline of fatalism in the West, combined with the wish to extirpate risk and to lesson personal exposure and responsibility, all limit the courage/rashness without which battle is less likely. More generally, wars have become less frequent for Western states, so they have become less normal and normative. Instead, they are increasingly perceived as aberrations. This is a cultural-intellectual shift that is as important as the earlier contribution of a sense and reality of the normality of war to the causes of conflict – indeed, to a feeling that wars did not require probing analysis or particular explanation.

This shift can also be seen with respect to weaponry. The states that signed the anti-land mine agreement in the late 1990s were those that did not expect to go to war, certainly to face an invasion, as opposed to taking part in a UN-sanctioned operation. Therefore it was easy for them to dispense with a weapon that was not needed and was suddenly deemed barbaric. Military recruiting advertisements in Britain and the USA in the late 1990s suggested that the purpose of the army was to protect people (often from natural calamities such as earthquakes), not to fight. During the Gulf War, there were complaints amongst American military personnel that they had never expected, when they joined the military, that they would actually have to go into a war zone. This was a direct result of recruitment programmes after Vietnam which suggested that the military was where one went to learn a career.

Anti-war sentiment is more than simply a matter of hedonism and familiarity. Nuclear weaponry has brought with it the possibility that war would lead to its use, and this utter destructiveness is widely viewed as an absolute deterrent, a moral as well as a prudential restraint on conflict. Without this, it is possible that the Cold War would have become hot – more specifically, that the Soviet Union would have used its superiority in land forces to invade West Germany, thus propping up both its system and its defences.

The prosperity of western Europe was a challenge to the logic of Communist rule, a central part in the propaganda war between the two systems. Modern hedonism focuses on consumerism, and this is the major motor of economic consumption and growth. As a result, developed economies have a major incentive to ensure peace. Although war and military preparedness benefits sections of industry, far more turnover, profit and employment is derived from consumer goods, and this is especially true of non-essential goods, the type that war is apt to hit the consumption of. Furthermore, pressure for expenditure on social welfare, health and education – aspects of the democratization of modern societies – lessens the availability of resources for the military, encouraging an emphasis on the peaceful settlement of international disputes. This had earlier been true of Britain and France during the period of appeasement. When domestic pressures are expressed in terms of demands for more schools, then this both detracts from any emphasis on confrontation in international relations and creates a domestic political sphere in which force is not central.

Nevertheless, not all are encompassed within such prosperity, while socio-economic shifts in the modern world also created and create strains. The interacting conflation of massive demographic growth, large-scale movement to the cities, major environmental changes, exposure to new consumerist expectations, the breakdown of traditional social patterns and the creation of a large and volatile political youth, have produced circumstances in which there are serious social pressures and a ready emphasis on gesture politics. Socio-economic shifts and challenges played a role in what has been termed 'the revolt of

Islam', a process that can be traced from eighteenth-century *jihads* to their modern counterparts, the Iranian revolution of 1978–9 being followed by a more hostile approach towards the outside world.[6]

Yet, again, it would be mistaken to draw a simple correlation from such changes to the outbreak of wars. Mexico has seen such developments, but its government does not pursue expansion to the south or revanche to the north. Indeed, Latin America has seen singularly little by way of international conflict in the last 30 years. There has been no war, defined as an international armed conflict involving at least 1000 casualties, in South America since 1941. There have been a number of militarized crises, but, for a variety of reasons, they were resolved short of war. This was despite major social changes and the number of states governed by the military. Such government could lead to tension, as in 1978 when Argentina rejected the terms of a British mediation settlement over three small islands in the Beagle Channel also claimed by Chile. A hurricane forced the Argentine and Chilean navies, heading towards each other, to return to base. Despite talk of war, papal mediation was accepted. However, Argentina refused to accept the papal confirmation of the islands as Chilean until after the military government fell as a result of its failure in the Falklands war of 1982. Nevertheless, there was no war between the two neighbours. The same absence of war is also true for the last decade of other countries experiencing major socio-economic changes and strains, for example Zambia.

Two explanations can be offered. First, regional hegemons, such as the USA and Brazil, can serve to restrict expansionist aspirations. The USA would not permit Mexican expansionism. Secondly, much of the socio-economic tension is directed into high levels of domestic violence that, generally, have only limited international repercussions. This is part of a general pattern since 1945 in which the incidence of interstate wars has been declining, but that of intra-state wars (and violence) has risen. Thus, in Pakistan the casualties in ethnic clashes in Karachi, between recent immigrants and longer-settled residents, run at a high rate, as do those from the war in Peru between government and the 'Shining Path' guerrillas, but neither can be compared to an international conflict. This is even more the case where crime is more explicitly the motive for high levels of domestic violence, as in contemporary South Africa.

The last paragraph, however, reopens an issue that reflects the central analytical problem with the question of the causes of war, namely the definition of war. Does a different definition apply at the end of the millennium? Can the divisions of trans-cultural, inter-cultural and civil war be re-examined profitably, not least in a context in which the end of the sovereign or nation state is frequently proclaimed, especially in western Europe.

The latter point is of limited value. Indeed, the collapse of the Western colonial empires from the 1940s, and of the Soviet empire and alliance system from the late 1980s, have greatly increased, not diminished, the number of independent states. In Western Europe, the pooling of sovereignty has acted to diminish the likelihood of conflict, and in Latin America arbitration, supported by American diplomatic, economic and military power, has had the same success. However, attempts to pool sovereignty or simply establish effective arbitration to prevent conflict have failed, both in the Arab world and in sub-Saharan Africa.

Trans-cultural and inter-cultural warfare is open to variable definition, as, for example, with the case of Pakistan and India: their conflicts can be presented in both lights. It is not simply the case that a functional definition in terms of decolonized powers says little about the role of different religious and political systems in creating distrust and exacerbating disputes between India and Pakistan, but also that it is unclear how far these different systems are crucial. In short, even if a trans-cultural situation can be discerned, should it be seen as vital in causing conflict and confrontation?

A similar point can be made with reference to Indo-China, not least relations between China and Vietnam. Again, the emphasis to be placed on ideology – in this case, Communism – in creating a common political culture is unclear, and it can be argued that traditional geopolitical rivalries are the central issue, as with the war between the two powers in 1979 and with persistent Chinese support for Cambodian opponents of Vietnamese hegemony. China did not want the Vietnamese Communists to succeed to the extent of reuniting Vietnam and throwing their weight around in Indo-China. What China wanted was for the war to go on for ever, wearing down American strength.

Despite formidable problems with definition and usage, the notion of trans- or inter-cultural conflict is still useful, because it focuses attention on the role of structural differences that are not an aspect of international relations as classically defined, in causing the customary differences between states to be handled in a way that leads to war, whether deliberately or not. That remains the case today, and, as in the past, this can be extended to the domestic sphere and employed to consider types of civil war. The nature of incorporation within states remains very varied, ranging from states that include substantial disaffected minorities acquired without any consultation, such as China and Tibet, to states where disaffection focuses on widespread social conditions, as in Peru. With the increase in the number of independent states, there should have come a proportionate increase in international rather than internal warfare, but this has not been the case, because many newly independent states have faced insurrectionary or terrorist movements.

Indeed, most modern conflicts are not struggles between clearly sovereign bodies. In the mid-1990s the model of war as a struggle between such bodies did not correspond to conflict and confrontation in the former Yugoslavia, the Caucasus, Zaire and its neighbours – Angola, Rwanda and Burundi – or Israel and Palestine. The definition of conflict, in terms of war or rebellion, remained problematic and politically charged at both the domestic and the international level. It is also far from clear how much the violence of the 1980s can be fitted into the West-versus-East model and thus subsumed into an analysis as part of the Cold War. This is true both of international conflicts and of civil violence.[7] More generally, the end of the Cold War is leading to reconsiderations of many aspects of the theory of international relations, although many of the analytical problems have not changed.[8]

Looking ahead is dangerous. It is striking how the grand projects of modernity – economic growth, secularism, democracy, 'rational government', state planning, international co-operation – have created or exacerbated tensions, as well as solved problems. They have neither assuaged ethnic, religious and national hatreds, nor provided a successful system of world government or policing. There have, of course, been successes. Economic growth has brought public and private wealth, producing the resources of peace as well as of war. Atomic weapons have not been used since 1945. The Soviet empire collapsed without major warfare, apart from in Afghanistan, a war in which the Soviets only committed a small portion of their military resources. German and Japanese rearmament has been consensual, limited and has not led to conflict: neither power possesses atomic weaponry. A Franco-German entente lies at the heart of the European Union. The United Nations has had successes as well as failures, although its critics tend to ignore them.

However, the UN has no more prevented conflict than older systems of collective security. Such systems have hitherto worked, if that, largely as short-term palliatives, serving the ends of particular leaders and states, and only effective as long as they could do so. In the 1810s Lord Castlereagh, the British Foreign Secretary, and Alexander I of Russia had both been aware of the limits of collective action, and this was also true of the American President Woodrow Wilson at the Versailles peace talks in 1919. He argued that it was likely to be a long time before the League of Nations could begin to make much difference.

Possibly, the most important current and future shift is growing reluctance to fight in many societies, certainly in comparison with the situation earlier this century, although the popularity of war toys, games and films suggest that military values are still seen as valuable, indeed exemplary, by many.[9] Partly thanks to growing professionalism and the abandonment of conscription in many Western states, the military there is less integrated into society, both into social structures and into concepts of society. This demilitarization of civil society leads to a decline in bellicist values: instead, they are expressed through sporting rivalries or as a response to media portrayals of violence. There has also been a civilianization of the military. It can no longer be an adjunct of society able to follow its own set of rules, but is expected to conform to societal standards of behaviour – a pressure that has caused scandals and court cases in the USA and the UK.

When accompanied by political commitments to social welfare, by pressures on defence budgets and by a decline in deference and hierarchy, there is a hostility to war that is greater than hitherto. The greater role of international trade and finance in national economies, the more widespread nature of international organizations, and the greater degree of domestic political openness in many states were, in a 1988 study, all positively correlated with a reluctance to go to war, and it is probable that these factors are at least as much the case today.[10] In news-presentation terms, it is harder to put a positive spin on war. Furthermore, politicians share with strategists an awareness of the dangers of war and the risks of confrontation, and this has been important in a partial demilitarization of international politics.

Yet, it is necessary to be cautious about extrapolating from this model to the situation throughout the world, while as the Gulf and Bosnia showed, globalism could readily lead to the use of force. Once roused, democracies can be very tenacious in war. Tribalism and the nature of domestic politics can ensure that the spilling of blood leads to a shift in attitude.

The suggestion that the 'West' has become less bellicist might seem ironic given its nuclear preponderance, the capacity of its weapons of mass-destruction, and the role of its industries in supplying weaponry to the rest of the world. It might almost be argued that this strength is a condition of the decline of militarism: that it ensures that there is no real threat to the territorial integrity of Western powers, a situation accentuated by their abandonment of colonial vestiges, such as Hong Kong in 1997. Such an explanation is overly reductionist and mono-causal. It also neglects the role of aspiration. Portugal and Spain were not threatened by South Asian and New World peoples and powers in the sixteenth century, but that did not prevent their unprovoked attack on, and conquest of, them.

Whatever the cause, the decline in bellicosity might seem an interesting reversal to the situation a half-millennium earlier. Then, it has been argued, there was something particularly relentless and determined about European war-making. This was, in part, responsible for European success in overthrowing developed civilizations in the New World.[11] The situation now is apparently different, and this raises several important issues. First, it is unclear whether any theory of war causation can have universal value. Secondly, an emphasis on geographical variations suggests that it is appropriate to emphasize cultural contexts, or to search for other explanations of variety. Thirdly, it is unclear how best such differences can be related to the systemic, inter-state and civil warfare, and the trans-cultural, intra-cultural and civil-warfare models. Fourthly, if there has been a shift over the last half-millennium, as suggested, then it is clearly necessary to clarify its chronology and turning-points. Lastly, it might be asked whether the decline in bellicosity does not owe something to the prevalence and vitality of other forms of 'aggression', for example what might be seen as economic and cultural imperialism.

If a difference in bellicosity between cultures in the present world is to be emphasized, then that, again, suggests the continued vitality of a model of trans-cultural as opposed to intra-cultural warfare. Thus, there is a difference, and not simply in resources or media attention, between trans-cultural conflicts such as the Gulf War of 1990–91, and intra-cultural wars, such as those in West and Central Africa in the 1990s. However, this is not a simple case of the continuation of earlier differences. In the nineteenth century, conflict within the European system had been characterized by formal declarations of war between sovereign states, while the crucial trans-cultural conflict, that of European imperialism, had been less clear-cut and, frequently, more a continuous process. In the post-colonial world, in contrast, trans-cultural conflict involving European powers has far more been a case of defined operations, whereas no such process of definition and limitation has affected many intra-cultural conflicts. The latter owes something to the nature of sovereignty. If statehood does not exist, as in the case of the Kurds or peoples within Burma, such as the Karens, then formal war with them is neither possible, in terms of the declaration of hostilities between sovereign states, nor desirable, as it would endow legitimacy on the non-sovereign combatant.

However, this is not the whole explanation. It is also the case that the autocratic, if not military, regimes that rule many states find little need to explain conflict to their people, certainly less so than democratic counterparts seeking domestic support. Furthermore, in the modern world autocratic regimes are more willing to live with conflict and to regard it as acceptable. Work on the propensities of democratic societies to engage in war largely relates to the period prior to 1990.[12] It is unclear that conclusions from earlier data-sets are valid in the different ideological and cultural context of the 1990s, and it is also possible to emphasize differences between democracies and to argue that some are likely to be less pacific. Georg Sørensen has suggested a contrast between North and South, with the latter participating in the global economy with less benefit to themselves.[13]

In general, democracies are characterized by the ability of governments to reflect, elicit and sustain consent. This is challenged both if consent is withheld, by either the majority or a significant minority, and if this situation leads to violence. The resulting weak states, many of them post-colonial, are especially prone to be the locales of war.[14] An absence of consent can also be related to a relative lack of tolerance such that ethnic and religious diversity are more likely to give rise to dispute and conflict.

An emphasis on the decline of bellicism in Western societies has to be matched by an understanding of the ability of small groups within society to wage effective terrorist wars. The nature of weaponry, logistics, tactics and strategy in these conflicts is such that low-intensity warfare can be both long-lasting and largely unrelated to general social attitudes.[15] Such warfare, and the responses to it, are difficult to define. Thus, in August 1997, when, in response to a terrorist bombing, the Israeli government threatened to seize suspected terrorists within the self-rule areas governed by the Palestinian Authority, the Palestinian police chief, Ghazi Jabali, declared 'that would mean war'. The Authority's president, Yassir Arafat, described Israeli sanctions, including a closure of the territories' borders, jamming of Palestinian airwaves and halting the transfer of tax revenue, as a declaration of war on the Palestinian people. In reply, the Israeli Prime Minister Benyamin Netanyahu demanded that the Arafat government make war on terrorism.[16] As a 'nation-in-arms', with a sense of encirclement and threat, the notion of war as a legitimate, indeed necessary, option is powerful within Israel.[17]

The possible diffusion of nuclear, and other highly destructive, weaponry threatens to alter the nature of low-intensity warfare. It also threatens to alter the potential effectiveness of deterrence and collective security. Had Iraq possessed the atomic bomb in 1990–91, the response to the invasion of Kuwait might well have been different.

It is not always clear how modern low-intensity warfare against terrorist movements can be differentiated from past or present episodes of warfare against criminal movements, such as the Mafia in Sicily or drug cartels in Colombia. Indeed, in some countries insurrectionary movements derive much of the revenue from criminal activities. This is true, for example, of Burma, Peru and Ulster. The Viet Minh had this down to a fine art. Dien Bien Phu was fought in part because they derived substantial sums from the opium crop in the valley – sums employed to buy weaponry. Rather than arguing that this is simply a matter of perspective – similar, for example, to the war-versus-rebellion difference – it is worth suggesting that criminality is an aspect of political movements that places an emphasis on force. The rejection of one type of restraint encourages a denial of other restraints. The IRA raises revenue by bank raids and extortion; RENAMO in Mozambique by ambushes and raids. In some states, such as China, Indonesia and Nigeria, sections of the armed forces intervene actively in the economy and are widely suspected of corrupt practices.

State-organized war is a largely Eurocentric notion that within the European system has for 300 years been surrounded by norms, rules and etiquette that make it an institution of international relations. By this definition armed conflict is a war when it creates a new set of rights and responsibilities under international law, and this is quite different from rebellions, piracy, booty raids, marauding and the like. Despite modern attempts to apply the Geneva Conventions in the latter type of conflict, operations systematically violate them. However, any attempt to exclude the latter type of conflict looks increasingly problematic. In the 1990s there has been a further breakdown in the institutional aspects of war. In Sierra Leone since 1991 and in Liberia since 1989 organized armed forces under central command have been largely replaced by drugged teenagers and outright looters who have little, if any, idea of the cause they are fighting for, except for their personal gain. Political objectives beyond the capture of power are hazy, and these 'wars' are financed primarily by criminal operations and forced extortions. There are no declarations of war, peace conferences, victory parades, heroes, chains of command, or (often) even uniforms that distinguish 'troops' from each other.[18] It is primarily in the number of victims that these wars resemble their European predecessors. 'War' therefore may be little different from organized crime or from riots, an all-encompassing process that makes analysis difficult. Thus, for example, it is unclear how far the Palestinian *intifada* against Israeli occupation that began in 1987 can be regarded as a war. Similarly, there may be a continuation between religious radicalism and conflict.

It is possible that low-intensity warfare will be that which is most common in the future, but, equally, across much of the world there is no effective restraint on the ambitions and activities of states, and the continued combination of issues over which to dispute, and bellicose leaderships, may lead to serious levels of warfare between regular forces. This is particularly the case in areas where leaders have seized and/or maintained themselves in power by force. Thus, British intelligence analysts failed to place sufficient weight on the nature of the Argentinian regime in 1982: 'a military establishment which obtained and retained its power illegitimately, secretly and treacherously should not have been assumed likely to act rationally and predictably . . . there was a need for analysts, diplomats and politicians to step away from their own experience and culture and recognize the emotional and the apparently irrational among the forces at work in Buenos Aires'.[19]

Autocratic leaderships are especially prone to belief in their own infallibility and mission. Hitler's belief in his infallibility and will led to his assumption of supreme command from the end of 1941. Caution was rejected as the advice of incompetents and defeatists, and it became dangerous to question his judgement. The consequent vying for favour and overly optimistic misinformation came to typify the German high command. Such a situation is not simply a matter of arrogance. There is also a need for leaders and ruling elites to retain their self-confidence, and in militaristic cultures this is most readily achieved by the display of force and the grasping of victory. Psychologists might also suggest that an element of sexual frustration and fulfilment may play a role.[20] Whatever the motivation, the victory required is not one that tends to offer conciliation to the defeated or reassurance to the neutral, and thus the seeds of fresh conflict are sown.

However, 'irrationality', a term generally used when the rationality of others is unwelcome, is not limited to authoritarian or dictatorial regimes. Indeed, studies of decision-making processes that focus on leaders emphasize the inconsistent and often questionable way in which they perceive situations. Personal experience, however limited, can play an important role, and there is a great capacity to fit developments into pre-existing schemas, however implausible.[21]

Furthermore, confrontation over resources in the context of rising demographic demands may encourage conflict, some of which will be a new version of the wars launched by revisionist powers.[22] Revolution and rebellion in the early-modern period have been traced to such confrontation.[23] Future conflict may be civil and international, and the latter may be not only regional, for example in the Persian Gulf, but also involve attempts to redistribute wealth at a global level. This could be linked to the recurrence of change and war linked to historical-structural cycles of world politics and economics. Indeed, the leading exponent of the long cycle analysis has recently suggested that it is misleading to feel confident that transitional warfare amongst the major powers has come to an end.[24]

Moreover, despite arguments that war has become obsolete,[25] and incompatible with the global nature of the modern world economy with its reliance on international trade, investment and currency flows, and, more prosaically, claims that the troubles of the post-Cold War world have been exaggerated,[26] there is little sign that states and rulers have learned from the failures of the past. These failures are the ultimate deterrent, but a tendency to explain away defeats ensures that this deterrent is too weak. A positive re-evaluation of the role of regional powers rather than superpower sponsors suggests that the end of the Cold War should not be seen as crucial.[27]

Furthermore, the demise of the Soviet Union, the decline of Russia and the rise of China, especially its dramatic economic growth, have combined to ensure that the most likely great power clash in the last half-century will be between China and the USA. This again would be an example of a trans-cultural conflict, for there is little sign that the authoritarian nature of Chinese political culture and the teleological emphasis of its Communism are weakening. Thus, arguments based on the decline of conflict between 'Western' powers have to be of scant value when considering rivalry between China and the USA. This rivalry may be based on 'issues', not least the need of the expanding Chinese economy for more resources, particularly oil, and a consequent accentuation of China's pursuit of territorial claims in the South China Sea, as well as its attempts to coerce Taiwan. However, such issues should not be separated from cultural factors that will encourage war, especially the authoritarianism of Chinese culture, its reluctance to accept a role for different views, especially from nearby states, and the belief in the role of struggle that reflects the impact of notions of class struggle and Social Darwinism on Communist thought. This ideological conviction and assault is not, and will not be, all one-way. The American conviction of the value of democracy (and of capitalism) is as universalist as the views of the French Revolutionaries, but their greater ability to disseminate and support such views carries with it a perceived global obligation to do so, especially if more specific state interests are involved. Thus, in 1996, the Americans deployed a powerful fleet in response to Chinese military pressure on Taiwan. Taiwan or South Korea may be the occasion and sphere for a future clash between what are two powerful states with very different political cultures, each convinced that the use of force may be necessary.

Furthermore, the balance of resolve that is important in such confrontations may be affected by strategic cultures that reflect ideas and attitudes spread and encouraged by governing elites.[28] Thus, a decision to fight may be a product of the interaction of bellicosity and what could be regarded as a misjudgement of the resolve of other powers.

A cautionary note is struck by consulting a hitherto unremarked analysis of the causes of war:

. . . the prevalence of public opinion may be the cause of hostilities between nations not being so common as in days of ignorance . . . when the individuals of those classes that most influence public opinion are aware that the pressure of taxation will be felt, more or less, in consequence, the community will not permit themselves, as in former days of ignorance or barbarism, to worry and attack their neighbours for mere pastime, or to gratify their caprice or warlike inclination . . . To argue, that because war has desolated Europe almost without intermission, longer than the memory of man or history can record, it will be as frequent in future, would be judging erroneously, and not making sufficient allowance for the present state of civilization and power of public opinion . . . As other nations become civilized . . . communities will be benefited, in general, by an interchange of commodities . . . As civilization extends itself, the art of war is brought to greater perfection, and the burdens attendant on such warfare press more heavily on the community . . . In an improved commercial and agricultural state, wars are seldom undertaken but for the sake of preserving independence, or of obtaining some great commercial or political advantage; as they necessarily tend to impoverish the community, which governs itself by public opinion, and acts according to its interests: hostilities, therefore, are not likely to be undertaken hastily, to be waged with acrimony, or extended unnecessarily.[29]

William Mackinnon, later a long-serving MP, published his *On the Rise, Progress and Present State of Public Opinion in Great Britain and Other Parts of the World* in 1828, when the world question posed by Revolutionary France and Napoleon was as defunct as the Cold War, and it was possible to look forward to the spread of 'advanced' ideas and practices. Over the following century, the rise of commerce, industry and the middle class did not prevent bitter and costly wars between 'civilized' states, nor indeed the brutal conquest of much that Mackinnon thought barbarous. One of his own sons was killed in the Crimean War.

EIGHT

Conclusion

An emphasis on cultural factors, on cultures and attitudes, is the central thesis of this short work. It is not intended as any denial that other forces play a major role, but, instead, rests on a conviction that bellicist values are important not only in creating a general context for international relations but also in sustaining the view that war is an instrument of policy, and in determining how disputes between, and within, states were treated. Bellicosity can be regarded as both cause and process, in so far as the two can be separated. By establishing that certain conditions and processes are more likely to increase the probabilities of armed conflict, this helps address the problem of discerning sources of war that transcend all contexts of time, location, situation and personality.

An emphasis on cultural contexts within which war is understood, even welcomed, as an instrument of policy is, also, in part, a reminder of the role of choice and, therefore, a qualification of the apparent determinism of some systemic models. A denial of determinism also opens up the possibility of suggesting that the multiple interpretations of contemporaries are valuable and possibly should be integrated into explanatory models. They permit an analysis, not to say atomization, of the state.

Contemporary interpretations varied, and vary, greatly, not least including a willingness to see what were and are presented as national interests as, in reality, those of a regime. Thus, the Jacobites wanted the Whig regimes of George I (1714–27) and George II (1727–60) of Britain to fight France in order that they would win French support and that the costs of the war would make the government unpopular.[1] A century later, Marx and Engels saw war as an unintentional device to secure the triumph of the proletariat, defeat helping to provoke revolution. For that reason, Lenin sought Russia's defeat in World War One, while in 1939–41 some left-wingers in Britain and France regarded World War Two as an imperialist struggle by class-dominated regimes.[2] Far from there being national unity in Britain in 1940, some left-wing mineworkers went on strike: Hitler, after all, was the ally of Stalin's Soviet Union.

An analysis that emphasizes bellicosity both puts a premium on intentionality and draws attention to the bellicose nature of what has been termed 'unspoken assumptions',[3] the values of ruling groups that do not need stating and are often inherent to their existence and role. As far as intentionality is concerned, bellicosity leads to war not through misunderstandings that produce inaccurate calculations of interest and response, but, rather, from an acceptance of different interests and a conviction that they can be best resolved through the use of force. It can be the resort of both satisfied and unsatisfied powers. The resort to war is a choice for unpredictability, not simply the uncertain nature of battle, but an inherent characteristic of the very nature of war.[4]

The unpredictability is challenged by the precepts and practices of military planning and training, which have become ever more insistent and persistent since the second half of the nineteenth century. They reflect the ambiguous nature of the relationship between the military and risk: the very resort to war entails risk, but diplomatic and military conduct is designed to reduce it. However, the acceptance that risk is involved and the willingness to confront it are culturally conditioned. Bellicosity does not require militarism in state and society, but it is greatly helped by the strength of militarist ideas and institutions.

To explain individual disputes is useful, but they are a habitual feature of a states system, and often there is only 'a very imperceptible line between peace and war'.[5] Furthermore, explanations are far from simple, not least if efforts are made to integrate structural and conjunctural factors. Discussing 'the science of world policy' on 10 October 1730, *Read's Weekly Journal*, a London newspaper, expressed scepticism about the likely success of 'state chymists', because policies faced

> ... the shortness and inconsistency of man's life and temper
> for the bringing any great project or design about, the emer-
> gency of undiscernible accidents that will be sure to inter-
> pose, the miscarriage of instruments that must be employed,
> [and] the competition and rencounter of adverse parties ...
> upon which miscarriages the historian concludes that men do
> not so much counsel things, as things counsel men.

In contrast, another London newspaper, *The Protester*, on 28 July
1753 had confidence that

> when these fluctuating objects shall be ascertained, method-
> ised and reposed in history, the reader, having none of the
> difficulties or diversions, which misled or confounded the
> spectator, will have the full and free use of his judgement, and
> will pronounce accordingly.

It is, however, difficult to share this confidence in pronouncing
judgement, and dangerous in hindsight to praise and condemn
contemporaries. As *Read's* observed, 'Who can so play his game
as to prevent all the blots that the dice of time and change may
put the best gamester upon'.

Response, as well as aggression, can be crucial to the outbreak of war. In 1755 Frederick the Great replied to a French
suggestion that Augustus III of Saxony-Poland be encouraged
to prevent the possible movement of Russian troops through
Poland in order to attack Prussia, by arguing that the Poles
would be able to resist for a fortnight only, that they would fail
and that the consequence would be the ruin of the state.[6] In
1772 Austria, Prussia and Russia gained much of Poland, in the
First Partition, without war, but in 1793 the Second Partition
led to an anti-Russian rebellion that resulted in large-scale hostilities. There was a major European war in 1914, but not 1912,
and war over Poland in 1939, but not over Czechoslovakia the
previous year.

Bellicose factors in leadership and society can be related to
the structure of international relations and to the perceived
alternatives available to leaders in reaching their objectives in
foreign relations. The former can owe something to the
response of other powers, but the extent to which the structure
shapes this response is questionable. The second is tied to the

type of assets that a government leader can (or thinks he can) directly control. Often, these happen to be aggressive, rather than conciliatory, ones, but this is less true in Western states today because, although the weaponry may exist for the projection of power, ideological and social assumptions and practices are less favourable. Bellicosity affects deterrence, conflict resolution mechanisms, the ability and willingness to reconcile the defeated, and the possibilities of international government.

Rather than focusing on individual conflicts, it is more important to understand the values that made compromise unacceptable, force appear necessary and even desirable, and war seem crucial to identity and self-respect. This remains the challenge today. The techniques of diplomatic management can help solve some crises, but others reflect a willingness, sometimes desire, to kill and be killed that cannot be ignored.

Selected Further Reading

I. GENERAL WORKS

G. Blainey, *The Causes of War* (London, 1973)

B. Ehrenreich, *Blood Rites: Origins and History of the Passions of War* (London, 1997)

K. J. Holsti, *Peace and War: Armed Conflicts and International Order, 1643–1989* (Cambridge, 1991)

D. Kagan, *On the Origins of War and the Preservation of Peace* (London, 1995)

L. H. Keeley, *War before Civilization: The Myth of the Peaceful Savage* (Oxford, 1996)

J. S. Levy, *War in the Modern Great Power System, 1495–1975* (Lexington, KY, 1983)

C. Reynolds, *The Politics of War: A Study of the Rationality of Violence in Inter-state Relations* (London, 1989)

H. Suganami, *On the Causes of War* (Oxford, 1996)

A.J.P. Taylor, *How Wars Begin* (London, 1980)

W. R. Thompson, *On Global War: Historical-Structural Approaches to World Politics* (Columbia, SC, 1988)

II. 1450–1800

T. J. Barfield, *The Perilous Frontier: Nomadic Empires and China* (Oxford, 1989)

J. Black, ed., *The Origins of War in Early Modern Europe* (Edinburgh, 1987)

T.C.W. Blanning, *The Origins of the French Revolutionary Wars* (Harlow, 1986)

R. B. Ferguson and N. L. Whitehead, eds, *War in the Tribal Zone: Expanding States and Indigenous Warfare* (Santa Fe, 1992)

J. R. Hale, *War and Society in Renaissance Europe, 1450–1620* (London, 1985)

J. H. Kautsky, *The Politics of Aristocratic Empires* (Chapel Hill, 1982)

P. Sonnino, *Louis XIV and the Origins of the Dutch War* (Cambridge, 1988)

J. E. Thomson, *Mercenaries, Pirates, and Sovereigns: State-building and Extraterritorial Violence in Early Modern Europe* (Princeton, 1994)

III. 1800–1900

B. Bond, *The Pursuit of Victory: From Napoleon to Saddam Hussein* (Oxford, 1996)
W. Carr, *The Origins of the Wars of German Unification* (Harlow, 1991)
N. Etherington, *Theories of Imperialism: War, Conquest and Capital* (1984)
D. M. Goldfrank, *The Origins of the Crimean War* (Harlow, 1994)
B. H. Reid, *The Origins of the American Civil War* (Harlow, 1997)
I. R. Smith, *The Origins of the South African War, 1899–1902* (Harlow, 1996)
J. Smith, *The Spanish American War: Conflict in the Caribbean and the Pacific, 1895–1902* (Harlow, 1994)

IV. 1900–2000

P.M.H. Bell, *The Origins of the Second World War in Europe*, 2nd edn (Harlow, 1997)
A. Clayton, *The Wars of French Decolonisation* (Harlow, 1994)
R.J.W. Evans and H. P. von Strandmann, eds, *The Coming of the First World War* (Oxford, 1994)
A. Iriye, *The Origins of the Second World War in Asia and the Pacific* (Harlow, 1986)
C. Jian, *China's Road to the Korean War: The Making of the Sino-American Confrontation* (New York, 1995)
J. Joll, *The Origins of the First World War*, 2nd edn (Harlow, 1994)
I. Nish, *The Origins of the Russo-Japanese War* (Harlow, 1985)
R. Ovendale, *The Origins of the Arab-Israeli Wars*, 2nd edn (Harlow, 1992)
A. Short, *The Origins of the Vietnam War* (Harlow, 1994)
S. M. Watt, *Revolution and War* (Ithaca, 1996)

References

PREFACE

1 'Heads of a Conversation with the Emperor at the Augarten on the
   Morning of 19 August 1782', BL, Add. 33526.

INTRODUCTION

1 The problem of cause in this context has been valuably approached from
   a philosophical standpoint in W. H. Dray, 'Some Causal Accounts of the
   American Civil War', *Daedalus*, XCI (1960), pp. 578–92, 'Concepts of
   Causation in A.J.P. Taylor's Account of the Origins of the Second World
   War', *History and Theory*, XVII (1978), pp. 149–74, and 'A Controversy
   over Causes: A.J.P. Taylor and the Origins of the Second World War', in
   Dray, *Perspectives on History* (London, 1980), pp. 69–96; and in H.
   Suganami, *On the Causes of War* (Oxford, 1996). For a recent study of the
   warlike nature of chimpanzees, see R. Wrangham and D. Peterson,
   Demonic Males: Apes and the Origins of Human Violence (London, 1997).
2 J. Dülffer, M. Kröger and R. H. Wippich, *Vermiedene Kriege. Deeskalation
   von Konflikten der Grossmächte zwischen Krimkrieg und Ersten Weltkrieg*
   (Munich, 1997).
3 Important work includes M. Mead, 'Warfare is Only an Invention – Not
   a Biological Necessity', *Asia*, XL (1940), pp. 402–5, repr. in *Classics of
   International Relations*, ed. J. A. Vasquez, 2nd edn (Englewood Cliffs, NJ,
   1990), pp. 216–20; R. P. Shaw and Y. Wong, *Genetic Seeds of Warfare:
   Evolution, Nationalism, and Patriotism* (London, 1989); and J. Haas, ed.,
   The Anthropology of War (Cambridge, 1990). More recently, see B.
   Ehrenreich, *Blood Rites: Origins and History of the Passions of War*
   (London, 1997); R. L. O'Connell, *Ride of the Second Horseman: The Birth
   and Death of War* (Oxford, 1997).
4 J. Keegan, *A History of Warfare* (London, 1993), pp. 387–92; W. H.
   McNeill, 'European Expansion, Power and Warfare since 1500', in
   Imperialism and War: Essays on Colonial Wars in Asia and Africa, eds J. A. de
   Moor and H. L. Wesseling (Leiden, 1989), pp. 19–20.
5 L. H. Keeley, *War before Civilization: The Myth of the Peaceful Savage*
   (Oxford, 1996); J. Haas and W. Creamer, 'Warfare among the Pueblos:
   Myth, History, and Ethnography', *Ethnohistory*, XLIV (1997),
   pp. 235–61.
6 D. Kagan, *On the Origins of War and the Preservation of Peace* (London,
   1995), p. 10.

7 A.J.P. Taylor, *How Wars Begin* (London, 1980), p. 14.

8 P. M. Bell, *The Origins of the Second World War in Europe*, 2nd edn (Harlow, 1997), pp. 5–7.

9 P. Curtin, *Economic Change in Precolonial Africa: Senegambia in the Era of the Slave Trade*, 2 vols (Madison, 1975), I, pp. 153–68.

10 J. Thornton, *Africa and Africans in the Making of the Atlantic World, 1400–1680* (Cambridge, 1992), pp. 100–01.

11 S. Subrahmanyam, *The Portuguese Empire in Asia, 1500–1700: A Political and Economic History* (Harlow, 1993), p. 49.

12 P. Spear, *Twilight of the Mughuls: Studies in Late Mughul Delhi* (Cambridge, 1951), p. 9.

13 Thornton, *Africa*, p. 122.

14 L. Scott and S. Smith, 'Lessons of October: Historians, Political Scientists, Policy-Makers and the Cuban Missile Crisis', *International Affairs*, LXX (1994), p. 660.

15 G. E. Dowd, *A Spirited Resistance: The North American Struggle for Unity, 1745–1815* (Baltimore, 1992), pp. 11–12.

16 A. J. Coates, *The Ethics of War* (Manchester, 1997), pp. 123–45.

17 S. R. David, 'Internal War. Causes and Cures', *World Politics*, XLIX (1997), pp. 552–76.

18 A.F.K. Organski and J. Kugler, *The War Ledger* (Chicago, 1980).

19 G. Modelski, 'The Long Cycle of Global Politics and the Nation-State', *Comparative Studies in Society and History*, XX (1978), pp. 214–35; W. R. Thompson, *On Global War: Historical-Structural Approaches to World Politics* (Columbia, SC, 1988); Thompson and K. Rasler, *War and State Making: The Shaping of the Global Powers* (London, 1989), and *The Great Powers and Global Struggle, 1490–1990* (Lexington, KY, 1994).

20 J. S. Levy, *War in the Modern Great Power System, 1495–1975* (Lexington, KY, 1983), and 'Alliance Formation and War Behaviour: An Analysis of the Great Powers, 1495–1975', *Journal of Conflict Resolution*, XXV (1981), pp. 581–613.

21 K. J. Holsti, *Peace and War: Armed Conflicts and International Order, 1643–1989* (Cambridge, 1991).

22 J. Goldstein, *Long Cycles: Prosperity and War in the Modern Age* (New Haven, 1988).

23 Thompson and G. Zuk, 'War, Inflation and Kondratieff's Long Waves', *Journal of Conflict Resolution*, XXVI (1982), pp. 621–44.

24 Modelski and Thompson, *Leading Sectors and World Powers: The Coevolution of Global Economics and Politics* (Columbia, SC, 1996), esp. pp. 157–8.

25 Levy, 'The Causes of War: A Review of Theories and Evidence', in *Behaviour, Society and Nuclear War*, ed. P. Tetlock et al. (Oxford, 1989), pp. 209–33; 'The Causes of War: Contending Theories', in *The Global Agenda*, eds C. W. Kegley and E. R. Wittkopf, 3rd edn (New York, 1988), pp. 59–69; 'Contending Theories of International Conflict: A Levels-of-Analysis Approach', in *Managing Global Chaos: Sources of and Responses to International Conflict*, eds C. Crocker and F. Hampson (Washington, DC, 1996), pp. 3–24.

26 C. Reynolds, *The Politics of War: A Study of the Rationality of Violence in Inter-state Relations* (London, 1989).

27 I. Geiss, *Die deutsche Frage, 1806–1990* (Mannheim, 1992), *The Question of German Unification, 1806–1996* (London, 1997). See also G. Schöllgen, *Die Mächte in der Mitte Europas: Stationen deutscher Aussenpolitik von Friedrich dem Grossen bis zum Gegenwart* (Munich, 1992).

28 M. Mishāqa, *Murder, Mayhew, Pillage and Plunder: The History of the Lebanon in the 18th and 19th Centuries* (Albany, NY, 1988), p. 227.

29 C. Boutant, *L'Europe au Grand Tournant des Années 1680: La Succession palatine* (Paris, 1985).

30 Taylor, *The Origins of the Second World War* (London, 1961).

31 D. Stevenson, *The Outbreak of the First World War: 1914 in Perspective* (Basingstoke, 1997), p. 42.

32 P. W. Schroeder, 'Napoleon's Foreign Policy: A Criminal Enterprise', *Consortium on Revolutionary Europe, Proceedings, 1989* (Tallahassee, 1990), pp. 105–6.

33 An important, skilful example of such an approach is R. N. Lebow, 'Play it Again Pericles: Agents, Structures and the Peloponnesian War', *European Journal of International Relations*, II (1996), pp. 231–58.

34 R. Cecil, *Hitler's Decision to Invade Russia, 1941* (London, 1975).

35 C. F. Doran, 'Power Cycle Theory and the Contemporary State System', in *Contending Approaches to World System Analysis*, ed. W. R. Thompson (Beverly Hills, 1983), p. 178.

36 Instructions to Feraty de Valette, 17 April 1725, Dresden, Hauptstaatsarchiv, Geheimes Kabinett, Gesandschaften 2797.

37 I. L. Janis, *Victims of Groupthink: A Psychological Study of Foreign-Policy Decisions and Fiascoes* (Boston, 1972).

38 George Tilson to Charles Whitworth, envoy at Berlin, 4 May 1722, BL, Add. 37389.

39 William Fraser to Sir Robert Murray Keith, envoy in Vienna, 7 June 1785, BL, Add. 35534.

40 John Shore to Earl Cornwallis, Governor-General, 9 September 1787, PRO 30/11/122 fol. 20.

41 William Kirkpatrick to Earl Cornwallis, 13 June 1787, PRO 30/11/121 fol. 60.

42 D'Eon, French envoy in London, to Praslin, French foreign minister, 20 July 1763, AE, CP, Ang. 450 fol. 498.

43 Joseph Yorke to Philip Yorke, 26 October 1753, BL, Add. 35363 fol. 338.

44 R. C. Snyder, 'Some Recent Trends in International Relations Theory and Research', in *Essays in the Behavioral Study of Politics*, ed. A. Ranny (Urbana, IL, 1962), p. 104.

45 K. N. Waltz, *Theory of International Politics* (Reading, MA, 1979). For 'classical' realism, H. J. Morgenthau, *Politics among Nations* (New York, 1948); R. O. Keohane, ed., *Neorealism and its Critics* (New York, 1986). For a criticism of Waltz, C. Reynolds, review of *The Origin and Prevention of Major Wars*, eds R. I. Rotberg and T. K. Rabb (Cambridge, 1989), in *International History Review*, XII (1990), pp. 651–2.

46 T.C.W. Blanning, *The Origins of the French Revolutionary Wars* (Harlow, 1986), pp. 26–7.

47 G. Blainey, *The Causes of War* (London, 1973), pp. 150, 114, 173–4, 245–8.

48 Q. Wright, 'The Nature of Conflict', *Western Political Quarterly*, IV (1951), p. 205.

49 E. R. May, ed., *Knowing One's Enemies: Intelligence before the Two World Wars* (Princeton, 1984); U. Trumpener, 'War Premeditated? German Intelligence Operations in July 1914', *Central European History*, IX (1976), pp. 58–85.

50 L. L. Farrar, ed., *War* (Santa Barbara, 1978), p. xiv; D. R. Rapkin, 'The Inadequacy of a Single Logic Integrating Political and Material Approaches to the World System', in *Contending Approaches*, ed. Thompson, p. 257.

51 E. D. Mansfield, 'The Concentration of Capabilities and the Onset of War', *Journal of Conflict Resolution*, XXXVI (1992), p. 21; Waltz, *Theory of International Relations* (Reading, MA, 1979).

52 Marquis de Silly to Duc de Richelieu, 4 January 1727, Paris, Bibliothèque Victor Cousin, Fonds Richelieu, XXXI, fol. 173.

53 Blanning, *French Revolutionary Wars*, p. 28; see also Levy, 'Misperception and the Causes of War: Theoretical Linkages and Analytical Problems', *World Politics*, XXXVI (1983), pp. 76–99; R. Jervis, 'War and Misperception', *Journal of Interdisciplinary History*, XVIII (1988), pp. 675–700.

54 Wright, 'Design for a Research Project on International Conflicts', *Western Political Quarterly*, X (1957), p. 267.

55 A. Einstein and S. Freud, 'Why War?', in *The Standard Edition of the Complete Psychological Works of Sigmund Freud*, ed. J. Strachey, XXII (London, 1964), pp. 199–215.

56 T. Hobbes, *Leviathan* (London, 1651), pt. 1, chap. 13.

57 B. Bueno de Mesquita, 'Risk, Power Distributions, and the Likelihood of War', *International Studies Quarterly*, XXV (1981), pp. 541–68.

58 Earl Cornwallis to William Pitt, 3 December 1791, PRO, 30/11/175 fol. 19.

59 Cornwallis to the Marquess of Lansdowne, 9 October 1791, BL, Bowood Collection, papers of the first marquess of Lansdowne, 40.

60 D. E. Kaiser, *Politics and War: Sources and Consequences of European International Conflict, 1559–1945* (Cambridge, MA, 1990); T. Ertman, *Birth of the Leviathan: Building States and Regimes in Medieval and Early Modern Europe* (Cambridge, MA, 1997).

61 V. B. Lieberman, *Burmese Administrative Cycles: Anarchy and Conquest, c.1580–1760* (Princeton, 1984).

62 Ata-Malik Juvaini, *Genghis Khan: The History of the World-Conqueror*, 2nd edn, ed. J. A. Boyle (Manchester, 1997), pp. 3, 80.

63 J. Pemble, *The Invasion of Nepal: John Company at War* (Oxford, 1971), p.12.

64 *Ibid.*, p. 47.

65 S. M. Watt, *Revolution and War* (Ithaca, 1996).

66 Additional instructions for Robert Liston, 26 February 1794, PRO, FO 78/15 fol. 46–7.

67 C. Jian, *China's Road to the Korean War: The Making of the Sino-American Confrontation* (New York, 1995).

68 M. Charlton, *The Little Platoon: Diplomacy and the Falklands Dispute* (Oxford, 1989); L. Freedman and V. Gamba-Stonehouse, *Signals of War: The Falklands Conflict of 1982* (London, 1990); A. Danchev, 'Life and Death in the South Atlantic', *Review of International Studies*, XVII (1991), pp. 305–12; and Danchev, intro. to *The Franks Report* (London, 1992).

69 J. Bulloch and H. Morris, *Saddam's War: The Origins of the Kuwait Conflict and the International Response* (London, 1991); Freedman and E. Karsh, *The Gulf Conflict, 1990–1991: Diplomacy and War in the New World Order* (Princeton, 1993); G. Feiler, 'Petroleum Prices, Politics and War', in *The Gulf Crisis and its Global Aftermath*, ed. G. Barzilai et al. (London, 1993), pp. 250–63.

70 J. P. LeDonne, 'Outlines of Russian Military Administration, 1762–1796. Part II: The High Command', *Jahrbücher für Geschichte Osteuropas*, XXXIII (1985), pp. 188–9. See also LeDonne, *Ruling Russia: Politics and Administration in the Age of Absolutism, 1762–1796* (Princeton, 1984), pp. 56–65.

71 E. Gibbon, *History of the Decline and Fall of the Roman Empire*, ed. J. B. Bury, 7 vols (London, 1897–1901), V, pp. 358–9, 319, VI, p. 175.

72 I have benefited from reading an unpublished typescript, 'Western Turkestan: The Emergence of the Uzbeks', by the late Joseph Fletcher. I would like to thank David Morgan for providing me with a copy.

73 Gibbon, V, p. 396, VII, p. 19.

74 W. Robertson, *The History of the Reign of the Emperor Charles V. With a View of the Progress of Society in Europe, from the Subversion of the Roman Empire, to the Beginning of the Sixteenth Century*, 3 vols (London, 1769; 1782 edn), I, pp. 134–5.

75 G. Sørensen, 'An Analysis of Contemporary Statehood: Consequences for Conflict and Cooperation', *Review of International Studies*, XXIII (1997), pp. 253, 267.

ONE · 1450–1650: AN AGE OF EXPANSION

1 A. Pagden, *European Encounters with the New World: From Renaissance to Romanticism* (New Haven, 1993).

2 T. J. Barfield, *The Perilous Frontier: Nomadic Empires and China* (Oxford, 1989); S. Jagehild and V. J. Symons, *Peace, War, and Trade along the Great Wall: Nomadic-Chinese Interaction through Two Millennia* (Bloomington, IN, 1989); A. M. Khazanov, 'Muhammad and Jenghiz Khan Compared: The Religious Factor in World Empire Building', *Comparative Studies in History and Society*, XXXV (1993), pp. 474–5; C. Halperin, *Russia and the Golden Horde* (London, 1987).

3 A. C. Hess, 'The Ottoman Conquest of Egypt (1517) and the Beginning of the Sixteenth Century World War', *International Journal of Middle Eastern Studies*, IV (1973), pp. 55–76.

4 J. Edwards, 'War and Peace in Fifteenth-century Castile: Diego de Valera and the Granada War', in *Studies in Medieval History Presented to*

R.H.C. Davis, eds H. Mayr-Harting and R. I. Moore (London, 1985), pp. 294–5.

5 W. Bracewell, *The Uskoks of Senj: Piracy, Banditry and Holy War in the Sixteenth Century Adriatic* (Ithaca, 1992).

6 J. F. Guilmartin, 'Ideology and Conflict: The Wars of the Ottoman Empire, 1453–1606', *Journal of Interdisciplinary History*, XVIII (1988), p.726.

7 Augustine, *City of God*, IV, 4; F. H. Russell, *The Just War in the Middle Ages* (Cambridge, 1975).

8 C. R. Boxer, *The Portuguese Seaborne Empire, 1415–1825* (London, 1969); S. Subrahmanyam, *The Portuguese Empire in Asia, 1500–1700: A Political and Economic History* (Harlow, 1993); Boxer, 'Portuguese and Spanish Projects for the Conquest of Southeast Asia, 1580–1600', *Journal of Asian History*, III (1969).

9 D. Birmingham, *Trade and Conflict in Angola: The Mbundu and Their Neighbours under the Influence of the Portuguese, 1483–1790* (Oxford, 1966).

10 J. Forsyth, *A History of the Peoples of Siberia. Russia's North Asian Colony, 1581–1990* (Cambridge, 1992).

11 A. Crosby, *The Columbian Exchange: Biological and Cultural Consequences of 1492* (Westport, CT, 1969), and *Ecological Imperialism: The Biological Expansion of Europe, 1500–1900* (London, 1986).

12 J. A. Fernández-Santamaria, *The State, War and Peace: Spanish Political Thought in the Renaissance, 1516–1559* (Cambridge, 1977), pp. 80–96; Pagden, *Spanish Imperialism and the Political Imagination: Studies in European and Spanish-American Social and Political Theory, 1513–1830* (New Haven, 1990), pp. 14–33; P. Seed, *Ceremonies of Possession in Europe's Conquest of the New World, 1492–1640* (Cambridge, 1995).

13 A. S. Donnelly, *The Russian Conquest of Bashkiria, 1552–1740: A Case Study in Imperialism* (London, 1968), p. vii.

14 W. E. Washburn, 'The Moral and Legal Justifications for Dispossessing the Indians', in *Seventeenth Century America: Essays in Colonial History*, ed. J. M. Smith (Chapel Hill, 1959), pp. 24–32.

15 S. Har-El, *Struggle for Domination in the Middle-East: The Ottoman-Mamluk War, 1485–1491* (Leyden, 1995); R. W. Olson, *The Siege of Mosul and Ottoman-Persian Relations, 1718–1743* (Bloomington, IN, 1975).

16 J. F. Richards, *The Mughal Empire* (Cambridge, 1993); S. Gordon, *Marathas, Marauders, and State Formation in Eighteenth-century India* (Delhi, 1994).

17 F. Wakeman, *The Great Enterprise: The Manchu Reconstruction of Imperial Order in Seventeenth-century China* (Berkeley, 1985).

18 R. Bireley, *Religion and Politics in the Age of the Catholic Reformation: Emperor Ferdinand II, William Lamormaini, S. J., and the Formation of Imperial Policy* (Chapel Hill, 1981).

19 S.C.A. Pincus, *Protestantism and Patriotism: Ideologies and the Making of English Foreign Policy, 1650–1685* (Cambridge, 1996), p. 442. A recent restatement of the traditional secular interpretations is offered by J. S. Levy and S. Ali in 'From Commercial Competition to Strategic Rivalry

to War: The Evolution of the Anglo-Dutch Rivalry, 1609–1652', in *The Dynamics of Enduring Rivalries*, ed. P. F. Diehl (Urbana, IL, 1997).

20 S. Gunn, 'The French Wars of Henry VIII', in *The Origins of War in Early Modern Europe*, ed. J. Black (Edinburgh, 1987); D.A.L. Morgan, 'The Political After-Life of Edward III: The Apotheosis of a Warmonger', *English Historical Review*, CXII (1997), pp. 869, 876; C. Vivant, 'Henri IV the Gallic Hercules', *Journal of the Warburg and Courtauld Institutes*, XXX (1967), pp. 176–97; M. Greenshields, *An Economy of Violence in Early Modern France. Crime and Justice in the Haute Auvergne, 1587–1664* (University Park, PA, 1994), pp. 233–4; E. H. Dickerman, 'Henry IV of France, the Duel and the Battle Within', *Societas*, III (1973), pp. 207–20.

21 H. Kamen, *Philip II of Spain* (New Haven, 1997), pp. 66–70; G. Parker, *The Strategic Problems of Philip II* (New Haven, 1998).

22 J. R. Hale, *War and Society in Renaissance Europe, 1450–1620* (London, 1985), p. 31.

23 J. Thornton, 'Legitimacy and Political Power: Queen Nijinga, 1624–63', *Journal of African History*, XXXII (1991), pp. 25–40.

24 P. Meyvaert, ' "Rainaldus est malus scriptor Francigenus": Voicing National Antipathy in the Middle Ages', *Speculum*, LXVI (1991), pp. 743–63.

25 R. Frame, *The Political Development of the British Isles, 1100–1400* (Oxford, 1990), p. 179.

26 D. Johnson, 'The Making of the French Nation', in *The National Question in Europe in Historical Context*, eds M. Teich and R. Porter (Cambridge, 1993), p. 42.

27 H. H. Rowen, *The King's State: Proprietary Dynasticism in Early Modern France* (New Brunswick, NJ, 1988).

28 Frederick II to Lord Marshal, 6 October 1753, *Politische Correspondenz Friedrichs des Grossen*, ed. R. Koser, 46 vols (Berlin, 1879–1939), X, p. 118.

29 W. Cobbett, ed., *Parliamentary History of England from … 1066 to … 1803*, 36 vols (London, 1806–20), XII, p. 167.

30 L. Y. Andaya, 'Interactions with the Outside World and Adaptation in Southeast Asian Society, 1500–1800', in *The Cambridge History of South-East Asia*, ed. N. Tarling (Cambridge, 1992), pp. 380–95.

31 D. Ayalon, *Gunpowder and Firearms in the Mamluk Kingdom: A Challenge to a Medieval Society* (London, 1956).

32 H. P. Varley, *Warriors of Japan, as Portrayed in the War Tales* (Honolulu, 1964).

33 Levy, 'Historical Trends in Great Power War, 1495–1975', *International Studies Quarterly*, XX (1982), p. 289.

34 E. H. Dickerman, 'Henry IV and the Juliers-Clèves Crisis: The Psychohistorical Aspects', *French Historical Studies*, VIII (1974), pp. 626–53; Dickerman and A. M. Walker, 'The Choice of Hercules: Henry IV as Hero', *Historical Journal*, XXXIX (1996), pp. 315–37.

35 C. Totman, *Early Modern Japan* (Berkeley, 1993), pp. 47–8. See also M. E. Berry, *Hideyoshi* (Cambridge, MA, 1982); and J. Elisonas, 'The

Inseparable Trinity: Japan's Relations with China and Korea', in *The Cambridge History of Japan. IV. Early Modern Japan*, ed. J. W. Hall (Cambridge, 1991), pp. 235–300.

36 W. J. Koenig, *The Burmese Policy, 1752–1819* (Ann Arbor, MI, 1990), p. 6.

37 P. Brightwell, 'The Spanish Origins of the Thirty Years War', *European Studies Review*, IV (1979), pp. 409–31, 'Spain and Bohemia: The Decision to Intervene, 1619', *ibid.*, XII (1982), pp. 117–41, 'Spain, Bohemia and Europe, 1619–21', *ibid.*, XII (1982), pp. 371–99.

38 Richards, *Mughal Empire*, pp. 33–4, 40–41.

39 O. Subtelny, *Domination of Eastern Europe, Native Nobilities and Foreign Absolutism, 1500–1715* (Gloucester, 1986); L. and M. Frey, *Societies in Upheaval: Insurrections in France, Hungary, and Spain in the Early Eighteenth Century* (Westport, CT, 1987); C. Russell, *The Fall of the British Monarchies, 1637–1642* (Oxford, 1990).

40 The extensive literature on the subject can be approached through Y.-M. Bercé, *Peasant Revolts in Early Modern France* (London, 1990).

41 H. Lloyd, *The Rouen Campaign, 1590–1592: Politics, Warfare and the Early-modern State* (Oxford, 1973).

42 B. F. Porshnev, *Muscovy and Sweden in the Thirty Years War, 1630–35* (Cambridge, 1995).

43 P. Lockhart, *Denmark in the Thirty Years' War, 1618–1648* (Cranbury, NJ, 1996).

44 Varley, *The Onin War* (New York, 1967); M. E. Berry, *The Culture of Civil War in Kyoto* (Berkeley, 1994).

45 Greenshields, *Economy of Violence*, pp. 233, 2. The complex medieval background can be approached through: G. Halsall, ed., *Violence and Society in the Early Medieval West* (Woodbridge, 1997); D. Kagay and L.J.A. Villalon, eds, *The Final Argument: The Imprint of Violence on Society in Medieval and Early Modern Europe* (Woodbridge, 1997); and A. J. Finch, 'The Nature of Violence in the Middle Ages: An Alternative Perspective', *Historical Research*, LXX (1997), pp. 249–68.

46 H. Zamora, *State and Nobility in Early Modern Germany: The Knightly Feud in Franconia, 1440–1567* (Cambridge, 1998); E. Muir, *Mad Blood Stirring: Vendetta and Factions in Friuli during the Renaissance* (Baltimore, 1993); D. M. Smith, *A History of Sicily* (London 1968), pp. 294–9; T. Astarita, *The Continuity of Feudal Power: The Caracciolo di Brienza in Spanish Naples* (Cambridge, 1993).

47 D. Bitton and W. A. Mortenson, 'War or Peace: A French Pamphlet Polemic, 1604–1606', in *Politics, Religion and Diplomacy in Early Modern Europe*, eds M. R. Thorp and A. J. Slavin (Kirksville, MO, 1994), p. 133.

48 G. F. Jewsbury, *The Russian Annexation of Bessarabia, 1774–1828: A Study of Imperial Expansion* (Boulder, CO, 1976), p. 2. See also M. Atkin, *Russia and Iran, 1780–1828* (Minneapolis, 1980).

TWO · 1650–1775: AN AGE OF LIMITED WAR?

1 For an attempt to offer a different approach, see J. Black, *The Rise of the European Powers, 1679–1793* (London, 1990). Important recent studies

include J. Kunisch, 'La guerre-c'est moi! Zum Problem der Staatenkonflikte im Zeitalter des Absolutismus', *Zeitschrift für historische Forschung*, IV (1987), pp. 407–38, and *Fürst-Gesellschaft-Krieg: Studien zur bellizisitischen Disposition des absoluten Fürstenstaates* (Cologne, 1992); L. Bély, *Les relations internationales en Europe, XVIIe-XVIIIe siècles* (Paris, 1992); and H. Duchhardt, *Balance of Power und Pentarchie, 1700–1785* (Paderborn, 1997). On Louis XIV's foreign policy see, in particular, R. M. Hatton, ed., *Louis XIV and Europe* (London, 1976).

2 M. Doyle, 'Kant, Liberal Legacies, and Foreign Affairs', *Philosophy and Public Affairs*, XII (1983), pp. 205–35, 323–53; J. S. Levy, 'Domestic Politics and War', *Journal of Interdisciplinary History*, XVIII (1988), pp. 653–74; G. Sørensen, *Democracy and Democratization: Processes and Prospects in a Changing World* (Boulder, CO, 1993); E. D. Mansfield and J. Snyder, 'Democratization and the Danger of War', *International Security*, XX (1995), pp. 5–38.

3 J. W. Smit, 'The Netherlands and Europe in the Seventeenth and Eighteenth Centuries', in *Britain and the Netherlands in Europe and Asia*, eds J. S. Bromley and E. H. Kossmann (London, 1968), p. 16.

4 R. Koser, ed., 46 vols (Berlin 1879–1939).

5 P. C. Curtin, 'Jihad in West Africa: Early Phases and Interrelations in Mauritania and Senegal', *Journal of African History*, XII (1971), pp. 11–24.

6 D. K. Richter, *The Ordeal of the Longhouse: The Peoples of the Iroquois League in the Era of European Colonization* (Chapel Hill, 1992); R. B. Ferguson and N. L. Whitehead, eds, *War in the Tribal Zone: Expanding States and Indigenous Warfare* (Santa Fe, 1992).

7 T. M. Barker, 'New Perspectives on the Historical Significance of the "Year of the Turk" ', *Austrian History Yearbook*, XIX–XX (1983–4), p. 4.

8 H. Davis et al., eds, *The Prose Works of Jonathan Swift*, 16 vols (Oxford, 1939–68), VI, pp. 23, 34.

9 S. Johnson, *Thoughts on the Late Transactions Respecting Falkland's Islands* (London, 1771), pp. 33–4.

10 *Ibid.*, p. 73.

11 Edward Finch, British envoy in Russia, to Lord Harrington, Secretary of State for the Northern Department, 1 November 1740, PRO, SP 91/26.

12 D. Napthine and W. A. Speck, 'Clergymen and Conflict, 1660–1763', *Studies in Church History*, XX (1983).

13 Anonymous, *A Seasonable Discours, Wherein is Examined What is Lawful during the Confusions and Revolutions of Government . . . as also, Whether the Nature of War be Inconsistent with the Nature of the Christian Religion* (London, 1689), pp. 53–61.

14 William Trumbull to the Earl of Sunderland, Secretary of State, 3 April 1686, PRO, SP 78/150 fol. 62; C. Pincemaille, 'La Guerre de Hollande dans le programme iconographique de la Grande Galerie de Versailles', *Histoire. Economie et Société*, IV (1985), pp. 313–33.

15 P. Burke, *The Fabrication of Louis XIV* (New Haven, 1992), pp. 94–5. See, more generally, J. Cornette, *Le Roi de Guerre: Essai sur la souveraineté dans la France du Grand Siècle* (Paris, 1993).

16 M. A. Thomson, 'The Safeguarding of the Protestant Succession,
    1702–18', in *William III and Louis XIV*, eds R. Hatton and J. S. Bromley
    (Liverpool, 1968), pp. 237–51.

17 Duke of Manchester to William Blathwayt, 16 September 1701, New
    Haven, Yale University, Beinecke Library, Manchester Box.

18 D. K. Wyatt, *Studies in Thai History* (Chiang Mai, 1994), p. 186.

19 Paul de Barrillon, French envoy in London, to Louis XIV, 4 January
    1685, AE, CP, Ang. 154 fol. 17–19.

20 A. Lossky, *Louis XIV, William III and the Baltic Crisis of 1683* (Berkeley,
    1954); J. Stoye, 'Europe and the Revolution of 1688', in *The Revolutions
    of 1688*, ed. R. Beddard (Oxford, 1991), pp. 197–8.

21 Marshal Noailles, memorandum, Vincennes, Archives de la Guerre, A1
    2997 fol. 89.

22 Marquis d'Argenson to Chevignard de Chavigny, 10 December 1744,
    AE, CP, Bavière 114.

23 Abbé de La Ville to the States General, 15 November 1750, Iden Green,
    papers of Edward Weston.

24 Sir Thomas Robinson to Robert Keith, envoy in Vienna, 11 March
    1755, Leeds, Archive Office, Vyner papers, 11835.

25 P. Conisbee, *Painting in Eighteenth-century France* (Oxford, 1981), p. 114.

26 P. Sonnino, *Louis XIV and the Origins of the Dutch War* (Cambridge,
    1988); C. J. Ekberg, *The Failure of Louis XIV's Dutch War* (Chapel Hill,
    1979), pp. 94–6. For the 1680s see R. Place, 'The Self-deception of the
    Strong: France on the Eve of the War of The League of Augsburg',
    French Historical Studies, 6 (1970) pp. 459–73.

27 N. V. Riasanovsky, *The Image of Peter the Great in Russian History and
    Thought* (Oxford, 1985), p. 303; D. A. Gaeddert, 'The Franco-Bavarian
    Alliance during the War of the Spanish Succession', PhD thesis, Ohio
    State University, 1969, pp. 198–9.

28 Lossky, *Louis XIV and the French Monarchy* (New Brunswick, NJ, 1994),
    p. 119; R. D. Martin, 'The Marquis de Chamlay, Friend and
    Confidential Advisor to Louis XIV: The Early Years, 1650–1691', PhD
    thesis, University of California at Santa Barbara, 1972, p. 28. See, more
    generally, J. H. Kautsky, *The Politics of Aristocratic Empires* (Chapel Hill,
    1982), e.g. pp. 15, 144–50, 230.

29 *The London Evening Post*, 23 April 1752.

30 Robert, fourth earl of Holdernesse, envoy in The Hague, to the Duke of
    Newcastle, 13 March 1750, PRO, SP 84/454.

31 Count Perron, Sardinian envoy in London, to Charles Emmanuel III,
    29 January 1750, Turin, Archivio di Stato, Lettere Ministri,
    Inghilterra 56.

32 Henry Fox to the Earl of Shelburne, 29 December 1761, BL, Bowood
    Collection, papers of the first marquess of Lansdowne, xv, fol. 65.

33 *The Times*, 26 May 1790; M. M. Shcherbatow, *On the Corruption of
    Morals in Russia*, ed. A. Lentin (Cambridge, 1960), p. 61; M. D'Aube,
    Maître des Requestes, Reflexions sur le Gouvernement de France,
    1734–8, Paris, Bibliothèque Nationale, nouvelles acquisitions françaises
    9513, p. 166.

34 S. C. Dutta, *The North-East and the Mughals, 1661–1714* (Delhi, 1984), p. 187.
35 P. P. Shafirov, *A Discourse Concerning the Just Causes of the War between Sweden and Russia*, ed. W. E. Butler (Dobbs Ferry, NY, 1973).
36 Mirepoix, Portrait de la Cour d'Angleterre, – November 1751, AE, Mémoires et Documents, Ang. 51 fol. 166.
37 Black, *America or Europe? British Foreign Policy, 1739–63* (London, 1998), pp. 74–80.
38 Johnson, *Thoughts*, pp. 1–2.
39 *Ibid.*, p. 44. See also, Anonymous, *An Inquiry into the Origin and Consequences of the Public Debt* (London, 1754), p. 25. E. Burke, *Reflections on the Revolution in France* (London, 1790), Everyman edn, London, 1910, p. 73.
40 J. Thornton, *The Kingdom of Kongo: Civil War and Transition, 1641–1718* (Madison, 1983); A. Hilton, *The Kingdom of Kongo* (Oxford, 1985).
41 B. K. Király, 'War and Society in Western and East Central Europe in the Pre-Revolutionary Eighteenth Century', in *East Central European Society and War in the Pre-Revolutionary Eighteenth Century*, eds G. E. Rothenberg, Király and P. F. Sugar (Boulder, CO, 1982), p. 11.
42 C. W. Ingrao, *In Quest and Crisis: Emperor Joseph I and the Habsburg Monarchy* (Lafayette, IN, 1979), pp. 158–9.
43 P. Spear, *Twilight of the Mughuls: Studies in Late Mughul Delhi* (Cambridge, 1951). I have benefited from Stewart Gordon's advice on the Marathas.
44 W. Cobbett, *Parliamentary History*, xv, p. 598.
45 Alexander Spotswood to Viscount Townshend, – 1727, BL, Add. 32694 fol. 4–5.
46 L. Petech, 'The Tibetan-Ladakhi-Moghul War of 1681–83', *Indian Historical Quarterly*, XXIII (1947), pp. 183, 193.

THREE · 1775–1914: WARS OF REVOLUTION AND NATIONALISM

1 L. Ranke, *Ursprung und Beginn der Revolutionskriege, 1791 und 1792* (Leipzig, 1879); H. A. Goetz-Bernstein, *La Diplomatie de la Gironde: Jacques-Pierre Brissot* (Paris, 1912).
2 J. Tulard, 'La Diplomatie française et l'Allemagne de 1789 à 1799', in *Deutschland und die französischen Revolution*, ed. J. Voss (Munich, 1983), pp. 43–8; E. Buddruss, 'Die Deutschlandpolitik der französischen Revolution zwischen Traditionen und revolutionärem Bruch', in *Revolution und Konservatives Beharren: Das Alte Reich und die französische Revolution*, eds K. O. Aretin and K. Härter (Mainz, 1990), pp. 145–50.
3 *Archives parlementaires de 1787 à 1860*, 127 vols (Paris, 1879–1913), XXXVII, pp. 410–11.
4 T.C.W. Blanning, *The Origins of the French Revolutionary Wars* (Harlow, 1986), pp. 96–123. See also J. H. Clapham, *The Causes of the War of 1792* (Cambridge, 1892); P. Howe, 'Belgian Influence on French Policy, 1789–1793', *Consortium on Revolutionary Europe 1986*, pp. 213–22.

5 *Archives parlementaires*, XXXVII, pp. 491–3.

6 See, especially, J. T. Murley, 'The Origin and Outbreak of the Anglo-French War of 1793', D.Phil, University of Oxford, 1959; J. Black, *British Foreign Policy in an Age of Revolutions, 1783–1793* (Cambridge, 1994).

7 Henry, third Lord Holland, *Memoirs of the Whig Party during My Time*, ed. Henry, fourth Lord Holland, 2 vols (London, 1852), I, p. 13; W. T. Laprade, *England and the French Revolution* (Baltimore, 1909), pp. 184–5.

8 J. T. Stoker, *William Pitt et la Révolution française, 1789–1793* (Paris, 1935), pp. 1, 205–6.

9 J. Gifford, *A Letter to the Hon. Thomas Erskine*, 6th edn (London, 1799), pp. 158–60, 177, *A Second Letter to the Hon. Thomas Erskine*, 4th edn (London, 1797), p. 35; J. Bowles, *French Aggression, Proved from Mr. Erskine's 'View of the Causes of the War'*, 2nd edn (London, 1797), p. 76.

10 Blanning, *Origins*, pp. 158–9; P. Jupp, ed., *The Letter-Journal of George Canning, 1793–1795* (London, 1991), p. 184.

11 Blanning, *Origins*, p. 159.

12 *Memorials and Correspondence of Charles James Fox*, ed. Lord John Russell, 4 vols (London, 1853–4), II, p. 379.

13 Bowles, *Farther Reflections Submitted to the Consideration of the Combined Powers* (London, 1794), p. 7.

14 Blanning, *Origins*, p. 123.

15 Lord Grenville, Foreign Secretary, to François, Marquis de Chauvelin, 24 January 1793, BL, Add. 34447 fol. 235.

16 Murley, 'Anglo-French War', p. 453.

17 P. Duparc, ed., *Recueil des Instructions données aux ambassadeurs et ministres de France depuis les traités de Westphalie jusqu'à la Révolution Française. Venise.* (Paris, 1958), p. 312.

18 P. W. Schroeder, *The Transformation of European Politics, 1763–1848* (Oxford, 1994), pp. 11–12.

19 Ibid., p. 354.

20 H. T. Parker, 'Why Did Napoleon Invade Russia? A Study in Motivation and the Interrelations of Personality and Social Structure', *Journal of Military History*, LIV (1990), pp. 131–46.

21 Schroeder, pp. 229–30, 249, 392–4.

22 S. Burrows, 'Culture and Misperception: The Law and the Press in the Outbreak of War in 1803', *International History Review*, XVIII (1996), pp. 793–818, quote, p. 815.

23 B. Perkins, ed., *The Causes of the War of 1812: National Honor or National Interest?* (Huntington, NY, 1962); D. R. Hickey, *The War of 1812: A Forgotten Conflict* (Urbana, IL, 1989).

24 J. M. Welsh, *Edmund Burke and International Relations* (Basingstoke, 1995), p. 130.

25 Schroeder *passim*, e.g. p. 581.

26 N. Rich, *Why the Crimean War?* (New York, 1985); D. M. Goldfrank, *The Origins of the Crimean War* (Harlow, 1994).

27 A. Blumberg, *A Carefully Planned Accident: The Italian War of 1859* (London, 1990).

28 G. Wawro, 'The Habsburg *Flucht nach vorne* in 1866: Domestic Political Origins of the Austro-Prussian War', *International History Review*, XVII (1995), pp. 221–48.

29 R. W. Johannsen, *To the Halls of the Montezumas: The Mexican War in the American Imagination* (New York, 1985).

30 J. L. Offner, *An Unwanted War: The Diplomacy of the United States and Spain over Cuba, 1895–1899* (Chapel Hill, 1992).

31 W. Carr, *The Origins of the Wars of German Unification* (Harlow, 1991).

32 N. Stargardt, *The German Idea of Militarism: Radical and Socialist Critics, 1866–1914* (Cambridge, 1994); F. Kühlich, *Die deutschen Soldaten im Krieg von 1870/71: Eine Darstellung der Situation und der Erfahrungen der deutschen Soldaten im Deutsch-Französischen Krieg* (Frankfurt, 1995).

33 A. Sked, *The Survival of the Habsburg Empire: Radetzky, the Imperial Army and the Class War, 1848* (London, 1979).

34 B. H. Reid, *The Origins of the American Civil War* (Harlow, 1997); G. S. Boritt, ed., *Why the Civil War Came* (Oxford, 1996).

35 R. Aron, *Penser la Guerre: Clausewitz* (Paris, 1976); P. Paret, *Clausewitz and the State* (Oxford, 1976); A. Gat, *The Origins of Military Thought from the Enlightenment to Clausewitz* (Oxford, 1989); B. Bond, *The Pursuit of Victory: From Napoleon to Saddam Hussein* (Oxford, 1996).

36 M. Ceadel, *The Origins of War Prevention: The British Peace Movement and International Relations, 1730–1854* (Oxford, 1996).

37 J. E. Thomson, *Mercenaries, Pirates, and Sovereigns: State-building and Extraterritorial Violence in Early Modern Europe* (Princeton, 1994); Black, *War and the World, 1450–2000* (New Haven, 1998).

38 M. Howard, *The Franco-Prussian War* (London, 1961), pp. 220–21.

FOUR · 1783–1914: WARS OF IMPERIALISM

1 J. Thornton, 'The Chronology and Causes of Lunda Expansion to the West, *c.* 1700–1852', *Zambia Journal of History*, I (1981).

2 N. Etherington, *Theories of Imperialism: War, Conquest and Capital* (1984).

3 E. Ingram, 'Timing and Explaining Aggression: Wellesley, Clive, and the Carnatic, 1795–1801', *Indo-British Review*, XXI/2, pp. 106–10.

4 J. Smith, *The Spanish American War: Conflict in the Caribbean and the Pacific, 1895–1902* (Harlow, 1994), pp. 43–4.

5 I. R. Smith, *The Origins of the South African War, 1899–1902* (Harlow, 1996).

6 W. L. Langer, 'The Origin of the Russo-Japanese War', in Langer, *Explorations in Crises* (Cambridge, MA, 1969), pp. 3–45; I. Nish, *The Origins of the Russo-Japanese War* (Harlow, 1985).

7 K. Epstein, 'Erzberger and the German Colonial Scandals, 1905–1910', *English Historical Review*, LXXIV (1959), p. 637; R. Horsman, *Race and Manifest Destiny: The Origin of American Racial Anglo-Saxonism* (Cambridge, MA, 1981); M. Banton, *Racial Theories* (Cambridge, 1987).

8 B. Williams, 'Approach to the Second Afghan War: Central Asia during

the Great Eastern Crisis, 1875–1878', *International History Review*, II (1980), pp. 216–17.

9 J. C. Herold, *Bonaparte in Egypt* (London, 1962), pp. 3–4.

10 A. Beer, ed., *Joseph II, Leopold II und Kaunitz: Ihr Briefwechsel* (Vienna, 1873), p. 260.

11 D. M. Lang, *The Last Years of the Georgian Monarchy, 1658–1832* (New York, 1957), pp. 182–5, 205–10; A. Bennigsen, 'Un mouvement populaire au Caucase au XVIIIe siècle: la "Guerre Sainte" au Sheikh Mansur', *Cahiers du monde russe et soviétique*, V (1964), pp. 159–97; J. Black, 'Sir Robert Ainslie: His Majesty's Agent-Provocateur? British Foreign Policy and the International Crisis of 1787', *European History Quarterly*, XIV (1984), pp. 253–83; S. J. Shaw, *Between Old and New: The Ottoman Empire under Sultan Selim III, 1798–1807* (Cambridge, MA, 1971), pp. 345–55.

12 J. K. Fairbank, *Trade and Diplomacy on the China Coast* (Cambridge, MA, 1953), and Fairbank, ed., *The Chinese World Order: Traditional China's Foreign Relations* (Cambridge, MA, 1953-6).

13 M. Atkin, *Russia and Iran, 1780–1828* (Minneapolis, 1980).

14 Recent work can be approached through R. D. Long, ed., *The Man on the Spot: Essays on British Empire History* (London, 1995); and J. Darwin, 'Imperialism and the Victorians: The Dynamics of Territorial Expansion', *English Historical Review*, CXII (1997), pp. 614–42. See also Atkin, *Russia*.

15 R. W. Olson, *The Siege of Mosul* (Bloomington, IN, 1975), p. 35.

16 P. J. Marshall, *Bengal: The British Bridgehead. Eastern India, 1740–1828* (Cambridge, 1987), p. 97.

17 P. Nightingale, *Trade and Empire in Western India, 1784–1806* (Cambridge, 1970), p. 40.

18 O. Pollak, *Empires in Collision: Anglo-Burmese Relations in the Mid-Nineteenth Century* (Westport, CT, 1979), esp. pp. 4–5; D. M. Peers, 'Rediscovering India under the British', *International History Review*, XII (1990), pp. 560–61.

19 Lord Grenville to Lieutenant-General Fox and to the Admiralty, 20 November 1806, BL, Add. 71592 fol. 28–9.

FIVE · 1914–45: TOTAL WAR

1 P. Kennedy, ed., *The War Plans of the Great Powers, 1880–1914* (London, 1979); L. L. Farrar, *The Short War Illusion* (Santa Barbara, CA, 1973); J. Snyder, *The Ideology of the Offensive: Military Decision Making and the Disasters of 1914* (Ithaca, 1984); S. E. Miller, S. M. Lynn-Jones and S. Van Evera, eds, *Military Strategy and the Origins of the First World War*, 2nd edn (Princeton, 1991); G. A. Tunstall, *Planning for War against Serbia and Russia: Austro-Hungarian and German Military Strategies, 1871–1914* (Boulder, CO, 1993).

2 E. C. Helmreich, *The Diplomacy of the Balkan Wars, 1912–1913* (Cambridge, MA, 1938); A. Rossos, *Russia and the Balkans: Inter-Balkan Rivalries and Russian Foreign Policy, 1908–1914* (Toronto, 1981).

3 See also F. Fischer, *War of Illusions: German Policies from 1911 to 1914*

(London, 1975), and 'Twenty-Five Years: Looking Back at the "Fischer Controversy" and its Consequences', *Central European History*, XXI (1988), pp. 207–33.

4 For these, see S. R. Williamson, *The Origins of a Tragedy: July 1914* (Arlington Heights, IL, 1981); J. Joll, *The Origins of the First World War* (Harlow, 1984); R.J.W. Evans and H. P. von Strandmann, eds, *The Coming of the First World War* (Oxford, 1994); K. Wilson, ed., *Decisions for War. 1914* (London, 1995). A more theoretical account is offered by J. S. Levy, 'The Role of Crisis Management in the Origins of World War I', in *Avoiding War: Problems of Crisis Management*, ed. A. L. George (Boulder, CO, 1991), pp. 62–102, and by P. W. Schroeder, 'Some Thoughts on the Use of Counterfactuals in History (with Particular Reference to the Origins of World War I)', unpublished paper.

5 B. Semmel, ed., *Marxism and the Science of War* (New York, 1981).

6 N. Ferguson, 'Germany and the Origins of the First World War: New Perspectives', *Historical Journal*, XXXV (1992), p. 733, and 'Public Finance and National Security: The Domestic Origins of the First World War Revisited', *Past and Present*, CXLII (1994), pp. 141–68.

7 F. R. Bridge, *From Sadowa to Sarajevo: The Foreign Policy of Austria-Hungary, 1866–1918* (London, 1972); Williamson, *Austria-Hungary and the Origins of the First World War* (London, 1991); J. Leslie, 'The Antecedents of Austria-Hungary's War Aims', *Archiv und Forschung*, XX (1993), pp. 307–94; S. W. Lackey, *The Rebirth of the Habsburg Army: Friedrich Beck and the Rise of the General Staff* (Westport, CT, 1995), pp. 158–62.

8 D.C.B. Lieven, *Russia and the Origins of the First World War* (London, 1983).

9 J.F.V. Keiger, *France and the Origins of the First World War* (London, 1983).

10 Z. Steiner, *Britain and the Origins of the First World War* (London, 1977); K. Wilson, *The Policy of the Entente: Essays on the Determinants of British Foreign Policy, 1904–1914* (Cambridge, 1985).

11 Joll, '1914: The Unspoken Assumptions', in *The Origins of the First World War: Great Power Rivalry and German War Aims*, ed. H. W. Koch (London, 1972), pp. 307–28.

12 N. Stone, 'Hungary and the Crisis of July 1914', *Journal of Contemporary History*, I (1996), pp. 153–70.

13 D. Stevenson, *Armaments and the Coming of War: Europe, 1904–1914* (Oxford, 1996); D. G. Hermann, *The Arming of Europe and the Coming of World War One* (Princeton, 1996); J. H. Maurer, *The Outbreak of the First World War: Strategic Planning, Crisis Decision Making and Deterrence Failure* (London, 1995).

14 A.J.P. Taylor, *War by Timetable: How the First World War Began* (London, 1969); L. Albertini, *The Origins of the War of 1914* (Oxford, 1952).

15 M. Trachtenberg, *History and Strategy* (Princeton, 1991), pp. 72, 96, 98; Levy, 'Preferences, Constraints, and Choices in July 1914', *International Security*, XV (1990–91), pp. 151–86; Stevenson, 'Militarization and Democracy in Europe before 1914', *International Security*, XXII (1997), pp. 147–8.

16 W. A. Renzi, *In the Shadow of the Sword: Italy's Neutrality and Entrance into the Great War, 1914–1915* (New York, 1988).

17 M. S. Seligmann, 'Germany and the Origins of the First World War in the Eyes of the American Diplomatic Establishment', *German History*, XV (1997), pp. 331–2. For the theoretical dimension, see R. M. Siverson, *The Diffusion of War: A Study of Opportunity and Willingness* (Ann Arbor, MI, 1991).

18 P. Preston, 'Mussolini's Spanish Adventure: From Limited Risk to War', in *The Republic Besieged: Civil War in Spain, 1936–1939*, eds Preston and A. L. Mackenzie (Edinburgh, 1996), p. 28.

19 S. G. Payne, *A History of Fascism, 1914–45* (London, 1995), p. 355.

20 P.M.H. Bell, *The Origins of the Second World War in Europe*, 2nd edn (Harlow, 1997); M. Howard, 'A Thirty Years' War? The Two World Wars in Historical Perspective', *Transactions of the Royal Historical Society*, 6th ser., III (1993), pp. 179–80, 182–4; P. Finney, ed., *The Origins of the Second World War* (London, 1997). Earlier works of value include N. Rich, *Hitler's War Aims* (New York, 1973–4); G. L. Weinberg, *The Foreign Policy of Hitler's Germany, 1937–39* (Chicago, 1980); W. K. Wark, *The Ultimate Enemy: British Intelligence and Nazi Germany, 1933–1939* (Ithaca, 1985); W. Carr, *Poland to Pearl Harbor: The Making of the Second World War* (London, 1985); R. Lamb, *The Drift to War* (London, 1989); D. C. Watt, *How War Came* (London, 1989); R.A.C. Parker, *Chamberlain and Appeasement: British Policy and the Coming of the Second World War* (London, 1993); A. Claasen, 'Blood and Iron, and "der Geist des Atlantiks": Assessing Hitler's Decision to Invade Norway', *Journal of Strategic Studies*, XX (1997). On the Soviets, G. Roberts, *The Soviet Union and the Origins of the Second World War: Russo-German Relations and the Road to War, 1933–1941* (London, 1995), and Roberts, 'The Alliance That Failed: Moscow and the Triple Alliance Negotiations, 1939', *European History Quarterly*, XXVI (1996), pp. 383–414.

21 M. Knox, *Mussolini Unleashed, 1939–1941: Politics and Strategy in Fascist Italy's Last War* (Cambridge, 1982); J. J. Sadkovich, 'The Italo-Greek War in Context: Italian Priorities and Axis Diplomacy', *Journal of Contemporary History*, XXVIII (1993), pp. 439–64.

22 R. J. Crampton, *A Concise History of Bulgaria* (Cambridge, 1997), p. 183.

23 P. Lowe, *Great Britain and the Origins of the Pacific War: A Study of British Policy in East Asia, 1937–1941* (Oxford, 1977); A. Iriye, *The Origins of the Second World War in Asia and the Pacific* (Harlow, 1986); N. Tarling, *Britain, Southeast Asia and the Onset of the Pacific War* (Cambridge, 1996); M. A. Barnhart, 'The Origins of the Second World War in Asia and the Pacific: Synthesis Impossible?', *Diplomatic History*, XX (1996), pp. 241–60.

24 N. J. Cull, *Selling War: The British Propaganda Campaign against American 'Neutrality' in World War II* (Oxford, 1995).

SIX · 1945–90: COLD WAR AND THE WARS OF
DECOLONIZATION

1 A. Clayton, *The Wars of French Decolonization* (Harlow, 1994).
2 D. H. Close, *The Origins of the Greek Civil War* (Harlow, 1995).
3 J. L. Gaddis, *We Now Know: Rethinking Cold War History* (Oxford, 1997).
4 L. S. Kaplan, *The United States and NATO: The Formative Years*
   (Lexington, KY, 1984).
5 M. Galeotti, *Afghanistan: The Soviet Union's Last War* (London, 1995).
6 R. Buzzanco, *Masters of War: Military Dissent and Politics in the Vietnam
   Era* (Cambridge, 1997), pp. 192–3, and a powerful scholarly critique
   from a serving officer, H. R. McMaster, *Dereliction of Duty: Lyndon
   Johnson, Robert McNamara, the Joint Chiefs of Staff, and the Lies That Led to
   Vietnam* (New York, 1997), e.g. pp. 322–5. See, more generally, A.
   Short, *The Origins of the Vietnam War* (Harlow, 1989).
7 W. Steenkamp, *South Africa's Border War, 1966-1989* (Gibraltar, 1989).
8 P. Kien-hong Yu, 'Itu Aba Island and the Spratlys Conflict', in *World
   Boundaries. III: Eurasia*, ed. C. Grundy-Warr (London, 1994), pp.
   183–95.
9 B. Morris, *Israel's Border Wars, 1949–1956: Arab Infiltration, Israeli
   Retaliation, and the Countdown to the Suez War*, 2nd edn (Oxford, 1997);
   M. B. Oren, *Origins of the Second Arab-Israel War* (London, 1992). See,
   more generally, R. Ovendale, *The Origins of the Arab-Israeli Wars*, 2nd
   edn (Harlow, 1992).
10 Z. Schiff and E. Ya'ari, *Israel's Lebanon War* (London, 1984).
11 R. Iyob, *The Eritrean Struggle for Independence: Domination, Resistance,
   Nationalism, 1941–1993* (Cambridge, 1995).
12 M. W. Daly and A. A. Sikainga, eds, *Civil War in the Sudan* (London,1993).
13 J. de St. J. Jorré, *The Nigerian Civil War* (London, 1972).
14 M. Kentridge, *An Unofficial War: Inside the Conflict in Pietermaritzburg*
   (Cape Town, 1990).
15 J. S. Levy and M. Froelich, 'The Causes of the Iran-Iraq War', in *The
   Regionalization of War*, eds J. Brown and W. P. Snyder (New Brunswick,
   NJ, 1985), pp. 127–43; E. Karsh, ed., *The Iran-Iraq War: Impact and
   Implications* (London, 1989).
16 K. P. Meyer and C. P. Danopoulos, eds, *Prolonged Wars: A Post-Nuclear
   Challenge* (Washington, DC, 1994).

SEVEN · 1990–: WAR TODAY

1 M. Janowitz, *The Military in the Political Development of New Nations*
   (Chicago, 1964), and *Military Institutions and Coercion in Developing
   Nations* (Chicago, 1977); V. R. Berghahn, *Militarism: The History of an
   International Debate, 1861–1979* (Cambridge, 1984), pp. 67–84.
2 R. D. Edmunds and J. L. Peyser, *The Fox Wars: The Mesquakie Challenge
   to New France* (Norman, OK, 1993), pp. 51–2.
3 J. Gow, 'After the Flood: Literature on the Context, Causes and Course
   of the Yugoslav War – Reflections and Refractions', *Slavonic and East

European Review, LXXV (1997), pp. 446–84; A. Lieven, *Flaying the Bear: Chechnya and the Collapse of Russian Power* (New Haven, 1998).

4 G. L. Mosse, *Fallen Soldiers: Reshaping the Memory of the World Wars* (Oxford, 1990).

5 P. Fussell, *Wartime: Understanding and Behaviour in the Second World War* (Oxford, 1978).

6 N. R. Keddie, 'The Revolt of Islam, 1700 to 1993: Comparative Considerations and Relations to Imperialism', *Comparative Studies in Society and History*, XXXVI (1994), p. 469.

7 M. Owusu, 'Rebellion, Revolution and Tradition: Reinterpreting Coups in Ghana', *Comparative Studies in Society and History*, XXXI (1989), p. 373.

8 J. S. Levy, 'War in the Post-Cold War Era: Structural Perspectives on the Causes of War', in *The Global Agenda*, ed. C. W. Kegley Jr, 4th edn (New York, 1995), pp. 64–74.

9 P. M. Regan, 'War Toys, War Movies and the Militarisation of the United States, 1900–85', *Journal of Peace Research*, XXXI (1994), pp. 45–58.

10 W. K. Domke, *War and the Changing Global System* (New Haven, 1988).

11 P. Bakewell, *A History of Latin America* (Oxford, 1997), pp. 99–100.

12 For example, R. J. Stoll, 'The Guns of November: Presidential Re-elections and the Use of Force, 1947–1982', *Journal of Conflict Resolution* (1984), pp. 231–46.

13 G. Sørensen, 'Kant and Processes of Democratization: Consequences for Neorealist Thought', *Journal of Peace Research*, XXIX (1992), pp. 397–414.

14 K. J. Holsti, *The State, War, and the State of War* (Cambridge, 1996), and *Political Sources of Humanitarian Emergencies* (Helsinki, 1997); R. Jackson, *Quasi States: Sovereignty, International Relations and the Third World* (Cambridge, 1990); R. W. Copson, *Africa's Wars and Prospects for Peace* (Armonk, NY, 1994); J. W. Harbenson, D. Rothchild and N. Chazan, eds, *Civil Society and the State in Africa* (London, 1994); Sørensen, 'An Analysis of Contemporary Statehood: Consequences for Conflict and Cooperation', *Review of International Studies*, XXIII (1997), pp. 253–69.

15 M. van Creveld, *The Transformation of War* (New York, 1991), pp. 206–8.

16 *The Times*, 2 August 1997, p. 12; 4 August 1997, p. 11.

17 U. Ben-Eliezer, 'A Nation in Arms: State, Nation and Militarism in Israel's First Years', *Comparative Studies in Society and History*, XXXVII (1995), p. 284.

18 A. Clayton, *Factions, Foreigners and Fantasies: The Civil War in Liberia* (Sandhurst, 1995).

19 D. E. King, 'Intelligence Failures and the Falklands War: A Reassessment', *Intelligence and National Security*, II (1987), pp. 338–9; Levy and L. I. Vakili, 'Diversionary Action by Authoritarian Regimes: Argentina in the Falklands/Malvinas Case', in *The Internationalization of Communal Strife*, ed. M. I. Midlarsky (London, 1992), pp. 118–46.

20 M.C.C. Adams, *The Great Adventure: Male Desire and the Coming of World War I* (Bloomington, IN, 1990); J. Bourke, *Dismembering the Male: Men's Bodies, Britain and the Great War* (Chicago, 1996).

21 D. W. Larson, *Origins of Containment: A Psychological Explanation*

(Princeton, 1985). The relevant literature includes L. S. Etheredge, *A World of Men: The Private Sources of American Foreign Policy* (Cambridge, MA, 1978), and M. G. Hermann, 'Explaining Foreign Policy Behaviour Using the Personal Characteristics of Political Leaders', *International Studies Quarterly*, XXIV (1980), pp. 7–46.

22 P. Kennedy, *Preparing for the Twenty-First Century* (New York, 1993); R. Kaplan, 'The Coming Anarchy', *Atlantic Monthly* (February 1994), pp. 44–76; T. F. Homer-Dixon, 'On the Threshold: Environmental Changes as Causes of Acute Conflict', and 'Environmental Scarcities and Violent Conflict: Evidence from Cases', in *Global Dangers*, eds S. M. Lynn-Jones and S. E. Miller (Cambridge, MA, 1995); Levy, 'Contending Theories of International Conflict', in *Managing Global Chaos*, eds C. Crocker and F. Hampson (Washington, DC, 1996), p. 18.

23 J. A. Goldstone, *Revolution and Rebellion in the Early Modern World* (Berkeley, 1991).

24 K. A. Rasler and W. R. Thompson, *The Great Powers and Global Struggle, 1490–1990* (Lexington, KY, 1994), p. 191.

25 J. Mueller, *Retreat from Doomsday: The Obsolescence of Major War* (New York, 1989); C. Kaysen, 'Is War Obsolete? A Review Essay', *International Security*, XIV (1990), pp. 42–69; R.L.O'Connell, *Ride of the Second Horseman: The Birth and Death of War* (New York, 1997).

26 Mueller, 'The Catastrophe Quota: Trouble after the Cold War', *Journal of Conflict Resolution*, XXXVIII (1994), pp. 355–75.

27 E. Karsh, 'Cold War, Post-Cold War: Does It Make a Difference for the Middle East?', *Review of International Studies*, XXIII (1997), pp. 271–91.

28 C. A. Kupchan, *The Vulnerability of Empire* (Ithaca, 1994).

29 W. Mackinnon, *On the Rise, Progress and Present State of Public Opinion in Great Britain and Other Parts of the World* (London, 1828), pp. 202–3, 297–9, 328.

EIGHT · CONCLUSION

1 Seigneur d'Iberville, French envoy in London, to Louis XIV, AE, CP, Ang. 259 fol. 152.

2 K. Marx, *The Revolutions of 1848*, ed. D. Fernbach (London, 1973), p. 109; S. F. Kissin, *War and the Marxists: Socialist Theory and Practice in Capitalist Wars*, 2 vols (London, 1989).

3 J. Joll, '1914: The Unspoken Assumptions', in *The Origins of the First World War: Great Power Rivalry and German War Aims*, ed. H. W. Koch (London, 1972), pp. 307–28; A. Offner, 'Going to War in 1914: A Matter of Honour', *Politics and Society*, XXIII (1995), pp. 213–41.

4 A. Beyerchen, 'Clausewitz, Non-linearity and the Unpredictability of War', *International Security*, XVII (1992–3), pp. 59–90; R. Beaumont, *War, Chaos and History* (Westport, CT, 1994).

5 Joseph Yorke to his father, Philip, Lord Chancellor Hardwicke, 6 May 1750, BL, Add. 35355 fol. 241.

6 R. Koser, ed., *Politische Correspondenz Friedrichs des Grossen*, XI, p. 282.

Index

honour 15
Hötzendorf, Conrad von 183
Hudson Bay 54
Huguenots 41, 71
Hungary 20, 51–2, 67, 85, 88, 109–10,
    146, 179, 186, 201–2, 209, 222
Hussein, Saddam 41
Hyderabad 21–2, 84, 110

imperialism 15, 218, 240
Independence Day 216
India 20–2, 28, 34, 57–8, 67, 74, 81,
    83–5, 104, 110–11, 138, 157–8,
    163, 170–1, 184, 209–11, 217,
    228
Indian Ocean 53–4
Indo-China 58, 152, 198, 203, 228
Indo-Pakistan Wars 204
Indonesia 203, 205, 210, 217, 221,
    234
Inkatha 214
intifada 235
Ipi, Faqir of 174
IRA 234
Iran 41, 215, 223, 227
Iraq 41, 52, 187, 198, 213, 215, 217,
    234
Ireland 59, 73, 184, 219
Islam 57, 61, 64, 82, 227
Israel 211–12, 233, 235
Italian Wars 39, 66–7
Italy 38–9, 140, 142, 147, 167, 185,
    188, 192–4, 196
Ivan III, of Muscovy 62
Ivan IV, 63

James II, of England 33, 94, 106
James IV, of Scotland 52
Japan 10, 58–9, 61, 67–9, 75–6, 152,
    154, 157, 188–9, 191, 196,
    198–200
Java 86
Jews 41, 191–2

jihad 82, 154, 168, 227
Johnson, Samuel 88–90, 105
Joseph I, 88, 93
Joseph II, 9, 164
Juvaini, Ata–Malik, 37

Kagan, Donald 15
Kant, Immanuel 26
Kashmir 204, 221
Kenya 213
Kirkpatrick, William 28
Knights of St John 52
Kondratieff cycles 18
Korea 16, 58, 68, 75, 163, 217, 237
Korean War 40, 204, 206–7
Kurds 41, 213, 232
Kuwait 41, 217, 234

Ladakh 114
Lansbury, George 172
Laos 154
Latin America 154–5, 159, 203,
    227–8
Latin American Wars of Liberation
    141
League of Nations 27, 186, 188, 230
Lebanon 19–20, 168, 198, 207, 211
Lenin, Vladimir 240
Leopold I 85, 92–3
Leopold II 122–3
Leszczynski, Stanislaus 95
Levy, Jack 18
Liberia 234
Libya 150, 167–8, 207, 210
Liston, Robert 39
Lithuania 63, 186
litigation 47, 77
Livonia 16
Lodis 49, 57
Lombardy 77, 93
Louis XI, of France 62, 71
Louis XII, of France 62
Louis XIV, of France 21, 23, 30, 33,